TCHAIKOVSKY:

A Biographical and Critical Study

THE CRISIS YEARS

(1874–1878)

TCHAIKOVSKY:

A Biographical and Critical Study

by

DAVID BROWN

Volume II
THE CRISIS YEARS
(1874–1878)

LONDON
VICTOR GOLLANCZ LTD
1982

© David Brown 1982

British Library Cataloguing in Publication Data
Brown, David, *1929–*
    Tchaikovsky: a biographical and critical study.
    Vol 2: The crisis years (1874–1878)
    1. Chaĭkovskiĭ, Peter Ilĭch
    2. Composers—Russia—Biography
    I. Title
    780'.92'4   ML410.C4

    ISBN 0-575-03132-8

Printed in Great Britain at
The Camelot Press Ltd, Southampton

To Elizabeth

CONTENTS

ILLUSTRATIONS

PREFACE

WITH THE OPERA, *Vakula the Smith*, composed in the middle months of 1874, Tchaikovsky's period of high nationalism came to an abrupt end. In many of the most important works of the next few years the personal element is consolidated, reaching its most intense expression in the Fourth Symphony and the 'lyrical scenes', *Eugene Onegin*, those two great pieces which are inextricably linked with the central crisis of Tchaikovsky's whole life: his marriage in 1877. This volume covers the years which lead up to this devastating event, and it concludes with Tchaikovsky's resignation from the Moscow Conservatoire a year later, a decision which marked the end of the most critical phase of his existence.

The editorial principles and practices established in Volume I are maintained here. The debt to those people who helped in practical ways in the first volume also extends to this one; my thanks, therefore, to Dr Anthea Baird and Mr A. Helliwell of London University, to my excellent typist, Mrs Miriam Phillips, and to my indispensable assistant in checking and proof-reading, my wife, to whom the whole work is dedicated. In addition, I am grateful to Mrs Alexandra Orlova for making available to me a photo-copy of the Soviet-published *Pisma k rodnïm*. This was printed in 1940, and offered the fullest text ever prepared of some of the most important letters the composer wrote to members of his family. The volume was suppressed before publication, however, and only a very few copies found their way into private collections in Russia. Mrs Orlova, who in 1940 was working in the Tchaikovsky Museum at Klin, managed to lay her hands on a copy and held on to it secretly for nearly forty years, finally smuggling it to the West when she emigrated in 1979. I am thus able to offer the fullest text yet printed in English of some of the most revealing documents Tchaikovsky ever penned.

UNIVERSITY OF SOUTHAMPTON   DAVID BROWN
NOVEMBER 1981

Main Literary Sources for Volume II

with Abbreviations

TLP 1–   Tchaikovsky (P.), *Polnoye sobraniye sochineny: literaturnïye proizvedeniya i perepiska* [Complete edition: literary works and correspondence] In progress (Moscow, 1953–)

TD   Tchaikovsky (P.), *Dnevniki* [Diaries] (Moscow/Petrograd, 1923)

TMKS   Tchaikovsky (P.), *Muzïkalno-kriticheskiye stati* [Critical articles on music] (Moscow, 1953)

TPB   Tchaikovsky (P.), *Pisma k blizkim* [Letters to his family] (Moscow, 1955)

TPJ 1–2   Tchaikovsky (P.), *Perepiska s P. I. Jurgensonom* [Correspondence with Jurgenson], 2 vols. (Moscow, 1938–52)

TPM 1–3   Tchaikovsky (P.), *Perepiska s N. F. von Meck* [Correspondence with Nadezhda von Meck], 3 vols. (Moscow/Leningrad, 1934–6)

TPR   Tchaikovsky (P.), *Pisma k rodnïm* [Letters to his relatives] (Moscow, 1940)

TTP   *P. I. Chaykovsky: S. I. Taneyev. Pisma* [Tchaikovsky/Taneyev. Letters] (Moscow, 1951)

BVP   Balakirev (M.), *Perepiska s P. I. Chaykovskim* [Correspondence with Tchaikovsky], reprinted in Frid (E.) [ed.], *M. A. Balakirev: vospominaniya i pisma* [Balakirev: Recollections and letters] (Leningrad, 1962)

DTC   Dombayev (G.), *Tvorchestvo P. I. Chaykovskovo* [Tchaikovsky's works] (Moscow, 1958)

KIVC   Kashkin (N.), 'Iz vospominany o P. I. Chaykovskom' [From my recollections of Tchaikovsky], printed in *Proshloye russkoy muzïki* (Petrograd, 1920)

KVC   Kashkin (N.), *Vospominaniya o P. I. Chaykovskom* [Reminiscences of Tchaikovsky] (Moscow, 1896)

PVC   Protopopov (V.) [ed.], *Vospominaniya o P. I. Chaykovskom* [Reminiscences of Tchaikovsky] (Moscow, 1962)

TZC 1–3   TCHAIKOVSKY (M.), *Zhizn P. I. Chaykovskovo* [Tchaikovsky's life], 3 vols. (Moscow, 1900–2)

YDGC   YAKOVLEV (V.) [ed.], *Dni i godï P. I. Chaykovskovo* [The days and years of Tchaikovsky] (Moscow/Leningrad, 1940)

One musical source is also abbreviated in references:

T50RF   TCHAIKOVSKY (P.), *50 Russian Folksongs*, arranged for piano duet by Tchaikovsky (Moscow, 1869)

I

FIRST PIANO CONCERTO TO
THIRD SYMPHONY

IN SEPTEMBER 1866, only eight months after Tchaikovsky had joined the staff of the Moscow Conservatoire, a 9-year-old lad was admitted to study piano. During the next year his course was interrupted, but in 1869 he resumed his studies, now including lessons with Tchaikovsky. This new composition student, Sergey Taneyev, was to become a composer of great distinction, not endowed with any truly original creative gift, but a fastidious and diligent craftsman with a technique second to none. Between master and pupil there quickly grew a friendship that was to endure until Tchaikovsky's death. The judgement of a man such as Taneyev, whose own taste and competence were so high, yet whose self-scrutiny was so severe, was naturally to be respected, and Tchaikovsky came to value greatly criticism from the younger man; indeed, Taneyev alone was to be encouraged to absolute frankness about the works of his former teacher. When Tchaikovsky resigned from the Conservatoire in 1878 it was this 21-year-old who succeeded him as teacher of harmony and orchestration. After Tchaikovsky's death Taneyev undertook to complete where possible his old friend's unfinished works.

To his compositional abilities Taneyev joined equally unusual competence as a pianist. He became Nikolay Rubinstein's pupil in 1871, and in January 1875, though still a student, he performed the Brahms D minor Concerto at an RMS concert in Moscow with Rubinstein himself conducting. As we shall see, Taneyev the pianist was to be of as much significance to Tchaikovsky as Taneyev the critic, and before 1875 was out he was to render his first service in this capacity: the introduction to Moscow of Tchaikovsky's new piano concerto.

Two others who shared in the early history of this work were Nikolay Rubinstein and Hans von Bülow, the latter one of the first European musicians to recognise Tchaikovsky's gifts. For his part, Tchaikovsky had been very impressed by Bülow when he had heard him in St Petersburg in 1864, and when the German pianist gave a recital in Moscow in March 1874, he was quick to voice his enthusiasm in the press. Bülow swiftly returned the compliment. Unlike Tchaikovsky, he did attend the Milan production of *A Life for the Tsar* two months later, and in the course of writing about the opera for the *Allgemeine deutsche Musik-Zeitung* in June, he made flattering mention of Tchaikovsky, commenting in particular upon the First Quartet and *Romeo and Juliet*. Little did he realise that a year hence he would be the soloist in the first performance of Tchaikovsky's most important work for solo instrument and orchestra.

It is not known what prompted Tchaikovsky to make his next large composition a piano concerto. When he returned to his teaching and journalistic duties in September 1874 after completing *Vakula*, he found a good deal in which he could take heart. Admittedly his illicit manoeuvring over the production of *Vakula* was to make for some discomfort, and until early November he was heavily absorbed in making the vocal score of the opera. But others of his existing works were enjoying growing success. The score of the First Symphony was to be printed at last, some at least of the St Petersburg group were taking a very flattering interest in the forthcoming performance of *The Tempest* in the Russian capital, and before the end of the year his two quartets were to be successfully performed at RMS concerts in St Petersburg (to warm approval for the second from Cui), while the first was also heard in Moscow. Even the growing fame of the contemptible *Oprichnik* was good for his self-confidence, if not for his musical conscience. There was therefore plenty of moral encouragement to future composition. The poet, Fyodor Berg, suggested an opera on the Hussites, but could offer Tchaikovsky no concrete plot, being attracted to the subject (so the composer said) simply because Hussites sang hymns. For the moment Tchaikovsky certainly wanted no more national subjects, 'though I would give much for a good libretto from non-Russian history,' he admitted to Modest on 10 November.[1] Not that he would have been likely to set about it immediately even if one had been to hand, for the same letter gives the first news that he had turned his attention to the concerto, though it reported no progress. Yet within little more than seven weeks, through assiduous effort rather than because composition came easily – and despite a short break in mid-December to attend the first performance of *The Oprichnik* in Kiev – it was finished, but not yet scored. His hope was that Nikolay Rubinstein would give the first performance at one of his concerts in the New Year. On 5 January 1875,

[1] *TLP*5, p. 372; *TPR*, p. 207; *TZC*1, p. 448; *TPB*, p. 91; *YDGC*, p. 109.

only three days after completing composition, he played it over to Rubinstein.

This occasion has become one of the most notorious incidents in the composer's biography. What happened was only disclosed by Tchaikovsky three years later, and since his confidante was Nadezhda von Meck, the account was probably heightened, though the bare essentials of it were confirmed by Kashkin. Yet there is no doubt that it was a very distressing episode that upset Tchaikovsky profoundly, and a fortnight after it had taken place he alluded to it darkly and bitterly to Anatoly, but without going into any details. To Mrs von Meck he was explicit. What Tchaikovsky had sought was not criticism of the concerto as composition, but simply advice on the piano writing. Rubinstein could certainly offer this, and Tchaikovsky had feared that he would have been offended if someone else had been approached instead. The Albrechts were giving a Christmas Eve party,[2] and Rubinstein proposed that they should meet beforehand in one of the downstairs rooms of the Conservatoire to go over the piece. Also present were Kashkin and Hubert:

I played the first movement. Not a single word, not a single comment! If only you could have known how foolish, how intolerable is the position of a man when he offers his friend food he has prepared, and his friend eats it and says nothing. Say something, if only to tear it to pieces with constructive criticism – but for God's sake, just one kind word, even if not of praise! Rubinstein was preparing his thunder and Hubert was waiting until the position clarified and the moment arrived to come down on one side or the other.... Rubinstein's eloquent silence had tremendous significance. It was as though he was saying to me: 'My friend, can I talk about details when the very essence of the thing disgusts me?' I fortified my patience, and played on to the end. Again silence. I got up and asked, 'Well?' It was then that there began to flow from Nikolay Grigoryevich's mouth a stream of words, quiet at first, but subsequently assuming more and more the tone of Jove the Thunderer. It appeared that my concerto was worthless, that it was unplayable, that passages were trite, awkward, and so clumsy that it was impossible to put them right, that as composition it was bad and tawdry, that I had filched this bit from here and that bit from there, that there were only two or three pages that could be retained, and that the rest would have to be scrapped or completely revised. 'Take

[2] The Russian Christmas Day occurs, according to the Western calendar, on 6 January.

this, for instance – whatever is it?' (at this he plays the passage concerned, caricaturing it). 'And this? Is this really possible?' – and so on, and so on. I can't convey to you the most significant thing – that is, the *tone* in which all this was delivered. In a word, any outsider who chanced to come into the room might have thought that I was an imbecile, an untalented scribbler who understood nothing, who had come to an eminent musician to pester him with his rubbish. . . .

Despite Tchaikovsky's suspicion of Hubert's ambivalence, it is clear that this colleague was at least profoundly embarrassed at Rubinstein's tirade, and did his best to soothe the composer, though without convincing Tchaikovsky that he was not on his assailant's side (there is no record of how Kashkin behaved on this occasion). 'I was not only stunned, I was mortified by the whole scene,' Tchaikovsky continued. '. . . I left the room silently and went upstairs. I could say nothing because of my agitation and anger. Rubinstein soon appeared and, noticing my distraught state, drew me aside into a distant room. There he told me again that my concerto was impossible, and after pointing out to me a lot of places that required radical change, he said that if by such-and-such a date I would revise the concerto in accordance with his demands, then he would bestow upon me the honour of playing my piece in a concert of his. "*I won't change a single note,*" I replied, "*and I'll publish it just as it is now!*" And so I did!'[3]

Tchaikovsky appears to have been as good as his word, and on 21 February the scoring was completed. There appears to be no truth in the assertion that Rubinstein was intended to be the original dedicatee, despite Modest's and Kashkin's statements to this effect. The dedication was first given to Taneyev, presumably because it was intended that he should be the soloist in the première of the work. Nevertheless it was Bülow who first played the concerto publicly and to whom it was finally inscribed. It is not known how he came to be chosen by Tchaikovsky for this rôle, nor why Tchaikovsky was prepared for the first performance to take place on the other side of the world during the extensive American tour upon which Bülow was to embark that autumn. One can only assume that, after Rubinstein's outburst, Tchaikovsky's confidence in the piece was so uncertain that he wanted its public fortunes to be tested where he knew he would not have to endure personally the humiliation of a disaster. Bülow, however, was immediately taken by the work, and on 13 June he wrote an exceedingly

[3] Letter of 2 February 1878. *TLP*7, pp. 64–5; *TPM*1, pp. 173–4; *TZC*1, pp. 456–8; *DTC*, pp. 440–1.

deferential letter to Tchaikovsky, thanking him for sending the concerto and for the very flattering dedication. The work was first heard in Boston on 25 October, further performances being so successful that the finale had to be repeated (so Bülow reported to Tchaikovsky, though his glowing account of critical reaction was certainly exaggerated). 'That never happens here!' Tchaikovsky noted sourly to Rimsky-Korsakov.[4]

The first Russian performance followed on 13 November in St Petersburg at an RMS concert, with Gustav Kross as soloist and Nápravník as conductor. Tchaikovsky attended and had some bitter things to say about the latter's direction of the orchestra. Nor did the St Petersburg critics think much of the work itself. Cui and Laroche reviewed it tepidly; only Famintsïn was enthusiastic. Tchaikovsky was much happier with the performance when, three weeks later, Taneyev introduced the work to Moscow at another RMS concert with – of all people – Rubinstein conducting. One wonders whether the latter had really been so merciless in his verdict. If so, he had by now clearly begun to doubt his earlier opinion, and Hubert's press notice was favourable. Tchaikovsky himself also reviewed the performance, and ended with a generous compliment to the artists: 'The present writer could not wish to hear a better performance of the piece than this one, for which he is indebted to the sympathetic talent of Mr Taneyev and Mr Rubinstein's mastery as a conductor.'[5] The distressing incident of last Christmas Eve was, it seems, to be considered closed. But within it continued to rankle, at least until, in 1878, Rubinstein openly admitted the error of his judgement by learning the solo part and from thenceforward becoming one of its most persuasive advocates.

Though Tchaikovsky had uncompromisingly resisted pressures from Rubinstein for revisions, he did respond later to suggestions from the pianist Edward Dannreuther, who gave the first English performance of the work at the Crystal Palace on 23 March 1876, and who immediately wrote to Tchaikovsky detailing his proposed improvements in the piano writing. The composer replied very favourably, and these were incorporated when the full score was printed in 1879. More followed in the edition of 1889, including a striking redistribution of the opening piano chords (Ex. 96). It is not known whether these last revisions were the composer's own, or were suggested by another person.[6]

---

[4] *TLP*5, p. 418; *TZC*1, p. 472.   [5] *TMKS*, pp. 292–3; *DTC*, p. 447.

[6] The matter of later revisions to the solo part is examined more fully in James Friskin, 'The text of Tchaikovsky's B flat minor concerto' in *Music & Letters*, vol. 50 (1969), pp. 246 ff.

Ex. 96

Tchaikovsky's First Piano Concerto incorporates three borrowed tunes, one in each movement. A little French ditty, 'Il faut s'amuser et rire', that had recently enjoyed great popularity in Russia, appears in the second movement; significantly it is said to have been a favourite in Artôt's repertoire.[7] The other two were Ukrainian folksongs, used respectively as the first subject in the first movement, and as the opening theme of the finale.[8] The former was, according to Tchaikovsky, a melodic tag sung by 'every blind Ukrainian singer';[9] he had noted it down at Kamenka.

Even with these two folktunes there could be no room in this new work for the deep-rooted nationalism of *Vakula*. Despite his earlier confessed dislike for the combination of piano with orchestra, Tchaikovsky was obviously fired by the dramatic possibilities within the confrontation of heroic soloist and eloquent orchestra. Problems there may have been with the piano writing (Tchaikovsky admitted he found devising passage work a great strain), but it is none

---

[7] For a speculative investigation of Artôt's (and the composer's own) presence in this concerto, see vol. I, pp. 198–200.

[8] The second of these was printed in Rubets, *216 pesen*, No. 11.

[9] Letter to Nadezhda von Meck of 21 May 1879. *TLP*8, p. 206; *TPM*2, p. 116; *DTC*, p. 450.

the less generally effective, if scarcely elegant, and the balance between soloist and orchestra is mostly well handled. That the work came sluggishly was manifestly not the result of sterility, but simply because the concerto situation was new to Tchaikovsky, and basic problems required solution. Moving from symphony to quartet had not been so difficult, for the new medium was an even more unified source of sound favouring even more a flow of smoothly unfolding thought, and requiring only a shift of emphasis – the reduction of rhetoric and the cultivation of lyricism within a more consistently linear texture. On the other hand, the dualism of soloist and orchestra, with its pressures for bold gesture, dramatic incident, and sharp contrasts, could not but impede, even disrupt any steadily evolving argument, while Tchaikovsky's favoured method for generating a development – the contrapuntal engagement of materials to build little slabs that might then be piled sequentially – could only be of limited use in such a work if it was heavily modified.

In the slow movement there was no particular problem, for here a simple flow of lyrical melody could fill much of the musical space. Certainly this posed no difficulty to Tchaikovsky, whose repetitive deployment of his two main themes (the initial one in D flat,[10] and the borrowed French tune) against mildly differing backgrounds reveals the Glinka disciple. Like the slow movement of the First Symphony, this one neatly combines two structural blueprints: here they are ternary in respect of speed scheme, simple rondo with regard to thematic recurrence and key. The tonal scheme is based upon a semitone shift, for the prestissimo introduces the French tune in D major, a key that has been anticipated in the middle of the preceding Andantino semplice. Nor is it only the key that is foreshadowed, for some of the strangely scampering fragments with which the piano ushers in the prestissimo have already been heard in decorous slow motion as the lead to the earlier D major section in which a third melodic idea had been briefly presented. As in the First Symphony of eight years earlier, there is rather more to this slow movement than might at first appear simply from the charm of its melodic material.

While in the 'aria situation' of the Andantino semplice it had been natural to think in enclosed musical sections, the sonata rondo scheme that was usual for the concerto finale required rather more than Tchaikovsky supplied in his alternation of two thematic blocks supplemented by brief self-contained chunks of transition containing only the lightest hint of quasi-developmental intent. Tchaikovsky's

[10] For a possible explanation of the variant in the opening bar of this theme, see vol. I, p. 199.

marshalling of these neatly processed lumps of material is tidy, and he offers some token of developmental activity by contrapuntally engaging some of his thematic materials above the extended dominant preparation that leads to the final titanic delivery of the broad second theme. The movement makes a simple and effective finale, but it largely avoids those questions of organic growth that Tchaikovsky had so boldly confronted in the first movement.

However, before examining his novel treatment of an old design, we must face the problem posed by the huge prefix he devised for this first movement. Outwardly what follows upon this section contains much of the broad design of a classical prototype. There is a solo/orchestral exposition, central orchestral ritornello followed by a solo/orchestral development and recapitulation: there is even a written-out cadenza before the coda. Yet this series of events is prefaced, not by an orchestral tonic-based ritornello parading a selection of material that is to be the basis of what follows, but by a large ternary structure founded upon a tune that never recurs – all set, after the first few bars, in the relative major.

Many critics have been embarrassed by this apparent solecism. No historical precedent can justify it, for though Tchaikovsky may have viewed it as a slow introduction after the classical model (his original marking was andante non troppo e molto maestoso; only later did he change andante to allegro), this fully formed thematic statement has nothing in common with such an introduction. Nor is it integrated into the following movement, as had been the introductions to *Romeo and Juliet* and the Second Symphony. Yet it is, in fact, integrally connected with what follows. The very first bars (Ex. 97i) expose the distinctive harmonic progression that is to open the second subject (Ex. 97h), and the following tune (Ex. 97g) opens as a compendious anthology of fragments that are to appear in the ensuing movement's main material, an anthology that is matched at the end of the movement when the second limb of the second subject (Ex. 97e) converts itself into a form that incorporates contours from the other main themes (Ex. 97j).

This might raise a suspicion that Tchaikovsky's model was Borodin's First Symphony, which had already provided him with the prototype for the scherzo of his Second Symphony. Here Borodin had opened the slow introduction to his first movement with a melodic line which, fragmented, had provided a fund of material to generate the following allegro; then, at the end, he had tacked on a slow coda in which an even more comprehensive selection of the preceding movement's material was assembled to produce an expanded version of the slow theme with which the symphony had opened. It may be objected

Ex. 97

that whereas Borodin's thematic synthesising is so precise that it must
have been consciously engineered, Tchaikovsky's is relatively amorphous, and might be merely casual. Yet the complex network of
relationships that is revealed by an examination of the main themes of
Tchaikovsky's first movement suggests that the relationships between
them are far from fortuitous, whether or not he had Borodin's example
in mind (it is worth noting that he was to devise the 'third subject' of his
Fourth Symphony's first movement by a similar process which was
patently deliberate (see below, p. 171). Indeed, if one takes the
Ukrainian folksong of this movement (Ex. 97c), the French ditty of the

second (Ex. 97d), the phrase ciphered from Tchaikovsky's own name (Ex. 97a), and the 'Artôt contour' (Ex. 97b) – see vol. I, pp. 198–200 – it can be demonstrated that almost every note of Tchaikovsky's own principal themes in this movement derives from these borrowed or precomposed materials. It is, in fact, difficult to believe that Tchaikovsky invented his own melodies with such cold-blooded calculation as Ex. 97 might suggest; rather these thematic relationships seem to have sprung from a particularly intensive application of those natural habits of mind that had produced the families of themes we have already noted in certain earlier compositions, including the recent *Vakula*. The opening theme of the concerto is as heavily involved in these relationships as any.

Perhaps this is the best justification that can be offered for this whole eccentric introduction. Though it does not possess that unqualified rightness that would make it a master stroke, yet no responsible critic seems to have condemned it with much conviction. It is certainly difficult to see how the concerto could have been launched with the slender idea of the first subject, and certainly this expansive opening theme does nicely balance the equally generous thematic statement that closes the finale of the concerto.

The following Allegro con spirito is not only one of the most effective but also one of the most thoughtful of Tchaikovsky's first movements, notable for its simple but enterprising exploitation of tonal instability as reinforcement to the more external drama of the concerto. Outwardly the exposition follows the model of *Romeo and Juliet*, with a ternary, tonally enclosed first subject and a second subject made from two distinct themes, the second not unlike its rocking counterpart in the earlier work. Tchaikovsky's solution of his eternal transition problem was his most radical yet: he not merely abandoned formal separation altogether (as in the original first movement of the Second Symphony) but actually overlapped the two subjects by twice inserting the opening bar of the impending second subject into the dying conclusion of the first. The required key shift occurs within the first part of the second subject, a wind theme with a restrained chromaticism and a propensity to modulate that fits it well for transitional service. These qualities also enable it, when alternated with the tonally stable second element (the muted string melody (Ex. 97e)), to bring a highly effective element of contrast into this whole new area in A flat, the unusual key choice for the second subject.

The resulting exposition (Ex. 98a) is Tchaikovsky's most original to date, with an arrangement of the thematic events and a tonal scheme that are as admirable as they are unorthodox. As for the recapitulation

Ex. 98

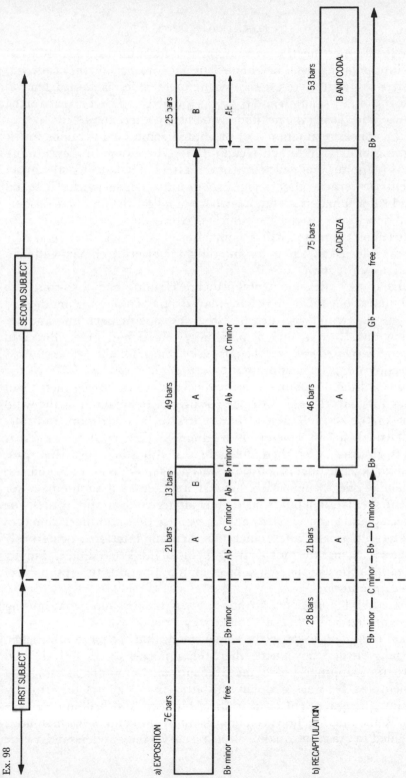

a) EXPOSITION

b) RECAPITULATION

(Ex. 98b), by omitting the first statement of the muted string theme (B) and interpolating the heightened tonal drama of the cadenza, Tchaikovsky engendered a significant increase in sustained tension before the final resolution into B flat is signalled by the recurrence of the long-excluded string theme, upon which the coda centres.

If the concerto situation had prompted some modifications in the designing of exposition and recapitulation, it required an even more radical reappraisal of developmental matters. Though the opening of the central ritornello might suggest, in its initial engagement of first and second subject material, that it is about to follow the practices of some earlier developments, the first subject is swiftly dismissed and attention is focused on the muted string theme, fresh light being shed upon it by its new role as an agent for building a powerful climax within a modulatory situation.

Tchaikovsky's developmental principle is simple and, for a concerto, novel; just as one theme may have played a part in shaping another, so now one theme may be turned into a new one or back into another existing one. It was such a possibility which had fired Glinka to compose *Kamarinskaya*, and Tchaikovsky himself had, of course, used the technique to striking dramatic purpose in *Romeo and Juliet*. As the ritornello of the development had proceeded, so the string theme had changed its nature; now, with the re-entry of the piano, it is the wind theme of the second subject that recurs to be even more radically transformed, for its opening is fragmented (Ex. 99b) to suggest a fresh beginning which then amalgamates with a new idea (Ex. 99c). Tchaikovsky's instinct to contrapuntal engagement is now applied, not to placing one theme neatly against another as a preliminary for sequential extension, but to fashioning an urgent overlapping dialogue between piano and orchestra on this new idea, thus building a climax of considerable weight, after which this thematic interloper dexterously converts itself into the muted string theme of this same subject. Finally the reappearance of the first subject material heralds the approach of the recapitulation.

The First Piano Concerto has drawn perhaps more patronising comment than any other of Tchaikovsky's major works. Such condescension quite fails to grasp the achievement that the piece represents, especially the first movement, where the composer successfully devised a structure appropriate to this difficult medium, not skirting the problem (as he was to do in the attractive Violin Concerto) by sustaining a movement on a train of lyricism and brilliant passage work. Remembering, however, how dismally the composer's first judge had failed to grasp the quality of the piece, we may understand a little

Ex. 99

why suspicion of the frankness and force with which Tchaikovsky declared himself in this work has deafened many to its finer qualities. Tchaikovsky himself was never in greater need of encouragement than on that dreadful Christmas Eve, for his own spirits had already sunk very low as the year drew to its close, and his colleague's brutal verdict plunged him into deeper gloom. Nobody in Moscow was really a close friend; even the St Petersburg group seemed to take more interest in him than his fellow-Muscovites. Yet he had to recognise that part of the cause lay in his own personality. 'I am very, very alone here,' he lamented to Anatoly on 21 January, 'and if it weren't for my constant work, I should simply succumb to melancholia. It's a fact that [my abnormality?] constitutes an unbridgeable chasm between me and the majority of people. It imparts to my character an aloofness, a fear of people, a timidity, an excessive shyness, a distrustfulness – in a word, a thousand traits which are making me more and more unsociable.'[11] One may wonder whether there was any particular significance in part of the letter he wrote a couple of months later to his other twin brother, the homosexual Modest: 'It makes me angry that you possess every single one of my shortcomings; that's a fact. I should like to find in you the absence of just one of my bad personality traits – and I simply can't. You are too like me, and when I am angry with you I am, in effect, angry with myself, for you eternally act as a mirror in which I see

[11] *TPR*, p. 214; *TZC*1, p. 455 (partial); *TLP*5, p. 390 (partial); *TPB*, p. 95 (partial).

reflected all my weaknesses.'[12] No wonder he was feeling more drawn
to the heterosexual twin, Anatoly. Yet his physical health was good, he
had to admit, and there were also some remissions from his spiritual
gloom. 'Now, with the approach of spring, these attacks of melancholia
have stopped completely,' he wrote to Anatoly more cheerfully on 21
March, 'but because I *know* that each year – or rather, each winter –
they will return more strongly, I have decided to quit Moscow for the
whole of next year.'[13] Where he would go he did not know, though he
had discussed with his brother-in-law, Lev Davïdov, who had recently
spent a few days in Moscow, the possibility of passing next winter with
him and Sasha in Geneva. Money was the problem, but winning the
prize with *Vakula* could solve this. However, such a visit to Switzerland
was to be delayed a year.

Thus Tchaikovsky began 1875 in the lowest of spirits. Towards the
end of January he did escape briefly to St Petersburg for a performance
of Anton Rubinstein's opera, *The Demon*, a work that he refused to
review since he had already seen the score and disliked it. For the rest of
the winter he laboured on with his various duties, probably putting the
finishing touches to his *A Short manual of harmony adapted to the study of
religious music in Russia*, which the Russian Synod had requested in May
1874, and which Jurgenson printed in 1875. He continued to compose,
but attempted no major task. As he had been embarking on the
concerto Bessel had asked for a set of songs, and this assignment was
postponed again by the composition of a second piece for soloist and
orchestra at the request of another virtuoso. Leopold Auer, who had
succeeded Wieniawski as professor of violin at the St Petersburg
Conservatoire in 1868, was already directly acquainted with
Tchaikovsky as a composer, having led the first St Petersburg
performances of both Tchaikovsky's string quartets, but he appears to
have had no personal dealings with Tchaikovsky until January 1875,
when they were introduced at Nikolay Rubinstein's. Tchaikovsky's
only mention of the *Sérénade mélancolique* is in a letter to Modest of 25
February, when he reported that he had 'already composed the violin
piece I promised *to Auer*'.[14] It is not known why the first performance
was given, not by Auer, but by Adolf Brodsky at an RMS concert in
Moscow on 28 January 1876. Auer first played the piece publicly when
he introduced it to St Petersburg ten months later, on 18 November.

Tchaikovsky's last two major works found echoes in this new piece.
The main key is that of the concerto, and the *Sérénade* even briefly

[12] *TPR*, p. 218; *TLP*5, p. 398; *TZC*1, p. 460.
[13] *TLP*5, p. 397; *TZC*1, p. 459; *TPR*, p. 217; *TPB*, p. 98.
[14] *TLP*5, p. 395; *TPR*, p. 216; *YDGC*, p. 114; *TPB*, p. 97; *DTC*, p. 462.

Ex. 100

proclaims D flat at its opening. The very first bar (Ex. 100) is straight from Oxana's challenge to Vakula in Act 2, Scene 2 of the opera (see Ex. 92), while a melody in the central faster section recalls the French chansonette of the concerto's second movement. Tchaikovsky attempted no major compositional feat in this work, contenting himself with an almost unbroken flow of lyrical melody from the soloist, darkly brooding at first, more radiantly tender when D flat is again reached and a new melody, shared canonically between soloist and cellos, builds itself around the Oxana phrase, and more impassioned in the più mosso e agitato which constitutes the central section of this simple ternary structure. The *Sérénade mélancolique* is an engaging piece, well worth an occasional performance.

The residue of Tchaikovsky's creative urges during this winter was channelled into a surge of song composition, for he not only furnished Bessel with a set of six romances, but also composed before the end of April two further collections of six songs apiece for Jurgenson's catalogue. Publication of all three sets followed swiftly. Since the Op. 16 romances of two years earlier Tchaikovsky had written only two songs, both at the instigation of the periodical *Nouvelliste*, which had included them in its issues of November 1873 and January 1874; the songs themselves had been composed by the middle of the preceding October. The first, 'Take my heart away', sets a Fet poem which dwells on disembodied amorous aspiration, and Tchaikovsky's response is matchingly amorphous, only the shock treatment of a couple of sudden tonal shifts enlivening the featureless agitation of his faceless music. By contrast 'Blue eyes of spring', a setting of Heine's 'Die blauen Frühlingsaugen' from *Neuer Frühling* in the translation by Mikhail Mikhaylov, has admirable lucidity of content, and Tchaikovsky, responding sensitively to this clarity, matched the simplicity of his vocal line with a comparable economy in the accompaniment, punctuating the singer's phrases with a gracious fragment of piano melody to compound a song of delicacy and charm.

These *Nouvelliste* supplements evidently enjoyed considerable success, for two years later the same periodical, perhaps also swayed by the recent impressive confirmation from Bessel's and Jurgenson's presses of Tchaikovsky's aptitude for fashioning attractive songs, commissioned two more. 'I should like in a single word' (again a Heine setting, this time of 'Ich wollt, meine Schmerzen ergössen' from *Die Heimkehr* in Mey's translation) and 'We have not far to walk' were completed in July 1875. It was now Heine's turn to be served with the inferior music. Compound metre was a natural choice for dactyllic verse, and when selecting $\frac{9}{8}$ or $\frac{12}{8}$ Tchaikovsky had found adequate room for rhythmic variety within and between the component phrases. But $\frac{6}{8}$ could be narrow and confining, and 'I should like in a single word', even more than the earlier *Nouvelliste* setting 'Take my heart away', moves forward in a series of short, metrically constricted utterances supported mostly by the most ordinary of patterned semiquaver figuration. There is more flexibility in the phrases of 'We have not far to walk', and in the piano accompaniment, too; furthermore the song has a plaintive little piano phrase to frame and intersect the whole. Gerald Abraham has drawn attention to the curious way in which this song anticipates Tatyana's 'Letter Song' in *Eugene Onegin*, and this is by no means the only context in Tchaikovsky's 1875 songs in which can be heard intimations of this musical world to come. Despite some falling off in the middle section, the *Nouvelliste* could take some pride in issuing this song. Yet it is the Heine setting of 1873 that takes the prize among these four musical supplements.

The eighteen songs that Tchaikovsky had composed in the first four months of 1875 had doubled his output of such works and had correspondingly clarified his song style – a style that always appears to be so emotionally committed, yet which, paradoxically, is so often anonymous. The secret of Tchaikovsky's effectiveness, even in his weakest romances, lay in his unfailing ability for devising vocal phrases that permitted a strong emotional delivery of the highly charged poetry that he normally chose. He well understood the human voice; given a good singer, none of these romances will ever fall flat in performance, however pallid the material from which it is built. Lacking the swift intuition with which Schubert could conceive a musical revelation of the inner life of a lyric, Tchaikovsky nevertheless possessed something of the facility with which the Austrian master could respond to verse, even when his deeper perceptions remained unstirred, and he could turn out a couple of romances in one day.

By now he had a small but effective armoury of practices and procedures to which he could resort in the absence of any other creative ideas. Most fundamental of these was the stepwise descending bass. The reader need turn but a few pages of these songs to realise how efficacious Tchaikovsky found it. Its great value was that it combined a natural capacity for suggesting growth with an ability to fit almost any melodic context. Also, by introducing chromaticisms into the descent, it was possible to turn aside tonally, deflecting the music perhaps into some unexpected key, or simply introducing an harmonic surprise to stir the listener's wavering attention. The harmonic structure might then be decorated by a simply patterned piano accompaniment in a manner somewhere between Schumann and Mendelssohn. As for overall design, a ternary scheme could always guarantee shapeliness to the whole, even when the price of this might require the words of the opening to return as well as the music. Otherwise the final portion of text could be made to carry the opening music, whether it was really suitable or not. Even when, as often happened, Tchaikovsky modified the latter portion of his first section when it returned, such a musical scheme was a blunt contradiction of any evolving experience there might be in the text. Thus it did little further violence to round off the song with a lengthy piano postlude that perhaps simply restated the prelude. Tchaikovsky's addiction to ternary schemes was perhaps the most serious flaw in his personality as a song composer.

It is useful to recognise the stereotyped romance that might quite easily be manufactured from an agglomeration of these conventional practices, for such awareness sharpens critical alertness to those songs in which Tchaikovsky showed himself more ready to quit the easy trail of ready-made solutions. Such songs are invariably his best. To be fair, even in those that are most dominated by formulae (such as the *Nouvellisto* contributions, 'Take my heart away' and 'I should like in a single word') there will still be at least one moment enlivened with genuine enterprise, if not insight, and there is never any denying Tchaikovsky's competence. Some even have positive merits. Not the turgid 'As o'er the burning ashes', the second song of Bessel's set, Op. 25, but 'Reconciliation', that precedes it, conveys a dignified resolve in its strongly profiled melody, while 'Mignon's song' (No. 3), a setting of 'Kennst du das Land?' from Goethe's *Wilhelm Meister* in a translation by Fyodor Tyutchev, fortifies longing with urgency to engender a richer experience. The success of his earlier attempt on 'Nur wer die Sehnsucht kennt' must have prompted Tchaikovsky to tackle another of Mignon's songs, but this time, instead of a broad cantilena, her words are favoured with shorter-breathed phrases (Ex. 101a). One need only glance at the first phrase of one of Glinka's most celebrated romances, 'I remember a wonderful moment' (Ex. 101b), to perceive where lay the real roots of Tchaikovsky's music in 'Mignon's Song'. Joined to Goethe's verse – and with the memory of how Schubert had treated this text – such an idiom sounds too sallow, nor does the return of the opening words to provide the final stanza resonate with the amplified yearning with which Tchaikovsky had so skilfully invested the end of his earlier song. This time the repetition sounds merely trite, damping the undeniable, if slightly second-rate fervency of Tchaikovsky's music.

Ex. 101

[Do you know the land where the myrtle and laurel grow, where the azure vault of the sky is deep and clear?]

[I remember a wonderful moment: you appeared before me,]

Of the four lyrics in this set expressing deep personal emotion, it is 'I never spoke to her' (No. 5) that receives the worthiest treatment. If few of Tchaikovsky's earlier romances had been fully melodic in the sense that they could have survived as equally convincing instrumental compositions, they had, notwithstanding, tended to organise the singer's part with considerable formality, balancing successive phrases rhythmically and grouping them so as to build into broader, well-integrated spans of music. Yet their preponderantly syllabic treatment, their prevailing tendency to use a limited range of shorter note values, and their readiness to fracture phrases in the interests of a more affecting delivery of the text had inclined their vocal style towards a declamatory manner, and it was a tendency that was strengthened considerably in certain of these 1875 songs. 'I never spoke to her' is such a fully declamatory song. The dismantling of the more discrete, more balanced periods of a formal romance like 'Reconciliation' is evidenced by the intrusion of the singer into the cadence of the piano's introductory phrase (Ex. 102a), the preliminary for an agitated outpouring in which the vocal line is much splintered into short gasps of two, three or four notes. Such urgency required more from the piano than interludes which were simply formal punctuation or mere polite rejoinders, and in 'I never spoke to her' the piano was made to provide willing substantiation and swift extension of the singer's sentiments. Nor could such a song finally come full circle to encapsulate a tidily processed emotional condition; instead agitation passes finally into ecstatic contemplation of the beloved who is the singer's 'ideal, delight and torment' as his impassioned declamation is brought to rest on a bed of still harmonies (Ex. 102b).

When setting 'The canary' (No. 4) Tchaikovsky attempted for the first time to annex for himself a little territory in that Russian musical Orient which Glinka had invented. It was an obvious thing to do in treating this dialogue on freedom between the Sultana Zuleika and her caged bird, but Tchaikovsky proved an uneasy inhabitant of this musical world; garnishing the melodic lines with triplet semiquavers and a liberal allowance of augmented and diminished intervals is insufficient to suggest properly the sensuous arabesques and exotic scales of the East. Nor did Tchaikovsky make any effort to illumine the subject more deeply, or outline the participants with any precision. In 'As they reiterated: "Fool!"' (No. 6) he was able to embrace far more easily the Russian folk character prompted by this narration of a drunken peasant who, having been repeatedly counselled to substitute water for wine to be rid of his drunkenness, goes to the river and asks whether its waters have the power to deliver him from his weakness.

Ex. 102

a. Andante semplice

p

Ya s neyu nikogda ne govo-

[I never spoke with her, yet

cresc.

- ril,   no ya iskal   povsyudu s neyu vstrechi;   bled - ne - ya   i drozha

everywhere I sought to meet her; pale and trembling, I followed her.]

pp

za ney sledil.   *espress.*

mf

b.   [Andante semplice] Poco più mosso

sempre f

moy   i – de – al,   ot – ra – du   i   muchen – ye,   moy   i – de – al, ot – ra –

cresc.

ff

[my ideal, delight and torment!]

Indeed they have a far more final solution to offer than that envisaged by the peasant's associates! But Tchaikovsky missed this irony when he neatly parcelled his rumbustious Russian phrases into a ternary-structured drinking song. Balakirev was to set the same text and perceive its meaning more deeply; one can only speculate upon what Musorgsky might have made of it.

There is nothing to explain why Tchaikovsky, having discharged his obligation to Bessel, should have promptly launched into a set of songs for Jurgenson. It may have been financial considerations, or perhaps Jurgenson simply saw what was being prepared for a rival and wanted some for himself. This seems highly probable, for he was prepared to give Tchaikovsky for each set of songs twice the 150 roubles paid by Bessel for his single set. Equally it may have been that Tchaikovsky sensed within himself a growing command of the possibilities of the form.

Certainly the first of these two Jurgenson sets shows a more consistent assurance than any of Tchaikovsky's three earlier collections. The stock procedures of the formula romance are less obtrusive (for instance, none of these six songs employs identical piano preludes and postludes), though they never disappear completely. Tchaikovsky had attempted once before to set the text of his first song, 'At bedtime', in a part-song of his early student days, and while he had not, of course, been capable of such things as the best of this song reveals (notably the beautiful opening), he had actually sustained his quality better in the earlier composition. 'Look, yonder cloud' (No. 2) is one of those songs in which Tchaikovsky employed very extensively a single brief thematic idea, pairing a $\frac{9}{8}$ section with another independent one in $\frac{3}{4}$, thus simultaneously broadening the field of experience and preventing the repetitions of the basic thematic unit from linking into a chain that might finally constrict the expressive world too tightly. 'Do not leave me' (No. 3) is more conventional, a tuneful ternary piece composed mainly in three-bar phrases, the more touching because there is no overburdening of the texture or of the expression, no posturing that would impose upon the slender material an expressive duty beyond its strength. 'Evening' (No. 4) is more appealing still. The Ukrainian Shevchenko's picture (in Mey's translation) of village life at the close of the day, with the girls returning home to their families as darkness gathers and the nightingale sings, obviously stirred Tchaikovsky deeply, and the simple declamation above an accompaniment, which, with the finest tact, pictures any detail upon which it can fasten, is touchingly direct. Beetles buzz gently in bar three of Ex. 103, and the maidens hasten homewards in bars ten to fourteen; rarely did Tchaikovsky succeed in incorporating quiet pictorialism so naturally into his music. The middle of this ternary song is, sadly, less fine, for the flow of distinctive detail in the accompaniment of the opening section falters, yielding to more conventional ornamentation, but the end is as lovely as the beginning, with the nightingale's flutings delicately gracing the last bars. 'Evening' is a charming creation, perhaps the most attractive of all these songs of 1875.

The last two numbers of Op. 27 are extensive dance songs, treating translations by Mey of poems by Mickiewicz which prompted Tchaikovsky, like Glinka before him, to adopt a mazurka metre in

Ex. 103

[A cherry orchard beside a cottage; beetles buzz above the cherry trees; the ploughmen draw the plough from the cornfield; and the singing girls hurry home for the evening.]

vishnya - mi gudyat; plug s ni - vï pa - kha - ri tash - chat;

poco più **f** **p**

i, raspe - va - yu - chi, devcha - tï do - moy na

vecheryu speshat.

p

sem . ya ikh

tribute to the poet's nationality. 'Was it the mother who bore me?' (No. 5), Mickiewicz's description of a tearful maiden agitatedly anticipating her beloved's return from the army, drew as straightforward and vigorous a treatment as did 'My spoiled darling' (No. 6), in which the

Russian composer seems to turn his mazurka into a waltz to catch all the gaiety of the young man's feelings as he gazes upon his sweetheart whom he longs to 'kiss, kiss, kiss all my life'.

The creative momentum, that had carried Tchaikovsky so creditably through his last set of songs, clearly slackened while he was compiling his second Jurgenson collection, Op. 28. One song, 'The corals' (No. 2), is outstanding, since the challenge and stimulus of a new type of subject – for Mey's translation from the Polish of Kondratowicz was a noble ballad that demanded an epic response – clearly roused Tchaikovsky's flagging inspiration. In fact, the first song of the set, 'No, I shall never tell', is also good. Something of the precision and refinement of 'Evening' lingers in the vocal opening, and though once again the identical prelude and postlude are in evidence, they have no part in the song itself, indicating, rather, through their melancholy, the forlorn state of the lover who would sooner die than confess his beloved's name, and whose tremulously agitated plaint is the subject of Grekov's translation from the French of de Musset. Here is another song containing hints of Tatyana's musical world in *Eugene Onegin*. They can be heard also in the equally lovelorn, but far more ordinary 'Why did I dream of you?' (No. 3), another of those romances that takes a single melodic phrase and builds largely from this. Once again features of the formula romance are strongly in evidence. 'He loved me so much' (No. 4) is rather better, for its melodic content is stronger and less constricted. Despite Tchaikovsky's own assertion that the text was by Apukhtin, there is some question hanging over its authorship. There is no doubt, however, that Apukhtin wrote the words of 'No response, or word, or greeting' (No. 5). It is sad that Tchaikovsky did not respond more fruitfully to his friend's text, for the endless 'dominant-into-tonic' type of progression and the prosaic melodic material make this the weakest song of Op. 28. Tchaikovsky was his own poet for the last song, 'The fearful minute'. Again he seems to probe towards Tatyana's musical world in this anguished address of a lover awaiting the fateful decision of the loved one. Less impoverished melodically than the preceding song, it nevertheless locks its passions within the more regular phrases, plainer harmonies and more measured accompaniments of the conventional romance.

'The corals' (No. 2) is a very different matter. It narrates a simple story: a young Cossack goes away to war bearing with him the prayers of his beloved and her enjoinder to bring her a string of corals on his return. After victory he seeks for the corals which are miraculously revealed to him. Hastily turning his steed homewards, he finds his beloved dead, and, grief-stricken, hangs the corals in tribute upon the frame of an ikon. There was no place here for the soft pleasantries of the drawing-room, and Tchaikovsky's music aligns itself squarely with that heroic strand which, like so much else in his Russian musical environment, owed its origins to Glinka's cornucopean score of *Ruslan*. Battle and horse-ride are graphically represented, but the deepest impression is created by the noble dignity of the remainder, dominated by the opening phrase (Ex. 104) that is as laconic as it is lapidary. This phrase represents the fateful corals, and it recurs in the centre as the warrior's thoughts return after battle to his quest, later erupting as he hears of his beloved's death, and flickering out in the very last bars.

Ex. 104

[As I went off with the Cossacks,

Hannah said: 'I have prayed to God with tears for you.']

This ballad is a powerful rejoinder to any who would assert that Tchaikovsky was incapable of music that was truly masculine.

Nevertheless 'The corals' is a solitary among these eighteen songs. Despite Tchaikovsky's defiance of Rubinstein's critical onslaught on his new piano concerto, his faith in the quality of his own self-declarations was badly bruised, and the impassioned sentimentality in so many of these other verses permitted him for a period to channel his personal feelings vicariously through the ecstasies and sufferings of his poetic subjects.

Yet it was characteristic of the man that, whatever his own troubles, he should still find time to exert himself on behalf of those dear to him who needed help. Modest was embarking upon a subsidiary career as a journalist in St Petersburg and was suffering a bout of self-doubt. As usual brother Pyotr proved a source of sound moral support. 'Perhaps you haven't a first-class talent [for writing], but you have a positive aptitude, taste, and you have that *understanding* which Laroche so values in you. *Understanding* is a great thing; sometimes very intelligent people lack it. Because of this understanding you will never write anything cheap or anything *false*.'[15]

If, by this, he helped Modest ease his anxieties (though within a month the ungrateful twin, evidently suspecting in his brother a preference for Anatoly, was reproaching him for indifference), he was also active in aiding Laroche, who was in a particularly distressing predicament. Anastasya, his wife, was dying of consumption. As a last resort he had taken her in January to the mineral springs at Aachen, leaving their young family in St Petersburg. Tchaikovsky well understood the misery this caused, and he played some small part in making arrangements for one of their children to travel to the West to bring comfort to the mother. Anastasya died in May; two months earlier Tchaikovsky had been even more grieved by the sudden death in Austria of Ferdinand Laub, his Conservatoire colleague who had led in the first performances of both his string quartets. A year hence Tchaikovsky was to compose his third and last quartet as a tribute to this violinist whose artistry he had so much admired.

It had been Tchaikovsky's intention to begin the summer with a short trip abroad, though his lack of funds quickly forced him to postpone this project until the end of the year. On 16 May *The Oprichnik* was first heard in Moscow, and this made him the more restless for term to end so that he might flee the city. In early April he had received an invitation from Olga, Nikolay's wife, to pass the summer with them at their home near Kharkov. It seems his brother had been upset that

[15] *TLP*5, p. 394; *TPR*, p. 216; *TPB*, p. 97.

Tchaikovsky had not visited them the previous summer when he had been in the vicinity. Conscience-stricken, Tchaikovsky determined to redeem himself in the company of the twins, but for a second year he defaulted, and when he left Moscow at the beginning of June, it was to Usovo that he directed himself. As he was about to leave he received an invitation from the Imperial Theatres to provide the music for a ballet, *Swan Lake*, for which he would be paid 800 roubles. Composition of this had, however, to wait upon other matters. After arriving at Shilovsky's estate he had first to finish the vocal score of *Vakula*; then, on 17 June, he set about a new symphony. Remembering how thriftily he had disposed his time when working on *Vakula* the previous year, he had no intention of so immersing himself in composition that he could not enjoy what Shilovsky's home had to offer. 'I've been at Usovo more than three weeks already,' he wrote on 1 July to the Sofronov brothers, who still divided between themselves the rôle of being his valet, 'and I'm spending the time quietly and pleasantly. Prince Vasily Golitsïn is staying here as well as me, and we're not bored. Every morning I have a bath in water from the well. Alexey, they've now built a splendid bath house here alongside the stables, and yesterday we steamed ourselves in it.... I'm now composing a new symphony, and I'm doing a bit at a time. I don't sit over it for hours on end, and I'm walking more.... Nothing's changed here. Even the dogs are the same, and they chase after me to have a walk.'[16] Despite his economical hours of work, the composition of the symphony had been finished by the time he left Usovo a day or two later, and the scoring was already begun.

From Usovo Tchaikovsky journeyed to Nizy, arriving there after a couple of days in Moscow. During his ten days at Kondratyev's estate he finished scoring the last two movements of the new symphony. Then, after some five more days in Moscow and three in Kiev, he reached Verbovka, another of the Davïdov estates close to Kamenka. While Lev managed the Kamenka estate for two elder brothers, Verbovka was his own property, bought in 1870, and it was here that Sasha and her family were spending the summer, together with Ilya Petrovich and Anatoly. Tchaikovsky was much drawn to Verbovka, especially with so many of his family around him.

On 13 August, a fortnight after his arrival, the symphony was finished. Yet his creative energies were far from spent, and with a month of the summer break still remaining, he had no intention of sinking into inactivity. Thus he promptly set about the new ballet. Kashkin, who was to make the piano score of the work, recollected that

[16] *TLP*5, p. 406.

Tchaikovsky had already composed Act 1 by the previous June, but clearly his memory deceived him in this. Yet one cannot but wonder whether Tchaikovsky had indeed done some preliminary work on it, for within a fortnight of completing the symphony, the music for the first two acts was certainly sketched. 'You see, I haven't been idle!' he wrote with some satisfaction to Taneyev on 26 August. 'However, I'm now experiencing some fatigue, and as from yesterday I'm giving myself a real holiday until I'm back in Moscow. I don't want even to think about music until then.'[17]

Altogether he spent about a month at Sasha's before making his last trip of the summer: a second call at Usovo. Because of bad railway connections the journey took nearly six days – or so a very disgruntled Tchaikovsky informed Lev Davïdov on 11 September. The dying summer, too, was giving him less cause for joy. 'The weather here [at Usovo] is filthy, and quite as cold as November. I spend the entire day picking mushrooms, of which a great number grow here.'[18] A day or two later he was back in Moscow to begin his winter chores.

After hearing his new work conducted by Nikolay Rubinstein at an RMS concert in Moscow on 19 November 1875, Tchaikovsky delivered his verdict upon it to Rimsky-Korsakov. 'As far as I can see this symphony presents no particularly successful ideas, but in workmanship it's a step forward,' he wrote,[19] adding, however, a less well-founded judgement on the relative merits of the five movements: 'I'm satisfied above all with the first movement and the two scherzos.' There can be no doubt that Nikolay Rubinstein's strictures on his most recent symphonic work, the First Piano Concerto, still rang in his ears, and he was determined that this new piece should not be open to charges of technical or structural inelegance, let alone incompetence. To this end he admitted to his compositional processes a fair measure of that studied neo-classicism which had most recently been directed into the Second String Quartet. The finale, indeed, is exactly of that work's world. Why Tchaikovsky should have begun his scoring operation with this movement is not known,[20] but music as bluff and uncharacterised as this required no critical decisions on matters of instrumental colour, and the orchestration, like the music itself, is thoroughly competent and equally unremarkable. The polonaise-mannered refrain of this rondo movement is partnered by two episodic themes, the first a

[17] *TLP*5, p. 410; *TTP*, p. 6; *YDGC*, p. 119 (partial).
[18] *TLP*5, p. 411; *TPR*, p. 222.
[19] *TLP*5, p. 417; *TZC*1, p. 271; *DTC*, p. 362; *YDGC*, p. 120.
[20] The score indicates the date upon which the scoring of each movement was completed. Finale, 21 July; fourth movement, 25 July; first movement, 7 August; second movement, 9 August; third movement, 12 August.

particularly dreary tune which recurs, after an arid fugato, to usher in the badly overblown coda. It was the 'tempo di Polacca' direction at the head of this finale that caused this symphony to be dubbed the 'Polish', a nickname quite inept for the remainder of the piece, and which appears to have originated in England with Sir August Manns, who conducted the Crystal Palace concerts.

The movement that opens the symphony is far more interesting, though its development succumbs to that same rhythmic turgidity and contrapuntal pedantry that weighs so heavily on the finale. Curiously it inherits from the First Piano Concerto not only the 'Artôt contour' but also the thrice-stated 'Tchaikovsky contour', though in this symphony their locations are exactly reversed, the former opening the slow introduction, the latter launching the first of the two themes that comprise the second subject (see Vol. I, Ex. 39e and f). This time there was to be no doubt about the rôle of the opening section, and the dominant pedal which, from the very first note, underlies this marcia funebre ensures that beneath the stately procession of halting phrases there lies a tension that constantly proclaims the introductory function of this extensive section. The progressive, if unsystematic evolution of the opening theme towards the first subject (Ex. 105) is yet another distant manifestation of the *Kamarinskaya* principle of thematic metamorphosis. All is held on a tight rein: all might be considered 'correct' in intention and founded upon honourable precedent, even to the poco a poco accelerando through which this massive dominant preparation finds release into the tonic of the Allegro brillante first subject.

Ex. 105

Fortunately the stiff formality of the introduction is balanced by a considerable rhythmic variety within the phrase structures. With the first subject, however, there is straightway a brief taste of that rhythmic constriction that is to cripple the finale, though, for the moment, it is largely held in check. While the first subject follows Tchaikovsky's now familiar pattern of two tonic statements of the main theme flanking a modulatory centre, the quasi-developmental tendencies of earlier examples are significantly curbed; such things were to be kept for their proper place, the development itself. As in *The Storm*, *Romeo and Juliet*, and the recent piano concerto, the exposition has three principal themes, but the last two are in no way intertwined to provide the second subject; instead, stated separately and further segregated by tonal differentiation, they make what amounts to an exposition of three subjects deployed in the tonic, relative minor and dominant respectively, the last prepared by a particularly sparkling passage over a dominant pedal. Doubtless Tchaikovsky looked upon the clear outlines and clear-headed organisation of this exposition with some pride, and he was to take up again this three-stage structure and evolve it with momentous consequences in his next, and greater symphony.

It is with the development that creative paralysis creeps in. Discipline of expression, thematic concentration, and a good measure of musical intellect are admirable qualities in a development, but Tchaikovsky's dogged pursuit of what he fondly imagined was proper developmental technique turns discipline into repression, concentration into constriction, and lively intellect into arid pedantry. It was doubtless the example of his favourite Schumann symphony, the 'Rhenish', that suggested to Tchaikovsky his five-movement structure, and in this development he was probably also modelling himself upon what he thought Schumann might have done if he had been composing the symphony. Had Tchaikovsky continued as he began – that is, by his already familiar procedure of neatly combining different thematic fragments – and had he then permitted his inventiveness to range over a wider field, a tolerable development might have resulted. Unfortunately his search for concentration led him to fasten upon the four-note figure *a* in the last two bars of Ex. 105d, a disastrous choice for the swift series of stretto entries which he now planned, for the complete lack of rhythmic variety and absence of any defined character in this melodic fragment could produce only pages of faceless and stodgy music, made even less bearable by Tchaikovsky's practice of stating twice over sections that were already tediously repetitive. Neither the use of this same figure in diminution, nor the addition of a similar stretto treatment of the first subject's opening could do much to alleviate the monotony of this stretch of the movement, with its seemingly endless crotchet plod.

Except for a generous expansion of the flat-keyed section between the second and third themes, much of the recapitulation is about as literal as may be, with a neat amalgamation of the figuration from the first subject's central section with the second subject; it is thus that Tchaikovsky short-circuits the restatement of the first subject, slipping in the oboe theme, which in the exposition had introduced the second subject in B minor, but which is now set in E minor to direct the recapitulation towards its expected tonic conclusion. The resurgence, in the coda, of the development's rhythmic tedium, coupled with a predictable dynamic inflation, leaves the listener with a final memory of the movement's more sterile features rather than of the attractive, if less than first-rate fare of much of the main material.

After the degree of fabrication in the first movement, the second (titled *Alla tedesca*, but really as much a waltz as anything Tchaikovsky so labelled) sounds particularly fresh. Feeling no other obligation than to carry this movement on a stream of melody (though the bassoon counter-melody that enters in bar eleven reminds us how attractive Tchaikovsky's counterpoint can be when allowed to be its own decorative self), he is at his most relaxed and winning, thinking almost entirely in four-bar phrases, yet avoiding completely that leaden four-square regularity which had already choked the first movement, and which is to spell death to the finale. Nothing demonstrates more clearly a composer's melodic strength than his final phrases, and the end of the first main section of this movement bears eloquent testimony to Tchaikovsky's mastery in such matters. Here, with the infiltration into the melody of the duple-time structure that had abruptly taken control of the harmonic rhythm in the preceding four bars (see bars 1–4 of Ex. 106b), the phrase slips out of the four-bar periods that had characterised the movement to this point, spreading itself instead over an integral span of nine bars, and finally permitting the figure that had formed the first half of the movement's much-heard opening phrase (Ex. 106a, bars 3–4) to discharge the natural cadential function that had been so long denied it, thus closing the entire section. Equally felicitous is the expansion, at the very end of the movement, of this little two-bar fragment into an eight-bar cadential phrase (Ex. 106c), internally subdivided into a 3 + 3 + 2-bar structure.

The trio of this movement finds Tchaikovsky devising material less notable for its musical substance than for its potential for attractively displaying orchestral colour. Even more designed for such use is the

fourth movement, the officially designated scherzo that draws upon
material from the prelude of the Peter the Great bi-centenary cantata
for its trio. This movement is easily under-rated, as Cui's verdict (it
'offers interest only as sound almost devoid of musical content'[21])
shows, for the swift kaleidoscopic undulations of rapidly alternating
string and wind scamperings with which it begins merely set the
background against which Tchaikovsky is to place a succession of

Ex. 106

[21] *DTC*, p. 363; *YDGC*, p. 124; *TZC*1, p. 481.

melodic fragments, neat but unselfconscious in their inter-relationships, and through which the movement gathers substance. The presence of the whole-tone scale in two passages confirms the impression gathered from the fleeting, sharp-coloured sounds, pert rhythms, and nicely spiced harmonies, that it is from the magic idiom of *Ruslan* (softened a little, perhaps, by Mendelssohn's fairies), and more specifically from Naina's world, that this movement really springs, though Tchaikovsky's invention owes no particular debt to any single feature of that enchantress's music. Tchaikovsky could not have borrowed more happily for the trio, for the held horn D seems specially designed to sustain those signs of Russian musical sorcery that the first section has so deftly exhibited, while the crisp melodic phrase, which, thrown about amongst the orchestra, is the whole basis of this central section, is always bound to whatever is harmonically compatible with this note, despite the phrase's determination to investigate as wide a range of harmonic regions as it may. This phrase is able to resurge in the movement's own coda and share in tying the final knots in this web of enchantment. Immensely elaborated, this delicate interplay of orchestral colours spun out upon a light skein of fleeting melodic fragments was to conjure the vision of the Alpine fairy flickering in the waterfall in the Manfred Symphony.

As beautiful, in a very different way, is the central slow movement. One cannot but wonder, remembering how *The Tempest* had been composed two years before in the idyllic conditions of Usovo, whether it was again the spell of Shilovsky's estate, coupled with the memory of the earlier work created there, that accounts for much of the character of this piece. Andante elegiaco it may be marked, but there is nothing funereal in this lovely music, though its darker tints might readily be thought nocturnal. The opening breathes a pastoral charm (is it entirely coincidence that the initial melodic fragment seems to echo the first phrase of the *Scène aux champs* from Berlioz's Symphonie Fantastique? (Ex. 107)), with birdsong surely prompting the little drooping-third figure that first enters in bar seventeen as part of a procession of thematic ideas that might be an anthology of those 'indistinguishable sounds of the night' that Tchaikovsky remembered so clearly from his evenings as Usovo two years earlier, here caught into phrases of much charm. Even more is that summer interlude of 1873 recalled when the main theme of the movement arrives, for this generous string passage grows straight from the lovers' music of *The Tempest*, touched neither with the indulgent languor nor with the unbridled ardour of Tchaikovsky's earlier Shakespearean lovers, but diffusing a simpler, chaster warmth that contrasts movingly with the lighter matters treated in the

Ex. 107

a.

b.

scherzos that flank this movement. Though less wide-ranging and
precipitate than Miranda's and Ferdinand's exploration of the realms
of passion, it nevertheless grows in richness, and the end is ravishing,
never more so than in the lingering cadence (see bars 4–6 of Ex. 108)
that precedes the final dozen bars that wind down the section – a
cadence which, exactly like the equally delectable end of the *Alla
tedesca*'s first section (see Ex. 106b), briefly infects the triple metre with
a duple-time structure. As for the following dozen bars, these are

Ex. 108

pointed with chromatic touches in the inner parts that are as exquisite as any Tchaikovsky ever devised. And if the opening of the movement had hinted at Berlioz's pastoral scene, the end even more seems to recall the conclusion of Beethoven's Scene by the brook in the Pastoral Symphony, where the snippets of birdsong are mingled with a cadential fragment (Ex. 109).

Ex. 109

Whether or not this movement drew its character from the world of Usovo, its natural companion among Tchaikovsky's earlier works is that self-confessed mood picture, 'Land of gloom, land of mists', the slow movement of the First Symphony. Like that impressive piece, it discloses on closer scrutiny that Tchaikovsky had given deeper consideration to the overall effect of the experience than the continuous flow of melody might at first hearing suggest; its totality is far more impressive, for instance, than that of the Second Symphony's slow movement. Indeed, its structure is dependent, at least in part, upon the scherzo that precedes it. For this Tchaikovsky had switched abruptly to the distant key of B flat, and, though the slow movement begins in D minor, the first of the two statements of the huge cantabile string passage, which, between them, are the real pillars of the structure, is set in B flat, thus extending the *Alla tedesca*'s tonal centre further into the heart of the symphony. With the need after this to return to D, there could be no question of simply repeating the pieces of melody that had gathered in the D minor opening, and their new modulatory and tonic-establishing function now admirably reinterprets their character as they ease the movement back to its real tonal centre for the second statement of the entire cantabile paragraph. Yet another haunting view of this patchwork of diverse ideas is provided in the coda. As for the following B minor scherzo, its mercurial keyshifts nicely balance the dislocation of the symphony's basic tonality effected by the earlier spread of B flat-centred music, for it engenders a state of relative tonal flux before the finale finally, and rather grimly, proclaims the tonic. The tonal strategy of the entire symphony shows evidence of careful and resourceful planning.

Of Tchaikovsky's major works to date, the Third Symphony is the most inconsistent and it is, on balance, the least satisfactory of all his symphonies, though not so devoid of 'particularly successful ideas' as the composer's own judgement would have us believe. Caught between the promptings of an uneasy musical conscience driving him towards a music whose diligent mechanisms might readily be recognised as respectable and highly intentioned, and a lyric force that would have him create according simply to his natural inner compulsion untroubled by pressures to create the sort of complex organic experience that lay behond his abilities, he was at least wise enough not to attempt an amalgamation of the two drives, but to allow his natural gift its full unfettered exercise in what he now clearly saw as the more relaxed central area of the symphony, reserving the laborious tussle with more weighty matters for the outer movements. Even more than the Second Quartet, the Third Symphony discloses the widening dichotomy within Tchaikovsky's style, and powerfully proclaims the musical tensions that matched those within the man himself. It could not have been more fortunate that the next work that was required of him was one in which those qualities so freely paraded in the splendid central movements of this symphony would be in demand to an even greater extent. When, immediately on completing the symphony, Tchaikovsky set about *Swan Lake*, the auguries for success were good.

2

THIRD QUARTET AND
SWAN LAKE

WHEN IN 1836 *A Life for the Tsar* was first produced, the composer was singularly fortunate in the 30-year-old singer who filled the hero's rôle. Six years later the same baritone, Osip Petrov, was to personate Ruslan in Glinka's second opera. This time he was less successful, but Susanin's part he made very much his own, and on that momentous night in 1850 when the 10-year-old Tchaikovsky had sat in the Alexandrinsky Theatre to experience for the first time the magic world of opera as exemplified in Glinka's first major work, it was the original Susanin who was yet again singing that rôle. Even by that time Petrov had some quarter of a century of professional life to his credit, and he had a further 28 years before him, remaining an honoured member of the Imperial Opera until his death in 1878. Many composers besides Glinka had cause to be grateful to him. For Dargomïzhsky he created the Miller in *Rusalka*, and Leporello in the posthumous first perform-ance of *The Stone Guest*; for Serov he created Oziya in *Judith* and Vladimir in *Rogneda*, for Rimsky-Korsakov Ivan the Terrible in *The Maid of Pskov*, for Musorgsky Varlaam in *Boris Godunov*. It was the enduring artistry of this 67-year-old singer that prompted Musorgsky to start upon *Sorochintsy Fair* in 1874; equally it was Petrov's death four years later that caused him to lose interest in this opera.

Tchaikovsky, too, was to benefit from his services, for it was Petrov who created the part of the Mayor when *Vakula the Smith* was first heard. Earlier in that same year, 1876, had occurred the fiftieth anniversary of Petrov's début, and Lyudmila Shestakova, Glinka's sister, instigated a grand celebration of this jubilee of the man who had not merely served her brother's cause so magnificently, but who had (to use Musorgsky's words) been 'the Titan who had borne upon his Homeric shoulders almost the whole of our dramatic music'.[1] On 3 May Petrov appeared yet again as that Glinka peasant hero whom he had first made

[1] Letter of 28 October 1874. Quoted in M. P. Musorgsky, *Pis'ma*, ed. E. Gordeyeva (Moscow, 1981), p. 149.

incarnate 40 years before, and three days later the RMS arranged at the St Petersburg Conservatoire a festival concert for which Tchaikovsky composed a special cantata. The great virtue of this occasional piece, especially when set beside its predecessors, the graduation cantata of 1865 and the Peter the Great bi-centenary cantata of 1872, is its brevity. No more than a single movement for solo mezzo-soprano, chorus and orchestra, this modestly tuneful tribute must have touched the great veteran whose voice 'embodying Russian art in sounds of passion, of beauty, of life' still brought 'love, zeal, and creative feeling to the altar of that art', as Nekrasov expressed it in the text he provided for Tchaikovsky's musical eulogy.

In Tchaikovsky's own life also there was a good deal to celebrate this winter. As he returned to Moscow from Usovo in mid-September Jurgenson issued a piano-duet arrangement of the Second Quartet, to be followed a month later by the printed parts both of this work and of the new piano concerto. Tchaikovsky's return also found Taneyev working hard at the solo part of the latter which he was to introduce to Moscow some ten weeks later. Tchaikovsky, greatly heartened by the zeal with which his young friend was preparing the piece, set about grooming the performance assiduously. 'I see Taneyev a lot,' he told Modest on 26 September. 'If only you knew how magnificently he is playing my concerto!'[2] The final result of these labours, heard on 3 December, did much to efface the sour impression left by Kross and Nápravník's St Petersburg performance three weeks earlier. Tchaikovsky had gone to the capital for this Russian première, where it is possible that his chagrin at the concerto's presentation was offset at least a little by the receipt of the 1500 roubles of prize money for his *Vakula*, which had just been nominated the winner in the opera competition.

Rushing back to Moscow, he sped straight from the railway station to a rehearsal of the new Third Symphony. The arrangements for preparing this work left him discontented, and there were some evident shortcomings in the performance that followed a few days later. In particular the exacting fourth movement 'was played far from as well as it could have been, had there been more rehearsals. The point is that our rehearsals last in all two hours. Admittedly there are three of them, but what can you do in two hours? However, I was generally satisfied with the performance,' he reported to Rimsky-Korsakov.[3] He was feeling particularly warm towards this composer, for the latter had deferentially sought his advice on his own efforts to broaden his

[2] *TLP*5, p. 414; *TPR*, p. 222; *TZC*1, p. 469; *DTC*, p. 443; *TPB*, p. 99; *YDGC*, p. 119.
[3] *TLP*5, p. 417; *TZC*1, p. 271; *DTC*, p. 362.

compositional technique. To this end Rimsky-Korsakov had spent the summer working on a mass of contrapuntal exercises: now he turned to Tchaikovsky for comment. In particular there were ten pieces in Bach style 'which I should very much like to show you so that you may tell me what you think of them, and make detailed comments'.[4] Public tributes to one's own works were delightful to the self-esteem, and Tchaikovsky had good cause to feel pleased with the reception of the new symphony. 'In particular the middle movements, and above all the Andante, drew sustained applause and evident satisfaction from the audience,' the correspondent of the *Moscow Gazette* reported.[5] But could such admiring plaudits really match a request for professional guidance from a fellow-composer, already established as one of the finest in Russia, with a formidable list of works to his credit? It was perhaps the sincerest and deepest compliment Tchaikovsky had ever received, and there is no mistaking the profound pleasure in the tone of the reply he hastened to send Rimsky-Korsakov:

You know, I simply prostrate myself reverentially in the face of your noble artistic modesty and astonishing strength of character. All these innumerable contrapuntal exercises that you've done, these sixty fugues and multitude of other pieces of stunning musical craft – all this is such an extraordinary feat from the man who wrote *Sadko* a full eight years ago, that I want to trumpet it to the whole world. I'm dumbfounded, and I don't know how to express my boundless esteem for your artistic personality. How slight, pale, complacently naive do I seem to be, when I compare myself with you.... I am indeed convinced that, with your great gift joined to that faultless conscientiousness with which you apply yourself to your task, there must come from your pen works that will leave far behind them everything that has been written in Russia to date.

I shall await the arrival of your ten fugues with the utmost impatience.... When I've looked them over carefully, I'll write you my very detailed opinion.[6]

Refreshed by the break from work that he had imposed upon himself at Usovo, Tchaikovsky promptly took up *Swan Lake* again on being back in Moscow. If we may judge from the affable account of his social and domestic life given to Modest a fortnight after his return, he had settled into his old routine cheerfully enough, and had been able to

[4] *TLP*5, p. 413.
[5] *TZC*1, p. 470.
[6] *TLP*5, p. 412; *TZC*1, pp. 467–8.

move to a better flat. Otherwise everything was as before – including his bitch, Bishka, to whose habit of periodically presenting him with six puppies he jokingly attributed his own practice of writing romances or piano pieces likewise in groups of six. Two months later he was still working diligently at the ballet, for he wished to finish it as soon as possible so that he might set about an opera.

Earlier in the year the other Shilovsky brother, Konstantin, had offered him a scenario, *Empress against her will*, which Tchaikovksy had with firmness but kindness rejected. Instead he suggested to Shilovsky that the latter should attempt an Egyptian subject, 'Joseph of the coat of many colours at Pharaoh's, or something of that sort'.[7] The fruit of this seems to have been *Ephraim*, a story related to the tale of Joseph and Potiphar's wife. Two other subjects are known to have caught Tchaikovsky's attention towards the end of 1875: *Francesca da Rimini*, to a libretto by Konstantin Zvantsev, and *Constantia*, upon which Modest was soon furiously drafting a scenario for his brother's perusal. Of these three possibilities, Modest's medieval concoction seems the most likely to have been attracting Tchaikovsky at this moment, but the proposed opera came to nothing. His interest in the other two subjects was to revive the next year, and *Francesca da Rimini* was ultimately to be embodied in an orchestral piece.

By now the toil of Tchaikovsky's onerous journalistic commitments had become quite intolerable, and before the end of the year he had made his last regular contribution to the *Russian Gazette*; there only remained the provision of five notices connected with the first-ever cycle of Wagner's *Der Ring des Nibelungen* at the opening of the Festspielhaus at Bayreuth in 1876. In partial preparation for this, Tchaikovsky was able to attend a small informal gathering in November at Klindworth's home. Because of his unique position as the man to whom Wagner had entrusted the preparation of vocal scores of his operas, Klindworth was able to give his Moscow colleagues a rare foretaste of Wagner's tetralogy, and he much impressed them all with his pianistic command of Wagner's elaborate textures. Tchaikovsky left no record of his own reactions to Wagner's music on this occasion, but he doubtless found little pleasure in it, certainly not as much as he gained from the visiting French composer whose Moscow début was among the subjects treated in his very last column as a regular music critic.

Camille Saint-Saëns already had one direct link with the Russian musical world, for when he had played the solo part in the first performance of his own Second Piano Concerto in Paris in 1868, the

[7] *TLP*5, p. 429.

conductor had been Anton Rubinstein. Saint-Saëns' first Moscow concert was on 13 December 1875, when he included his recent two-piano Variations on a theme of Beethoven, with Nikolay Rubinstein as his partner. Tchaikovsky was much taken with this piece, as also with the equally new *Danse macabre* heard at a special RMS charity concert five days later. He liked, too, the Third Piano Concerto which Saint-Saëns himself played, but was less enthusiastic about *Le Rouet d'Omphale*.

The composer himself he found as congenial as his music. Together they attended a performance of Gounod's *Faust*, an occasion which provided Tchaikovsky with the opportunity to deliver a last critical broadside at his old adversary, the Italian opera company that had so often provoked him to despairing anger. 'Possessing a touch of that individuality which Pyotr Ilich always found attractive in people, and also a certain knack for instant friendship ... he [Saint-Saëns] straightway charmed Pyotr Ilich and became very close to him – so close that our composer at that time saw in this friendliness something that must have significance in the future,' recorded Modest.[8] So quickly were the barriers broken between them that Tchaikovsky was moved to participate in some impromptu clowning with his new French friend. 'As young men,' Modest continued, 'both had not only been very attracted to the ballet, but had also some natural skill for that sort of dancing. And so once, wishing to show off their art to each other, they performed on the stage of the Conservatoire's hall an entire little ballet, *Galatea and Pygmalion*. The 40-year-old Saint-Saëns was Galatea, and performed the rôle of the statue with remarkable assiduity, and the 35-year-old Tchaikovsky took upon himself the part of Pygmalion. Nikolay Rubinstein provided the orchestra.'[9] It seems sad that there were no actual witnesses of this spectacle.

Tchaikovsky's hopes that his friendship with Saint-Saëns might bear fruit in the future were disappointed. Less than three months later Modest met Saint-Saëns in Lyon and attempted to further his brother's fortunes by demanding of the French composer when he was going to perform *Romeo and Juliet*. It is apparent that Saint-Saëns had agreed to do this service for Tchaikovsky, but to Modest he was now evasive. Tchaikovsky himself, for all his concern to cultivate the interests of his own works, was deeply embarrassed by Modest's blunt approach. 'Why, he might believe that I'm dying of a passionate wish to be *played* in Paris. Even assuming that this is in fact true, Saint-Saëns must in no way come to know of it,' he rebuked his brother.[10] There seems to have

[8] *TZC*1, pp. 473–4.   [9] *TZC*1, p. 474.
[10] *TLP*6, p. 33; *TPR*, p. 234; *TZC*1, p. 485; *TPB*, p. 107.

been more than is immediately apparent in this reluctance to pursue that connection with Saint-Saëns which had begun with such outward ease and cordiality in Moscow, for Tchaikovsky deliberately avoided meeting the Frenchman when he himself was in Paris only a month later. Thus their relationship rapidly atrophied. 'When, some long time afterwards, they met again, they were as strangers, and such they always remained,' Modest concluded.[11]

Tchaikovsky's spirits seem to have been good as 1875 drew to its close. For the past three years it had been the custom of the conservatoire members to celebrate their director's name-day, 18 December, and this year Weber's *Der Freischütz* was mounted by the students in Nikolay Rubinstein's honour, the performance being followed by a supper and dance. Tchaikovsky threw himself so actively into the more athletic part of the evening that the following morning he was ill. Four days later Artôt reappeared in Meyerbeer's *Les Huguenots* at the Bolshoy. She had put on weight dreadfully and her voice had faded, but her artistry still sufficed to win her a rapturous reception, not least from her former suitor. It was the same when he heard her sing Amneris in Verdi's *Aida* some two months later.

At some point during 1875 Tchaikovsky had himself made a small contribution to the operatic life of Moscow by translating, at Nikolay Rubinstein's request, da Ponte's libretto to Mozart's *Le nozze di Figaro*. He had rewritten the recitatives, not hesitating to make adjustments to suit Russian singers, and excising the more scabrous passages. The finished work was to be first heard on 17 May 1876 performed by students of the Conservatoire. During December 1875 Tchaikovsky not only composed his tribute to Petrov, but also embarked upon a new set of piano pieces. As we have seen, he had already composed four vocal supplements for the periodical *Nouvelliste*; now its editor, Nikolay Bernard, requested a whole series of twelve piano pieces, each to represent one month of the year and to be published in the appropriate issue. Tchaikovsky set about this commission with some diffidence, fearing that he might not be able to remain simple and brief enough without sliding into banality. With that unusual concern we have already noted in his attitude to other publishers, he instructed Bernard to have no hesitation in requesting revisions if he thought any of the pieces unsuitable for his purpose. As it was, *The Seasons* (as the set is now rather inappropriately called) was to become Tchaikovsky's most famed piano work.

Tchaikovsky spent most of January 1876 outside Russia. Modest, convinced that he would never be good for anything in government

[11] *TZC1*, p. 474.

service, had abandoned this with the intention of becoming tutor to a seven-year-old deaf mute, Nikolay Konradi. Because Modest was quite unequipped for such a responsibility, the boy's father had arranged that the potential tutor should go abroad to Lyon where there was a school that specialised in a method for teaching deaf mutes to talk. There was no particular urgency for Modest to accept the post; in any case, Konradi senior had agreed that Modest should not commit himself to undertake his son's education until he had had some experience of the Lyon establishment. Long before, Tchaikovsky had already agreed to take his younger brother on a trip abroad at this very season, and it was apparent there was still time to carry out this intention before Modest had to proceed to Lyon. Thus, on the very first day of 1876, the brothers left Russia for Western Europe. Modest had never been abroad before, and his own memories of the trip were the happier for the evident delight his elder brother found in observing the novice traveller reacting to new experiences and places. Below Tchaikovsky's outer contentment there had, however, been initially some dejection, as he revealed to the other twin some twelve days later in a letter that also charted the course of their travels:

Don't worry about my melancholia. It's not the first occasion it's descended upon me, and it'll go away just as it's done before. By now I'm almost completely recovered, and I feel very well.... Modest and I travelled to Smolensk and Warsaw. Naturally we were a day and a half late arriving in Berlin. Modest liked Berlin very much, and we stayed there two days. He heard *Les Huguenots*, and in addition we both went to a performance of *Round the world in eighty days*. ... We arrived here [in Geneva] exactly a week after leaving Moscow. Lev [Davïdov] and the girls met us. We had assumed that we would stay in a nearby *hôtel*, but Sasha wouldn't hear of it, and though it's crowded, we're nevertheless lodging here with them. We're passing the time very pleasantly though, apart from two or three strolls around the town, we haven't been out. I don't like Geneva much.... Sasha's put on a bit of weight around the middle [she was, in fact, pregnant], but she's very cheerful and well. The children are as nice as they were in Verbovka. Here [in Geneva], Tanya has lost the air of being an idle miss, and consequently makes a very pleasant impression. *Bebinka* [Vladimir Davïdov] has grown. He tyrannises me and Modest cruelly, and of course we're only too happy to carry out his orders....

On Sunday we're leaving. I want to spend several days in Paris *incognito* – so, Tolya, please don't mention this in musical circles. The point is that I want to have nothing whatsoever to do with music during any of this trip, and in consequence I shan't visit Saint-Saëns, or Viardot, or any such people. Thus these beings mustn't know of my stay in Paris.[12]

Despite his declared intention of avoiding everything musical on this expedition, Tchaikovsky's short stay in the French capital was to afford him one of the most overwhelming musical experiences of his whole life. He and Modest had left Geneva on 15 January; five days later, at the Opéra-Comique, the two brothers saw Bizet's *Carmen*. Among the audience at the very first performance of the opera on 3 March 1875 had been Vladimir Shilovsky, who had been sufficiently impressed to despatch promptly a copy of the work to Tchaikovsky in Russia. Modest declared that never before had he seen his brother so taken by a piece written by a contemporary composer. Yet the deep impression made upon him by Shilovsky's vocal score was as nothing compared to the impact of the work when staged:

> Rarely have I seen my brother so deeply moved by a performance in the theatre. Though he was already familiar with the music of the opera, the fact that this was the occasion when he first became acquainted with the beauties of the scoring explains this [strong reaction]. In addition, Mme Galli-Marié's stunning performance of the part of Carmen proved to be a significant factor in making this impression. As a singer she was not outstanding, for her vocal equipment was far from first-class – but, on the other hand, as an actress she had the most compelling gifts. In her performance, Carmen, while retaining all the vitality of her type, was at the same time shrouded in a certain indescribable magic web of burning, unbridled passion and mystic fatalism.[13]

Recent legend and a touch of the occult seem to have played their part in the spell this opera cast over Tchaikovsky. Bizet had died only seven months before, three months to the day after Célestine Galli-Marié had created the part of Carmen, and the story of how, at the performance on the very eve of Bizet's death, she had been filled with foreboding during the card scene, and had subsequently fainted, had acquired some embroidery by the time it came to Tchaikovsky's ears. 'Pyotr Ilich, I remember,' continued Modest, 'told me at that time that, at the last performance before Bizet's death, Galli-Marié in the

[12] *TLP*5, pp. 427–8; *TPR*, p. 225; *TPB*, pp. 100–1 (lacking first three sentences).
[13] *TZC*1, p. 479.

[fortune-telling] scene actually turned up only spades. Being superstitious, she was so shaken that she was taken ill and couldn't finish the act. After this it seemed that involuntarily, while she was singing the monologue, there floated into her imagination the figure of the master who had perished prematurely – and this, perhaps, made her performance so moving, beautiful, and capable of reducing the audience to tears.'[14] Nevertheless, the profound impression of the music itself remained with him. 'As a matter of fact, I know nothing which in recent years has really seriously captivated me except *Carmen* and Delibes' ballet [*Sylvia*],' he wrote to Nadezhda von Meck on 8 December 1877.[15] 'It's music without pretensions to profundity,' he added a month later, 'but so delightful in its simplicity, so lively (not contrived but sincere) that I got to know it all almost by heart from beginning to end.'[16] Nearly three years later, on 30 July 1880, he elaborated his views:

In my opinion, it [*Carmen*] is a *masterpiece* in the full meaning of the word – that is, one of those rare pieces which are destined to reflect most strongly the musical aspirations of an entire epoch.... It is as though he [Bizet] says to us: 'You don't want anything majestic, heavy and grandiose, you want something *pretty*, and here's a *pretty* opera for you.' And, indeed, I know of no music that would have a stronger claim to be the embodiment of that element which I call *prettiness, le joli*. It's delightful and charming from beginning to end. There's an abundance of piquant harmonies, of completely new combinations of sound – but all this isn't simply an end in itself. Bizet is an artist who pays tribute to our present age, but he is fired with true inspiration. And what a wonderful subject for an opera! I cannot play the last scene without weeping; on the one hand, the people enjoying themselves, and the coarse gaiety of the crowd watching the bullfight, on the other, the dreadful tragedy and death of two of the leading characters whom an evil destiny, *fatum*, has brought together and driven, through a whole series of agonies, to their inescapable end.'[17]

To mark the occasion of his first direct acquaintance with Bizet's masterpiece, Tchaikovsky purchased a picture of the composer and

[14] ibid.

[15] *TPM*1, p. 100; *TZC*2, p. 55. In fact, this phrase was probably not in the original letter (destroyed by Modest), but in a letter to Kashkin of the same date (see *TLP*6, p. 260).

[16] *TPM*1, pp. 137–8; *TLP*6, pp. 330–1; *TZC*2, p. 75.

[17] *TLP*9, pp. 196–7; *TPM*2, pp. 382–3; *YDGC*, p. 237 (partial).

inscribed it with the date of that unforgettable experience. It was, said Modest, *Carmen* which decided his brother that his own next opera was likewise to be on a real-life subject from recent times. Thus it contributed to Tchaikovsky's final choice of Pushkin's *Eugene Onegin* a year later.

Far less pleasurable was the parting from Modest when, two days afterwards, Tchaikovsky quit Paris and headed back towards Russia. Modest was obviously apprehensive, and the elder brother had to administer his usual portion of counsel and moral support. Passing through Cologne, Tchaikovsky arrived in Berlin the next evening, furious to discover that he was too late to hear what promised to be a particularly fine performance of *Lohengrin*. On 26 January he was in St Petersburg where he paused ten days to attend the rehearsals and first performance in the Russian capital of his Third Symphony. During this stay there was serious discussion of a suggestion that he should spend two years abroad. The scheme that would have made this possible stemmed from an idea hatched by the composer, Mikhail Azan-chevsky, who had become director of the St Petersburg Conservatoire in 1871; a fund was to be established that would provide selected medal winners of the Conservatoire with an opportunity to improve their skills abroad. As a medallist himself, Tchaikovsky was eligible for such an award, though it might have been expected that the skill and eminence he had already attained would have placed him above serious consideration. Yet it was clear that he was held to be fully eligible, and was himself very tempted by the prospect. He had shed his musical journalism; now, for a moment, he glimpsed an unexpected avenue of escape from the stifling routine of the Conservatoire into an existence that would permit him not merely to compose at every prompting of his creative forces, but also to bury himself alone whenever he wished by escaping abroad. But he remained divided about it, as he admitted to Modest: 'I both want and fear it [the opportunity], for I nevertheless love holy *Russia terribly*, and fear that I shall pine for her.'[18] Finally, however, no agonising decision was required of him, for the matter was taken no further.

As for the remaining occupations of his stay, he enjoyed a full social life with his friends and family, and was much fussed over by Cui, who invited him and Taneyev, who was also in St Petersburg, to dinner. This wooing seems to have had its ulterior motive. Cui had just written a scathing review of Tchaikovsky's last three sets of songs; now his own opera, *Angelo*, was in rehearsal, and he was doubtless seeking to mollify Tchaikovsky in the hope of a favourable verdict. Two years earlier Cui

[18] *TLP*6, p. 18; *TPR*, p. 228; *TZC*1, p. 481; *TPB*, p. 103; *YDGC*, p. 124.

had played the first act to Tchaikovsky, who had not found it at all to his liking, and it had no greater appeal for him now that he saw it in rehearsal. His own musical fortunes were further advanced during this visit. Besides important discussions on the forthcoming production of *Vakula*, his Second String Quartet was performed at an RMS chamber music evening on 1 February, and four days later the Third Symphony was given. This time he was more than satisfied with Nápravník's conducting; the work 'went off very well and had a considerable success. I was called for and was applauded warmly,' he informed Modest.[19] On 7 February he was back in Moscow. In his luggage was part of a new string quartet which he proposed to dedicate to the memory of Ferdinand Laub.

Tchaikovsky had begun work upon his Third String Quartet in January while in Paris. Like its two predecessors, it was written quickly, and within little more than a month of starting composition, he could report it finished. Its performance, a private one during a soirée at Nikolay Rubinstein's on 14 March, followed barely a fortnight later. The company was enthusiastic, the composer less certain about its merits. 'I think I've rather written myself out,' he declared to Modest the next day. 'I'm beginning to repeat myself, and cannot conceive anything new. Have I really sung my swan song, and have nowhere further to go? It's terribly sad. However, I'll endeavour to write nothing for a bit, but try to recoup my strength.'[20] Exactly two weeks later, on 28 March, the work was heard at a concert arranged at the Conservatoire in honour of the Grand Duke Konstantin Nikolayevich, who was visiting Moscow. Two further fully public performances followed within the next six days. The audiences were much struck by the new piece. 'It pleased everyone *very* much. During the Andante (andante funebre e doloroso) many, so I'm told, were in tears. If this is true, then it's a great triumph,' the composer could now inform Modest more cheerfully on 5 April.[21] Critical reaction, too, was favourable, though Cui was to think the thematic material 'wishy-washy'. Nevertheless, the work continued to make a deep impression, and it is no surprise that, on the composer's own death seventeen years later, it was this elegiac offering to another musician that was chosen as tribute to its own creator in memorial concerts in St Petersburg, Moscow, and Kharkov.

Of the first movements of Tchaikovsky's three string quartets, that of

[19] *TLP*6, p. 20; *TPR*, p. 229; *TZC*1, p. 482; *TPB*, p. 104; *YDGC*, p. 124.
[20] *TLP*6, p. 28, *TPR*, p. 232, *TZC*1, p. 484, *DTC*, p. 496, *TPB*, p. 105; *YDGC*, p. 126 (partial).
[21] *TLP*6 p. 33; *TPR*, p. 235; *TZC*1, p. 485; *DTC*, p. 496; *TPB*, p. 107.

this last one is the finest. More complex and subtle in structure than that of the first, less featureless and fabricated than that of the second, this Allegro moderato is sustained above all on a melodic stream which, for the most part, declares the identity of its composer with clarity. If the main theme of the slow introduction (a section which also turns out to be a frame to the whole movement) seems to spring from the same root as that of the piano concerto's slow movement, the main body of the movement is an immense valse triste of a pervading melancholy that touchingly hallows the memory of Tchaikovsky's departed friend. In part the melodic world of this first movement is that of ballet, never more unmistakably so than in the violin/cello duet that crowns this introduction. Perhaps it would seem, from the very first sounds, that this introduction is to repeat the chromaticism of its predecessor's beginning, but instead the incipient pathos is twice dissolved into a cadence, and the full main theme of this andante sostenuto is adumbrated in ardent fragments. Yet the opening four bars (Ex. 110a) prove to be more than just an affecting opening statement; they have seminal import, for, transformed (Ex. 110b), they usher in the Allegro moderato, their end in bar four remodelled to make the B flat an explicit dominant, not the tonic it had been formerly. Tchaikovsky's varied treatment of this idea – for its shadow falls across a number of contexts in this exposition – is as felicitous as it is resourceful. Its image re-emerges some bars later (Ex. 110c, bars 1–4) with the answering phrase now directed to a dominant conclusion. It appears for the third time in the transition (Ex. 110d), again with the same answering phrase, though where before there had been four-bar phrases, there are now two-bar. Yet again it infiltrates its way into the second subject (Ex. 110e), thus contributing one clearly identifiable factor in that excellent natural balance between thematic variety and kinship that Tchaikovsky achieves in this whole exposition. The exposition's codetta, with its new concluding phrases whispered like precious and intimate afterthoughts, with the cello reluctant to let the final cadence close the exposition, is particularly beautiful (Ex. 111).

Though the development resorts to a good deal of the mechanical repetitiveness of the Second Quartet, it avoids the parsimony of the earlier work, displaying greater, if intermittent inventiveness, especially in the lead back to the recapitulation. Nor does the latter simply repeat the exposition with the minimum of modification. Instead, it breaks the transition to admit a new theme, a peculiarly wistful little 'duple-time waltz' that intrudes initially in the remotest possible key, A major. E flat is firmly restored by the second subject, only to be again subverted, as soon as the recapitulation is done, by the

Ex. 110

pull of brighter sharp-key regions. The home key is proclaimed in the remainder of the extensive coda and conclusively confirmed by the return of the opening andante sostenuto, its course soon adjusted to follow a firm tonic road.

The scherzo is simply a brief, delectable interlude between the weightier utterances of the first movement and the even more burdensome grief of the slow movement. It is a further confirmation of the capacity Tchaikovsky had already displayed in the scherzo of the Third Symphony for devising music that is airy in texture, insubstantial, perhaps, in content, yet sparkling, infectious, and never, it seems, anything but surefooted. Though the very opposite, both in intention

Ex. 111

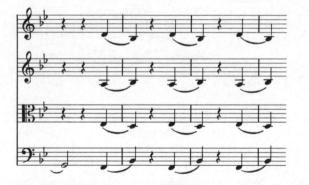

and expressive gravity, of the following slow movement, it is arguably a
better piece. It was this Andante funebre that most fully embodied the
quartet's avowed grief, and its lugubrious rhetoric was not lost on the
first audiences, as we have observed. Regrettably, however, it has more
manner than substance, seeking, even more than the slow movement of
the Second Quartet, to fray the nerves as much as touch the heart. The

opening phrase (Ex. 112), which lives primarily through the harmonic abrasiveness engineered by the first violin's inverted dominant pedal, is overstated, while the monotonous requiem chant that follows, with its endless tolling B flat in the second violin, is a funereal token that is undeniably emotive but, as music, sadly frugal. Only the beautiful G flat cantabile theme that occupies the middle of the movement passes beyond the outward show of lamentation to stand as a truly worthy tribute to Tchaikovsky's departed colleague.

Ex. 112

When Tchaikovsky confessed his fears that in this quartet he was beginning to repeat himself, he probably had in mind especially the last movement. This is a headlong and unusually proportioned rondo in which the first and last episodes, by far the longest single sections in the piece, evoke the same lively Russian world as the folksong of the piano concerto's finale. This time, however, there is no broad second tune, the whole piece displaying instead an unremitting energy, with the central episode seeming to shift towards the world of Mendelssohn's scherzos without muting more than a little the ubiquitous vigour of the remaining music. This is an engaging movement that provides the whole quartet with an attractive exit, only momentarily touched with a more serious intimation when, just before the coda, the bustle is suddenly stilled and a brief fragment of the pizzicato accompaniment in the first movement's introduction recalls the basic elegiac preoccupation of this memorial quartet. And surely it is not coincidence that the single fragment of cello melody which closes this tiny but arresting quasi andante outlines exactly the contour produced by the first four pitches which may be extracted from the name: Ferdinand Laub? (Ex. 113)

Ex. 113

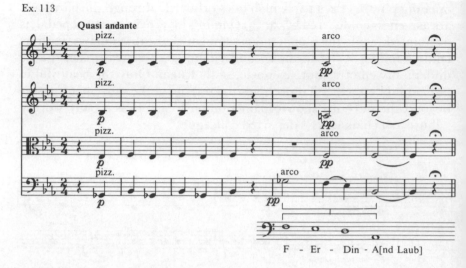

F - Er - Din - A[nd Laub]

Tchaikovsky wrote no more string quartets. It is difficult to decide how much this is a matter for regret. Though they offer some beautiful things, none of his three examples can, in toto, count among his very best works, and it is hard to believe that, with the trends developing in his music towards a more violent rhetoric and a more strained emotional forcefulness, he could much longer have contained any really sustained stretch of characteristic invention within a dynamic and textural scale suitable for four string players. Yet the first movement of this Third Quartet remains a notable and characteristic achievement, and, of their kind, the scherzo and finale are admirably realised conceptions. As music the Fourth Quartet would doubtless have elicited more gratitude than is aroused by his next substantial chamber work, the sterile Piano Sonata in G.

The dread voiced by Tchaikovsky after hearing his Third Quartet played ('Have I really sung my swan song, and have nowhere further to go?') was one that was frequently to recur in his letters. Yet it did not stem in this instance from lack of compositional schemes for the future, and even as he was working on the quartet his mind was busy with other projects. There was certainly encouragement to forge ahead. Though he himself alleged to Modest that the reviews of his Third Symphony, including Laroche's, had been cold, this was quite untrue; they had been very approving, and Laroche's was particularly warm. He had the stimulus of knowing that Anton Door, a former Conservatoire colleague and the dedicatee of the *Valse caprice* for piano, Op. 4, had been introducing some of his music to Vienna. Even more, there were Bülow's letters from America in which the pianist reported not merely on the fortunes of the piano concerto but also upon the markedly warm reception accorded Tchaikovsky's First String Quartet when it was performed in Boston on 13 January 1876. Tchaikovsky could not but compare Bülow's attitude to his work with that of Anton Rubinstein, and he poured into his reply to Bülow's last letter from the other side of the world all the bitterness he felt at his former teacher's unrelenting posture:

> This god of Olympus has never shown towards my works anything but supreme contempt, and I'll confess to you in complete confidence that I have always been deeply wounded by this. Regarding the quartet whose success you report, let me tell you of a little incident that will make you understand how great is this contempt. When, some years ago, I approached the publisher Bessel (of St Petersburg), offering him the quartet free of charge, he called upon Rubinstein to learn from him whether this work was worth publishing. 'No,' my former teacher replied, and thereupon (just like that!) Bessel sent me a rejection slip of the most formal and humiliating sort. And this is always the way in which this great artist has behaved towards my works.[22]

Faced with Rubinstein's implacable antipathy to his music, and the critical ambivalence of prominent critics like Cui and even his friend Laroche, the veneration of this great musician, not one of his fellow-countrymen but a son of the leading musical nation of Europe, was of inestimable value to his morale.

Work on *Swan Lake* ceased, of course, while he worked on the quartet, but even during this busy phase his thoughts were still fastened upon two of the libretti that had been attracting him in December. 'I'm vacillating between *Ephraim* and *Francesca*, and I think the latter will be my first choice. It appears that before (do you remember?) I was unjust to this very skilfully constructed libretto. Now I'm beginning to like it,' he informed Modest on 22 February, eight days before finishing the quartet.[23] Tchaikovsky's indecision about these libretti was to continue for a long while yet. At the end of June he was still assuring Konstantin Shilovsky that he would use *Ephraim*, and he seems to have held it as an option until he set about *Eugene Onegin* in the summer of 1877. The choice of *Onegin* also saw the final demise of *Francesca da Rimini* as a possible opera subject, for though Tchaikovsky had nearly a year

[22] *TLP*6, pp. 21–2.
[23] *TLP*6, pp. 24–5; *TPR*, p. 231; *TZC*1, p. 483 (partial); *TPB*, p. 105; *YDGC*, p. 125 (partial).

earlier composed an orchestral piece on Dante's pathetic heroine, his interest in Zvantsev's libretto revived briefly when he was engaged on the operatic quest that finally led him to Pushkin's novel in verse. Kashkin recorded that there was, however, a fundamental obstacle to *Francesca da Rimini* – that Zvantsev, a passionate Wagnerian, insisted that it should be set according to that composer's operatic principles, a condition utterly repugnant to Tchaikovsky.

The process that brought *Swan Lake* into the world is almost as hidden as that of the Third Symphony, though it was certainly more protracted. There is enough sparse evidence in Tchaikovsky's letters to show that he continued working on it throughout the winter of 1875–6. 'I'm diligently composing the ballet,' he declared to Modest on 26 September 1875,[24] shortly after returning, with two acts sketched, from Vladimir Shilovsky's estate at Usovo. Some at least of the instrumentation was done as he went along, for in the full score the second Scène (No. 3) of Act 1 is dated 25 October 1875. In late November he wrote to Rimsky-Korsakov that he was hurrying to finish it as soon as he could; a further month (23 December), and he mentioned to Anatoly that he was doing more scoring of the piece. Yet it is impossible to believe that there did not remain much to be done. The next report on progress is contained in a letter to Anatoly of 29 March, three months later and one month after the Third Quartet was finished. 'I'm up to my neck in scoring the ballet which I must complete without fail by St Thomas week [in 1876 this began on 24 April]. Because there remain two and a half acts to finish off, I've decided to devote Passion Week and Holy Week to finishing this endlessly boring, long-drawn-out affair.'[25] By this time the Conservatoire term was over, and he could see that if he remained in Moscow he would be inundated by people who believed that he now had time on his hands. The only solution was to flee the city without delay. On 4 April a preliminary rehearsal of several numbers from Act 1 was held in the hall of the theatre's school, Tchaikovsky's music being represented by a single violin. The composer found the whole proceedings rather ridiculous, though he was delighted by the general reception of his new work. 'Everyone in the theatre's in raptures about my music,' he informed Modest the next day. 'At the end of this week I'm going to Kostya Shilovsky's in the country.'[26] Konstantin's estate was at Glebovo; there, on 22 April, the ballet was finished.

Some ten months later, on 4 March 1877, *Swan Lake* was produced at

[24] *TLP*5, p. 414; *TPR*, p. 222; *TPB*, p. 99; *TZC*1, p. 469; *YDGC*, p. 119.
[25] *TLP*6, p. 30; *TPR*, p. 233; *TZC*1, p. 484; *TPB*, p. 106; *DTC*, p. 225 (partial).
[26] *TLP*6, p. 33; *TPR*, pp. 234–5; *TPB*, p. 107; *DTC*, p. 225 (partial).

the Bolshoy Theatre in Moscow as a benefit performance for Pelageya Karpakova, the ballerina who created the part of Odette. It was realised for the stage by a certain Julius Reisinger, who was ballet master at the Bolshoy from 1871 to 1878. If there is little information about the actual composition of the ballet, there is even less about the preparations for production. Had it been an opera, Tchaikovsky would certainly have involved himself deeply in these matters; on ballet performance, however, he had no kind of professional competence that could aid the theatre staff, and the preliminary rehearsal he had attended in April 1876, at which he had witnessed Reisinger's impromptu efforts at choreography, had given him no taste for entangling himself more deeply in such affairs. His letters during this period contain not a hint of the ballet's route to production; the only mention is of a private playing of Kashkin's piano transcription of the first two acts, an event which took place at Tchaikovsky's own home on 28 September. Tchaikovsky invited both Jurgenson and Albrecht, a sign that he must at that time have been feeling some pronounced satisfaction with the work. Yet he does not seem to have been particularly concerned about the ballet's fate. As Modest put it, his brother suffered none of 'that nervous tension and those upsets such as he experienced when his operas were staged, and in consequence didn't particularly take to heart the far from brilliant success of his work. The impoverished décor (scenery and costumes), the lack of outstanding performers, the poverty of the ballet-master's imagination, and, finally, the orchestra which, though not bad in itself, was in the charge of Mr Ryabov who, up till then, had never had to deal with such a complicated score – all this in toto enabled the composer with justification to lay the blame for failure upon other people.'[27]

There were certainly plenty of candidates for censure, starting with the three designers, Ivan Shangin (Act 1), Karl Waltz (Acts 2 and 4), and Paul Gropius (Act 3). Above all there was Reisinger, whose limitations as a choreographer seem to have been almost boundless. Tchaikovsky also had sound reason for feeling that not all the musical failings of the work, whatever these might be, could be laid at his door, for in addition to the incompetent rendering of what he had actually written, some of the music that was heard was not even his. 'While the ballet was going into production several numbers were dropped as being awkward to dance, or were replaced by extracts from other ballets,' Kashkin remembered. 'In addition, the ballet-master insisted that there must be a Russian dance for whose presence there was very little justification. All the same, the composer gave way, and the dance

[27] *TZC*1, p. 527; *DTC*, p. 225.

was written.... Though the success of *Swan Lake* was not particularly brilliant, it was not negligible, and it held the stage for many years until the scenery disintegrated completely.'[28]

Kashkin also threw some light on the musical fortunes of the work. 'Yet it was not only the scenery that disintegrated; the music also suffered grievously. Substitution was extended more and more, and towards the end nearly an entire third of the music of *Swan Lake* was replaced by extracts from other ballets which were, to boot, very mediocre.'[29] In fact, despite Kashkin's testimony, there appears to have been only one insertion of alien music at the first performance (a Pas de cinq by some unnamed composer, performed immediately after the Pas de six in Act 3). Nevertheless there was a proliferation of such cuts with successive performances. Much of this mangling occurred when the ballet was newly produced by Reisinger's successor, a Belgian called Joseph Hansen, in Moscow in 1880.

Press reaction was mixed, but heavily inclined to censure rather than praise. Kashkin, who, having made the piano score, had good cause to know the ballet well, was the most favourable. 'Tchaikovsky's music contains many beautiful moments and, as music for a ballet, it is perhaps even too good; but it would be a mistake to rank it with the same composer's other works,' he informed the readers of Tchaikovsky's old journal, the *Russian Gazette*.[30] Other critics complimented Tchaikovsky on his handling of the orchestra, but expressed varying degrees of doubt about the music itself, one finding it mostly dull and monotonous, 'interesting, perhaps, only to musicians',[31] another alleging it revealed 'Mr Tchaikovsky's usual shortcoming: a poverty of creative fantasy and, in consequence of this, thematic and melodic monotony'.[32] In short, even some of those whose job it should have been to be discriminating in such matters found the music of *Swan Lake* beyond their comprehension.

We have no information on what relationship the *Swan Lake* produced in 1877 bore to the little children's ballet Tchaikovsky had devised for his nieces at Kamenka in 1871, nor do we know whether he himself provided the initiative that led to the choice of subject for his first full-length ballet. Though unlikely, it is not impossible that Tchaikovsky himself drafted the plot. Credit for this is normally assigned to Tchaikovsky's friend, Vladimir Begichev, and to Vasily

[28] *KVC*, p. 103; *DTC*, p. 226; *TZC*1, p. 528.
[29] *KVC*, p. 103; *DTC*, p. 226.
[30] *DTC*, p. 226; *YDGC*, p. 141.
[31] *TZC*1, p. 529; *DTC*, p. 226.
[32] *TZC*1, p. 529; *DTC*, p. 227; *YDGC*, p. 142.

Heltser, one of the finest dancers of the Moscow ballet, but the name of neither appeared on the programme for the first production. The plot may have antecedents in Germany (*Swan Lake* is set in that land), but elements of the story could equally be derived from Russian tales of the supernatural. Since Tchaikovsky's death the plot has been subject to modifications. To be fair to those who have to incarnate such works for the stage, a ballet will demand from the producer and choreographer a far greater inventiveness in creating incidental action than does an opera, unless the composer has incorporated a wealth of instructions in his score.

Tchaikovsky did not, and because so much that he did not specifically sanction has accrued to the plot in the last hundred years, it seems essential first to identify the bare bones of the action as he himself envisaged it. It is significant that when Jurgenson printed the full score in 1895, eighteen years after the first performance, the stage directions remained as they had been in Kashkin's piano reduction issued in the very month of the première. Apart from trifling additions in the manuscript score, Tchaikovsky did not confer official status upon anything added to his own original prescriptions. In fact, nothing really crucial is omitted from his score instructions, and if these skeletal stage directions are supplemented by extracts from the 'libretto' distributed to the audience at the first performances, we come as close as we may to the original ballet scenario as imagined or agreed by the composer (extracts from the libretto are enclosed in square brackets):

Act i.
Scène (No. 1). [*The action takes place in Germany.*] *Part of a splendid park; in the background a castle. A graceful bridge spans a stream.* Prince Siegfried and his friends are seated at tables, drinking wine. A crowd of peasants enters to congratulate the Prince [on his coming of age]. His tutor, Wolfgang, enjoins them to amuse his pupil by dancing; the peasants agree. The Prince orders wine for their entertainment. Servants carry out his orders. Flowers and ribbons are distributed among the women. Waltz (No. 2). [The dances proceed animatedly.] Scène (No. 3). A footman runs in and announces the imminent arrival of the Princess, the Prince's mother. The servants put everything in order: the tutor tries to assume the air of a man who is busily occupied. Enter the Princess. She urges her son to marry.... [Although the Prince, not wanting to marry yet, is vexed by his mother's proposition, he is ready to submit, and respectfully asks his mother whom she has chosen to be his life's companion. 'I have chosen no one yet,' replies his mother, 'for I want you to make your own choice. Tomorrow I am having a grand ball to which will come noblemen and their daughters. From among these you will have to choose the one who pleases you, and she will be your bride.'] The Princess leaves. The Prince observes: 'There's an end to our carefree life....' Benno, a knight, consoles

him. All sit, and the banquet is resumed. Pas de trois (No. 4) and Pas de deux (No. 5). [The peasants dance, sometimes in groups, sometimes singly.] Pas d'action (No. 6). The tutor gets drunk, dances, and arouses everyone's amusement by his clumsiness. He pirouettes and falls down. [*In the first production this was elaborated thus:* One of the peasant girls particularly attracts him, and after declaring himself in love with her, he tries to kiss her, but the minx evades him and, as always happens in ballets, he kisses not her, but her betrothed.] Sujet (No. 7). It begins to get dark. One of the guests proposes they should perform finally a goblet dance. Danse des coupes (No. 8). Finale (No. 9). A flock of swans appears in the sky. . . . ['You know, it would be hard to hit them,' says Benno, egging on the Prince as he draws his attention to the swans. 'Nonsense,' replies the Prince. 'I could hit them for sure. Fetch my gun.' 'Don't,' pleads Wolfgang. 'Don't. It's time for bed.' The Prince makes as though, indeed, he will not do it, but will go to bed. But as soon as the old man, being reassured, leaves, he beckons to his servant, takes his gun, and hurries off with Benno in the direction in which the swans have flown.]

ACT 2.

Scène (No. 10). [*A wild, mountainous place: forests on all sides. In the background a lake, on the right bank of which is a half-ruined stone building, something like a chapel. A moonlit night.* A flock of white swans is swimming on the lake. The flock swims towards the ruins, led by a swan with a crown on its head.] Scène (No. 11). The Prince [with Benno] enters. The Prince recognises the swan. He prepares to fire; the swans disappear. Odette appears. The maiden asks the Prince: 'Why do you persecute me? . . .' Odette tells her story: ['My mother was a good fairy. Against the will of her father she fell passionately, madly in love with a noble knight, married him, but he destroyed her: she died. My father married another, neglected me, and my wicked stepmother, who was a sorceress, came to hate me and almost destroyed me – but my grandfather took me to live with him. The old man loved my mother terribly, and so mourned and wept for her that his tears formed this lake, and there, to its lowest depths, he retreated and hid me from the world. Now, recently, he has begun to indulge me, and gives me complete freedom to enjoy myself. Thus during the day my friends and I turn ourselves into swans, and joyfully cleaving the air with our breasts, we fly high, high almost up to the very sky, and at night we play and dance here, near my grandfather. But all the time my stepmother has left neither me nor even my friends in peace.] An owl appears. ['Look, there she is!' . . . 'She would have destroyed me long ago,' continues Odette, 'but my grandfather watches me vigilantly, and won't let me come to any harm.'] Odette [reveals]: 'If I marry, [the sorceress will lose her power to harm me, but until then only this crown protects me from her evil.' 'O forgive me, my lovely one, forgive me!' cries the confused Prince, falling on his knees.] Scène (No. 12). A flock of swan-maidens [and children] appears [and reproaches the young huntsman.] Odette [speaks]: 'Stop! that's enough. He is a friend. . . .' The Prince throws away his gun ['I swear that from henceforth I shall never raise my hand to kill any bird.'] Odette [replies]: 'Calm yourself, sir knight. . . .' Danses des cygnes (No. 13). [There begin dances in which the Prince and Benno join. Sometimes the swans form beautiful groupings, sometimes they dance singly.] Odette dances alone. [The Prince is constantly close to Odette; during the dances he falls madly in love with her, and implores her not to reject his love] (Pas d'action). Odette and the Prince [dance. Odette laughs: 'I'm afraid to believe you, noble knight. I fear that it is only your imagination deceiving you. Tomorrow, at your mother's feast, you will see many lovely young maidens, and will fall in love with someone else. You will forget me. . . . I will not hide from you that . . . I have also fallen in love with you, but a terrible foreboding grips me.' 'I shall love you, only you, all my life.' . . . 'Very well. Tomorrow must decide our fate. . . .'] Scène (No. 14). Odette and the swans disappear into the ruins . . . [A flock of swans swims out into the lake, while above a great owl flaps heavily.]

ACT 3.
[Scène] (No. 15). [*A luxurious hall in the Princess's castle, everything prepared for a feast.*] The aged Wolfgang gives the servants orders. Guests appear. There enter the Prince, the Princess and their suite, pages, dwarfs, etc. . . . Danses du corps de ballet et des nains (No. 16). The master of ceremonies gives the sign for the dances to begin. The dwarfs dance. Scène: La sortie des invités et la valse (No. 17). The sound of a trumpet announces the arrival of fresh guests. The master of ceremonies advances to meet them, and a herald announces their names to the Prince [*in the libretto:* to the Princess]. There enter an old count, his wife and daughter. They bow to their hosts, and the daughter dances a waltz with one of the knights. Again the sound of a trumpet and appearance of guests. The old couple sit down, and at the invitation of one of the guests, their daughter dances another waltz. The whole scene is repeated, and everyone dances a waltz, including the corps de ballet. Scène (No. 18). The Princess takes her son aside, and asks him which of the maidens has pleased him . . . [The Prince replies sadly: 'So far not one of them has pleased me, mother.' The Princess's shoulders heave with vexation; she beckons to Wolfgang and angrily informs him what her son has said. The master tries to persuade his pupil, but a trumpet sound rings out and] Baron Rotbart and Odile come forward. The Prince is struck by the resemblance of Odile to Odette, and consults with Benno about this. Pas de six (No. 19). [For some time the Prince feasts his eyes upon Odile as she dances, then himself joins in the dancing.] Danse hongroise: Czardas (No. 20), Danse espagnole (No. 21), Danse napolitaine (No. 22), and Mazurka (No. 23). Scène (No. 24). The Princess rejoices that Odile has pleased her son, and questions Wolfgang about it. The Prince invites Odile to dance a waltz with him. The Prince kisses Odile's hand. The Princess and Rotbart advance to the middle of the stage: the Princess announces that Odile is to become the Prince's bride. Triumphantly Rotbart takes his daughter's hand and gives it to the Prince. For a moment the stage darkens . . . [An owl's cry is heard, Rotbart's disguise falls away and he is revealed in the form of a devil. Odile laughs. . . . The window flies open noisily, and a white swan with a crown on its head appears. In horror the Prince flings away the hand of his newly betrothed and, clutching his breast, rushes headlong out of the castle. General confusion.]

ACT 4.

Entr'acte (No. 25). Scène (No. 26). [*The scene is as in Act 2. Night.*] Odette's friends are wondering where she can have gone. Danses des petits cygnes (No. 27). [Without her they are miserable, and try to divert themselves by dancing and] teaching the cygnets to dance. Scène (No. 28). Odette rushes in and unburdens her grief to her friends. 'He is coming,' her friends tell her.... ['He?' cries Odette in alarm, and runs towards the ruins, but then suddenly stops and says: 'I want to see him for the last time.... Go, sisters, and wait for me.' They all [the swans] enter the ruins.] The scene darkens, a storm begins. Thunder rumbles. Scène finale (No. 29). The Prince rushes in. 'O forgive me!' cries the Prince.... ['It is not in my power to forgive you. All is finished: we are seeing each other for the last time.' ... Tearing herself from the Prince's embrace, she runs towards the ruins. The Prince catches up with her, grasps her hand, and exclaims desperately: 'Not thus, no! Willy-nilly, you shall remain with me for ever!' Quickly he tears the crown from her head and hurls it into the seething lake, which is already overflowing its banks. An owl flies screeching overhead, bearing in its talons Odette's crown which the Prince has cast away. 'What have you done? You have destroyed both of us! I am dying,' cries Odette,] falling into the Prince's arms. [... The waves sweep over the Prince and Odette, and they swiftly disappear beneath the waters. The storm dies down.... The moon's pale light breaks through the scattering clouds.] The swans appear on the lake.

Swan Lake incorporated several pieces of existing music. One of the themes associated with the swans (quite certainly the oboe tune first heard in the finale to Act 1) is said to have come from Tchaikovsky's earlier children's ballet, while the Pas d'action (with violin and cello obbligati) in Act 2 was based upon the final duet for Huldbrand and Undine from Tchaikovsky's ill-fated second opera. Two relics from his first opera, *The Voyevoda* (also destroyed), were the Entr'acte to Act 4 (originally also the final Entr'acte in the opera) and the E major opening of the Scène finale of the ballet, where the Prince and Odette are reunited (taken from the couples' reunions in the *Voyevoda*'s last act). In both these *Voyevoda* appropriations Tchaikovsky retained his original keys, and he also preserved the five-flat key-signature of Bastryukov's farewell in Act 1 (later also used as Andrey's farewell in Act 4 of *The Oprichnik*) when he resorted to it to suggest the Danses des petits cygnes in Act 4 of the ballet (Ex. 114).

And, just as some pieces of *Swan Lake* existed before Tchaikovsky set to work upon the ballet, so others were added after the initial work was completed. As Kashkin's testimony has already revealed, Tchaikovsky supplemented the suite of national stylisations with a Russian dance at the request of the choreographer so that the prima ballerina, Pelageya Karpakova, might don a national costume and join in the divertisse-

Ex. 114

a.

Bastryukov

Raz - mï - chem   mï - go - re

p

[We will wash away our grief]

b.   Moderato

p

ment (in 1878 Tchaikovsky reworked this piece as the *Danse russe* in the Twelve Pieces (moderate difficulty) for piano, Op. 40). In addition, at the fifth performance was incorporated a Pas de deux composed because Anna Sobeshchanskaya, the ballerina sharing with Karpakova the rôle of Odette, wanted a dance of greater virtuosity than it was within Reisinger's capabilities to devise. Sobeshchanskaya journeyed to St Petersburg to seek the assistance of Petipa, who invented the required dance, founding it upon music by Minkus. On her return Tchaikovsky substituted music of his own, modelling it upon the rhythms and structure of Minkus's dance. This addition was swiftly dropped and the music disappeared, though a rehearsal version for two violins exists. Only the orchestral parts for the second variation have been discovered.

After the Hansen production was withdrawn from the repertoire in 1883, *Swan Lake* was never again mounted in Tchaikovsky's lifetime. It was with the new and mutilated version prepared by Petipa and Lev Ivanov, assistant ballet master in St Petersburg, for the Maryinsky Theatre, and first performed there on 27 January 1895 at a benefit performance for Pierina Legnani, that the ballet was set on course towards the overwhelming popularity it enjoys today. The idea for a new production came from Ivan Vsevolozhsky, who had been director of the Imperial Theatres since 1881. In 1888 Vsevolozhsky had devised, with Petipa, the scenario for Tchaikovsky's second ballet, *The Sleeping Beauty*, while the conductor at the première of that work had been Riccardo Drigo, a very mediocre Italian composer slightly remembered still for a single trifle, the Serenade from his ballet, *Les Millions d'Arlequin*. All three men (with Ivanov) were again involved in Tchaikovsky's third and last ballet, *The Nutcracker*, and it was this same group that proposed in 1894, probably as the result of a very successful memorial performance in March of Act 2 of *Swan Lake*, to do posthumous service to Tchaikovsky's now-neglected first ballet.

Vsevolozhsky began by persuading Modest Tchaikovsky to revise the libretto. Modest's agreement to do this cannot be construed entirely as treachery to his late brother's work. Whether any of the revisions he now made in the story had been discussed with his brother during his lifetime is uncertain, and attempts to suggest that the musical changes made in the 1895 production had been agreed by the composer before his death carry little conviction. However, there were undeniably things in the original libretto that were unsatisfactory. The connection of Rotbart and his daughter with the wicked stepmother was unspecified and, in consequence, his motive for obstructing the Siegfried–Odette union was not evident. Modest clarified this, excising all reference to the stepmother (and to the good grandfather, who was even more expendable), making Odette and her companions the victims of Rotbart (who now took over the owl incarnation), their swan-like state not a guard from evil but a consequence of Rotbart's enchantments, and the latter's intrusion into the betrothal feast a credible result of his determination to retain power over Odette. Indisputably this improved matters, and many of Modest's other changes – for instance, the substitution of the aspiring brides and their parents for the old baron, his wife and daughter, or Odette appearing unheeded at the window before the Prince pledges himself to Odile – were innocuous, even perhaps beneficial. Harmless, too, was the loss of Odette's crown as talisman. Modest's real offence was to turn the tragic end into romantic apotheosis, with Siegfried, having stabbed himself to death and thus destroyed Rotbart, united for ever with Odette in 'the temple of eternal happiness and bliss'. Tchaikovsky did not, in fact, consider the last act of the ballet to be the best: that was Act 2. Yet it is difficult to believe that he could possibly have sanctioned this new cosy conclusion to a work whose original end possessed great pathos and power.

If Modest was not blameless, Drigo was infinitely more guilty. A case could certainly be made for reducing the length of some of the set dances. Even Laroche, who became the most enthusiastic partisan for *Swan Lake*, took this view, and the operation could have been carried out simply by reducing the numerous repetitions of sections. Drigo went much further than this, savagely cutting some numbers; even less defensible, he changed the order of others, and introduced three new pieces selected from Tchaikovsky's Eighteen Pieces for piano, Op. 72 (Nos. 11, 12 and 15), which he orchestrated specially for this production. This was inexcusable, for the sequence of musical numbers was already admirably, and very carefully organised.

From the beginning *Swan Lake* was a very remarkable and bold achievement, for though Tchaikovsky composed it for a ballet whose tradition was already long and honourable, and whose current technical standard was high, there was a deplorable disparity between the skills of the company and the condition of the repertoire, which was both conservative and musically trivial (though, to be fair to Moscow in the 1870s, it did favour ballets with more substantial plots than did St Petersburg). In ballet the lead had passed to France where, in 1870, a new stage in the history of the form was inaugurated by Delibes' *Coppélia*. Tchaikovsky did not know this ballet when he was composing *Swan Lake*, and *Sylvia*, which he came to admire so much, was not produced until nearly two months after he had written the last note of his own first ballet. According to Anna Bryullova, the mother of Kolya Konradi, Tchaikovsky confessed to having been a complete novice when writing *Swan Lake*, dependent entirely upon the ballet-master's directions, even down to the finest details of rhythm, tempo, and number of bars. Patently this was gross exaggeration, though Kashkin recorded that Tchaikovsky had long consultations with Reisinger before setting about composition. Problems his music certainly posed for the dancers, but these arose not from Tchaikovsky's incompetence, but simply from the novelty of some of the things he expected of them, things that later dancers have come to consider the most natural of requirements.

The main problem was that, for the nineteenth-century Russian audience, the ballet was above all a decorative spectacle – certainly not, even in Moscow, a dramatic enactment. Every potential scenario had to submit to this condition. Ballroom scenes, peasant festivals, national dances, rituals of enchantment, feasts which would justify elaborate visual entertainment of the guests – all these were the stock situations which, in large undigested slabs, were imposed upon the plot, or around which it was fabricated. In *Coppélia* much of this divertissement element had been concentrated in the last act, where it was excused as the festival to celebrate the presentation of the bell. Petipa produced this ballet in St Petersburg in 1884, and it was surely the example of this work that decided those who compiled the plot for *The Sleeping Beauty* to reserve likewise the greater part of the formal dance numbers for the last act ('Aurora's wedding'). In *Swan Lake*, however, these static set-pieces were distributed throughout the work, being excused in Act 1 as the entertainments and festivities of a rustic drinking party, in Act 2 as part of the swans' natural recreation during which the Prince and Odette could be brought together, and in Act 3 as the formal dances and diversions of a courtly ballroom. Even Act 4, which presented little natural opportunity for such ornament, incorporated its Danses des petits cygnes before Odette's distraught entrance. Given these inescapable audience expectations, *Swan Lake* was a remarkable attempt to incorporate a drama that was more than a convenient series of incidents for mechanically shifting from one divertissement to the next. True, the endless dances in Act 1, and the national stylisations near the end of Act 3 might with profit be truncated, but the drama of the last act, once it begins, is allowed to proceed with the minimum of embellishment and the maximum of musical substance. *Swan Lake* may be far from a model of what a ballet plot should ideally be, nor was Tchaikovsky's instinct infallible, but as a product of the Russia of its time, when the grandest ornaments of the repertoire were the confections of Minkus and Drigo, it was almost visionary in its perception of the dramatic possibilities within the form.

For if Tchaikovsky had been, and would always remain a composer of severe limitations when it came to opera, as a composer of ballets he had ideal musical equipment, and remarkable natural instinct. Opera at the highest level demanded precise characterisation, an ability not simply to identify with a limited range of stock types, but a capacity, so marvellously displayed by Musorgsky, to catch the very essence of individual human beings, to match the words through which their feelings were projected not merely with music which adequately fitted the text, but which caught those individual inflections which exposed the soul within the body, which embodied in graphic and succinct musical phrases the essential, individual traits or emotions of the character. Ballet, on the other hand, required none of this punctilious delineation, none of this scrupulous and refined detail. In ballet the dramatis personae were little more than types, insubstantial and airy when embodied in stylised dancing, dependent almost entirely upon the actor's skill of projection in the case of those personified by mimes. What was required of the composer was an ability to create and sustain atmosphere: above all, a facility for suggesting and supporting movement, especially by inventing a copious flow of dance music, conventional, even rudimentary in structure, and almost rigidly regular in the length of its periods and constituent phrases, but animated by an abundant inventiveness, above all rhythmic, within the individual phrase. Glinka had possessed something of this capacity, as his *Valse fantaisie* had admirably demonstrated; Tchaikovsky owned it in yet greater measure.

The waltzes in which this score is rich show this above all. One need look no further than the first eight bars of each of the various waltzes set out in Ex. 115 to grasp this point. In every case the accompaniment is

Ex. 115

always of the simplest, always explicitly triple time, yet the themes themselves show effortless rhythmic variety, partly through details of phrasing prescribed by Tchaikovsky, mainly by fertilising the basic triple metre with duple-time inflections. Given no barlines and no accompaniment, the innocent listener might well assign Ex. 115a and f a $\frac{2}{4}$ time signature, as in Ex. 115b and g. Ex. 115c projects forceful offbeats until bar four for a moment restores firmly the true first-beat accent. Ex. 115d follows two unequivocal $\frac{3}{4}$ bars with two which give a surface sound of being three $\frac{2}{4}$ bars. Only Ex. 115e is absolutely regular until the very end (though Tchaikovsky's slur between bars four and five does soften this rigid symmetry). Tchaikovsky had a positive genius for the waltz, not merely in the seemingly inexhaustible fertility of his melodic invention, but also in his ability to order different waltz themes to make a larger entity. 'Symphonic' artifice is eschewed, except for the piling of sequences to effect a transition or give the coda weight. Always everything is square, symmetrical, and section is bluntly juxtaposed to section.

The very first waltz (No. 2 of Act 1), perhaps the most imposing set-piece of the whole ballet, is built almost entirely from sixteen-bar units, the great majority of these made by repeating an eight-bar phrase. These sixteen-bar units, themselves repeated where necessary, are assembled into larger members of binary or ternary design, these members in their turn being strung together to make a gigantic simple rondo scheme with a second episode in a very contrasted flat-key region, and a last section which summarises the material of the opening with much sequential treatment to generate the weight and tension appropriate to a coda climax. Throughout the waltz some phrases pointedly echo the rhythmic structure of earlier ones, others equally pointedly offer contrast. If, in judging the success of an extensive musical movement, the criterion is the aptness of the form to the material, then this first waltz of *Swan Lake* is arguably the most successful instrumental movement Tchaikovsky had composed to date.

There is commendable variety of character in the dance music itself. The only justification for the national stylisations in Act 3 was that they widened the range of the dance element, and in general Tchaikovsky responded well to the challenge of these alien rhythms and tempera-ments (ironically, though perhaps rather inevitably, it is the local dances, the Mazurka and the Russian Dance itself, that make the least impression in the company of such fresh bursts of colour from more distant lands). The Neapolitan dance is founded, if we may believe the evidence of Nadezhda von Meck, upon a genuine Neapolitan tune; Tchaikovsky was to use the tune a second time in the *Chanson napolitaine*, No. 18 of the Children's Album, Op. 39. The brief dance of the dwarfs in Act 3, with its slightly awkward, then fidgety movement, and plaintive scoring, is nicely characterised, though mild compared to the spicy dishes of Chernomor's world in *Ruslan*, from which Tchaikovsky's invention derives its character. There is an engagingly naive freshness in the famous 'cygnets' dance from the Danses des cygnes in Act 2. In the long and highly inconsistent string of dances that makes up the second half of Act 1, the slow section of the Pas de deux (No. 5) is a violin solo that, in its rather vapid context, almost takes one aback with its heart-melting sweetness. There is an especial fascination, too, in the bitter-sweet dissonances that accompany the main waltz theme of Act 3 (Ex. 116). At the opposite extreme from these slightly sultry sounds is the fresh, open-air Russian world of the Danses des petits cygnes (No. 27) in the last act (see Ex. 114b), the most truly national piece in the whole ballet.

However, by no means all the formal dance music is on this level, either in character or as music. Some is quite ordinary, a little even

Ex. 116

trite. This is especially marked in some of the quick dances in $\frac{2}{4}$ whose narrow bars constricted the scope for rhythmic variation (we have already noted, in the large batch of songs Tchaikovsky composed in 1875, how relatively crippling rhythmically he found compound duple as opposed to compound triple metre). The Pas de trois (No. 4) in Act 1 tails off; its canonic second section is appealing, but the 'polka' third and fifth sections are of no distinction. More sadly, inconsistency marks the Pas de six (No. 19) in Act 3, during which the Prince is lured into betraying Odette. The opening has some coquetry, the second variation both allure and force, and the fifth some seductiveness, but the first variation is little more than pert, nor do the remaining limbs of the piece do much to reinforce the potency of the spell to which the Prince is falling victim. For the composer the problem of such movements was that they were merely a succession of separate sections for individual dancers or groups – a suite of dances strung together, far less cogent musically than such rounded set-pieces as the Waltz (No. 2) that had followed upon the ballet's opening Scène, or the goblet dance (No. 8), a grand polonaise that is placed immediately before the Act 1 finale, thus balancing exactly that earlier great dance. And if the finale in its turn balances the Scène with which the act had opened, it also anticipates with excellent effect the music that is to begin Act 2.

This finale contains the only clear reminiscence tune in the whole ballet, the oboe theme (Ex. 117) that is to be associated with the swans

Ex. 117

and especially Odette. For musical integration of larger stretches of music Tchaikovsky relied more upon the simple repetition of whole sections. The bustling music that had opened Act 1 returns aptly in the middle of the act as festivities recommence after the departure of the Princess. In Act 2 the waltz that ushers in the Danses des cygnes (No. 13), during which the relationship between the Prince and Odette develops, recurs in the middle of this suite of dances and, compounded with an agitated motif from the lovers' Pas d'action, turns up yet again before the coda. The opening Scène (No. 10) is heard again as the swans retreat to the ruins, thus providing the neatest of frames for the act which, Tchaikovsky rightly believed, was as a whole the most satisfactory of the four. Certainly it is tauter than Act 3, though this provides an accumulation of earlier musical incident towards the end by launching the final Scène (no. 24) with some of the Princess's earlier music (opening of No. 18), continuing with a portion of the waltz that had loomed large near the beginning of the act (from which, in fact, the Princess's music is derived), and recalling agitatedly the swans' reminiscence theme as the Prince pledges himself to Odile (this had also been heard as Odile and Rotbart had first entered). The use of the multiple entries of guests to determine the structure of the earlier Scène (No. 17) was a happy, if fairly obvious decision. As for the last act, it had little need of such widely spaced structural props. Its brevity, and the dramatic concentration of the dénouement, drew from Tchaikovsky a large symphonic tableau which fills the last part of the act with the most concentrated musical fare in the whole ballet, and in which the swans' reminiscence theme at last comes fully into its own.

Though details of the action may be accomplished within the context of a formal dance, the substantial parts of the plot are furthered in the scènes, movements whose general character is appropriate to the prevailing spirit of the plot at the point where each occurs. Here the musical invention is neither subservient to the metrical patterns or the regular phrase lengths of a dance, nor organised with the stiff formality of the set-piece. Such movements are able to change mood with some abruptness when required to by a twist in the tale, and to build, when the occasion demands, climaxes of great expressive force. Sometimes a scène achieves a clear musical shape by using one section as a refrain to produce a ternary structure (as in the very first Scène of the ballet) or a simple rondo (as in the second (No. 3), or the unlabelled Scène (No. 15) that opens Act 3), at others permitting the plot itself to provide the frame for the music. It is in the second Scène (No. 3) of Act 1 that the infiltration of 'symphonic' elements into *Swan Lake* first becomes pronounced, seen here most obviously in the fugato conclusion where the Prince ponders upon the more serious matters that must now chase away his former carefree life. Even more is one aware of such things in the series of scènes that opens Act 2, which treat each portion of a swiftly evolving action to a separate and appropriate musical section, each founded upon a distinct musical phrase that saturates the section and provides the integrating element in music that substantiates the movement and tensions of the stage drama by its restless key shifts. Much of this is splendidly apt – for instance, the swans harassing the Prince at the beginning of No. 12, worrying him with a nervous little phrase in a passage whose unstable tonal course uncovers their own fluttering anxiety.

A movement like this, or the powerful symphonic picture with which the ballet ends, would be proof enough of Tchaikovsky's seriousness of intent in *Swan Lake*. 'I undertook this labour [the composition of the ballet] partly for the money which I need, partly because I have long wanted to try my hand at this kind of music,' he had written to Rimsky-Korsakov on 22 September 1875, immediately after returning to Moscow from Usovo with the first two acts sketched.[33] Despite terse, sometimes weary, even, on one occasion, disparaging reports about the work during composition, he cared for it deeply, and patently lavished much thought upon its composition.

Just how thoughtful he was, and just how much subtlety he thought could be profitably achieved in this work is amply shown by the careful planning of the tonal scheme. John Warrack has drawn attention to the use of key colour to illumine the musical drama. In fact, the representation of the forces of evil by flat keys, of the pure world of Odette and the swan-maidens by sharp ones, is used with notable consistency in all three acts which deal with such matters. Thus both

[33] *TLP*5, p. 412; *DTC*, p. 225 (partial).

Act 2 and Act 4 are almost exclusively in sharp keys; the fact that
Tchaikovsky wrote some of the more extreme sharp-key movements or
passages in flat-key notation was merely a convenience to the musicians
who had to read the notes. Even the orchestral introduction to the
whole ballet presages the workings of evil by ending, after a B minor
beginning (very much the swans' key), in D minor. Because Act 1 takes
place in the ordinary world of mortals it ranges freely amid both sharp
and flat keys, but Act 2 is set in the realm of the 'good ones', the swans,
beginning in B minor as they swim to the ruins (with a whole-tone
touch in the bass at one point (Ex. 118) to alert us to the imminence of

Ex. 118

subversive enchantment), dropping one sharp (to G major) as the
Prince enters, momentarily but abruptly veering towards a flat key (C
minor) as the Prince prepares to shoot, reverting equally suddenly to
neutral ground (C major) as the swans disappear, and moving back
towards the initial two-sharp realm when Odette begins to address the
Prince. As she narrates her evil fate, there is an assertive move to B flat.
Whether the next section is really B major or C flat, written in more
convenient notation, may be open to debate, but when the key
signature is dropped at the appearance of the evil stepmother owl, there
is no doubt about the validity of the thick crop of flats that invades the
music. It is clear that, as Odette tells of the marriage vow that may
break the enchantment, Tchaikovsky intends an enharmonic change to
F sharp minor. From this point, with the swans taking possession of the
stage and the Prince succumbing to Odette's beauty, Tchaikovsky
moves the music sharpwards, reaching F sharp (written G flat) in the

Pas d'action, which ends excitedly in D sharp (written E flat) before all join in the G sharp (written A flat) waltz. From here the sharps fall away rapidly, and the act ends exactly as it had begun, in B minor with the swans swimming away into the ruins.

In Act 3, where the power of Rotbart's evil spreads and finally destroys Odette and the Prince's bid for happiness, the prevailing drift is towards flatter keys, except (as Mr Warrack points out) in the national stylisations, which are outside the main action and therefore outside the dramatic key system. The act opens in a neutral C major, inclines flatwards as the dances begin, then plummets to A flat as the music that is to introduce Rotbart and Odile is heard for the first time to herald the arrivals of earlier guests. For the Pas de six (No. 19), during which Odile seduces Siegfried, there is a sudden shift to a relatively innocuous F major, with each successive section descending farther into flat regions as the Prince is lured into Rotbart's net. Curiously, when Tchaikovsky added the rather mediocre Pas de deux for Odile and the Prince after the Pas de six, he abandoned his key principle, setting it in D major. It can only be assumed he felt by now that his careful tonal strategy was lost on the audiences who turned up for his new ballet. After the lengthy interlude of the national dances the Princess, unaware of the threat to her son's happiness, rejoices at the prospect of his betrothal in an innocent C major, and the music even lifts sharpwards as the Prince invites Odile to dance, only to plunge again to A flat as Rotbart's design is finally accomplished with a momentary signal from the Russian musical supernatural (held horn note against detached chords: see also Exx. 15, 34c, and 83 in Vol. I) to mark the instant the spell finally holds Siegfried captive (Ex. 119).

The last act, returning to the world of Odette and the swans, sees an overwhelming resurgence of sharp keys. By happy chance, the *Voyevoda* entr'acte that Tchaikovsky took over satisfied this condition admirably (again, some passages are notated in flats for the performer's ease). The swans dance in A sharp (written B flat) minor, Odette rushes on in D sharp (written E flat) minor, the Prince in E major, and the act ends in a strong B major. Only at the beginning of the storm, the last sally of Rotbart's power to keep the lovers apart, is the pull of a flat key (D minor) briefly felt.

The popularity of *Swan Lake* seems indestructible, for it has, above all, the overwhelming and universal appeal of a tragic tale of young lovers trapped into their pathetic fate by outside forces as inexorable as those which took Romeo and Juliet to their doom. *The Sleeping Beauty* may excel *Swan Lake* in its variety, its colour, its structure and in the sheer and consistent dramatic richness of its music, but it can elicit

Ex. 119

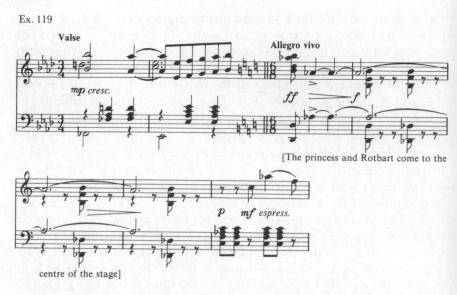

[The princess and Rotbart come to the

centre of the stage]

none of that particular emotional response that the earlier ballet commands. This, above all, is what counts with the wider public. Nor has any tragic ballet since surpassed *Swan Lake* in combining atmosphere (whether gay or sinister), feeling (whether joyful or sorrowful), movement (whether swift or languorous), with the civilised grace and refinement of the elegant, artificial world of a highly stylised dance idiom. Like the blending of eroticism and religion, there is a peculiar fascination and strength in the fabric which weaves vivid threads of naked reality within the elegant, orderly tissue of a highly formalised enactment – as, for instance, Stravinsky was to do in *Oedipus Rex*. And just as, in that latter-day Russian masterpiece, the listener can be surprised, even stunned by the emotional force of the end, when fate has done its worst and Oedipus stands no longer a remote king-figure but a pathetic, broken human, as vulnerable as the rest of common humanity, so the suddenness with which all decoration falls away at the end of *Swan Lake* and the lovers' tragedy hurtles to its conclusion has a force that can be quite shattering in its nakedness, even brutality. Of all Tchaikovsky's heroines, only Tatyana in *Eugene Onegin* has a greater appeal to our tender sympathies than the insubstantial yet, through the eloquence of Tchaikovsky's music, strangely live Odette.

3

THE CRISIS BEGINS:
FRANCESCA DA RIMINI

THE WINTER OF 1875–6 had not been, it seems, a particularly bad one for Tchaikovsky's state of mind. Modest had specified the latter half of 1874 as marking the beginning of his brother's increasing depression, and certainly the winter of 1874–5 had been unhappy in some respects, most of all for Rubinstein's merciless condemnation of the piano concerto – an attack which had sorely exacerbated Tchaikovsky's sense of isolation in Russia's second city. Yet within a year the success of this work with American audiences and its generally respectful, if temperate reception in Russia had done much to ease that particular wound, while the enthusiastic response of his compatriots to his new Third Symphony, his success in the opera competition with *Vakula*, the deep impression created by the Third Quartet, and evidence of increasing international dissemination of his music had all given him much that might cheer his present spirits and raise high his expectations for the future. Clearly there were still bad patches – the melancholia that he had briefly suffered as he was leaving for Western Europe at the turn of the year, for instance – but such things were not new, and seem to have been no worse or more frequent than before. Now, however, all this was about to change abruptly. Far from bringing that general lifting of the spirits that the arrival of spring and the prospect of an ending to the Conservatoire session usually signified, the second quarter of 1876 saw a slump in Tchaikovsky's morale which continued with little remission throughout those precious months during which he had the greatest leisure to compose. The coming summer was to be utterly sterile.

The onset of this crisis was marked by bouts of fever. These had begun even before Tchaikovsky had left Konstantin Shilovsky's Glebovo estate a couple of days after finishing *Swan Lake*, and within a fortnight he had an attack so violent that the doctor feared the beginning of typhus. He had recovered sufficiently to pay a flying visit to St Petersburg in mid-May to expedite arrangements for mounting

Vakula. Already the production staff were worried about the realisation of some of the supernatural effects, while the singers chosen for Vakula and the Devil had refused point-blank to be flown either off or on to the stage in Act 3. Ever mindful of Modest's welfare, Tchaikovsky took the opportunity of visiting the Konradis while in the Russian capital, and was much relieved to find that he could warmly approve of them. For a moment he returned to his musical journalism, penning a background account of the founding of the first Bayreuth festival in preparation for the reports he was to write on Wagner's tetralogy when it inaugurated the new Festspielhaus in August. Tchaikovsky, in his turn, was the subject of a series of articles, for at the end of May there appeared in a periodical, *The Musical World*, the first of four contributions on *Vakula* written by Konstantin Galler, a minor composer and folksong collector. These articles upset Tchaikovsky, for though well-intentioned, their dry style could do little to rouse eager anticipation for his work. Though for the moment his health was better, he had been advised to take a cure for gastric catarrh at Vichy, and this became one of the two main objectives of his summer schedule. The other was to attend the first Bayreuth festival. Before embarking on these enterprises, however, he intended to make a round of visits within Russia itself, starting with Nizy. Thus on 7 June, having rounded off yet another Conservatoire session, he set out for Kondratyev's estate.

The summer started badly and thus it remained for most of its course. Tchaikovsky had intended to spend two weeks with Kondratyev, but he remained only three days. On his very first visit in 1871 he had found the servants at Nizy insubordinate; this time their behaviour roused him to such a pitch that he could bear it no longer. On 14 June he explained all to Modest. 'Every night Alexey, *the footman*, arranges servants' drinking parties, as a result of which sleep is quite impossible. One night, driven to my wits' ends, I left the wing where I was housed and created an unutterable scandal. I woke the master of the house and told him firmly that if Alexey was not banished the next day, I'd leave. They didn't banish Alexey and consequently I find myself in Kiev.'[1] Two days later he arrived at Kamenka. Here disappointment awaited him. Sasha was to return at last from Geneva, but Tchaikovsky had miscalculated the date of her arrival, and instead of finding his sister back home, he had to pass a cheerless fortnight with only walking and Lev's company to provide any pleasure. He would have liked to compose, but his creative faculties seemed paralysed. Then came news that Sasha, still in Geneva, was ailing, and that her new baby was ill and weak. The affairs of the estate made it difficult for

[1] *TLP6*, p. 43; *TPR*, p. 239.

Lev to leave, and he asked his brother in-law to hasten to Geneva to be with Sasha and make whatever arrangements were necessary for her well-being and for the trip to a mountain spa which the doctor had recommended for her. By the time of Tchaikovsky's departure, however, Sasha's plans were changed yet again. She had determined to return home, and when Tchaikovsky left Kamenka on 30 June, his destination was Vienna, where he expected to meet his sister. In the end he had to wait six days in the Austrian capital, during which he had one genuine pleasure, an 'ideal performance' of Rossini's *Guillaume Tell*,[2] but otherwise found nothing to divert him. His impression of the city was very different from that of 1870, when he had passed two happy days there with his brother Nikolay. 'I don't like Vienna and I found having to spend several days there by myself the height of boredom,' he wrote to Modest,[3] forewarning him that he would be later than anticipated in Lyon. By contrast the three days he was able to pass in this French city were delightful. 'I think Modest has set about his job as conscientiously as he has sensibly,' he was to report to Sasha. 'I found the affection that unites master and pupil very touching. Kolya inspired me with a very tender feeling; I find him a very gentle and sensible lad.'[4] It was a very reluctant Tchaikovsky who, on 13 July, left Lyon for Vichy to start his cure.

If Nizy had been upsetting, Kamenka a disappointment, and Vienna a bore, Vichy proved to be intolerable. Tchaikovsky's letters record his wholesale aversion to the place, and the oppressive melancholy that he experienced there. To Modest, so tantalisingly close in Lyon, he wrote almost daily during his first week there, chronicling his stay, his daily round, and pouring out his misery:

I don't know what's going to happen, but today such a *terrible*, deadly melancholy oppressed me that it's extremely doubtful whether I shall stay here for long [he began his very first letter]. You can't imagine what an execrable place Vichy is, nor how complete is the absence of anything here that might divert or comfort me.... I arrived late yesterday evening; at the last station I was joined by a gentleman who suggested I should stay at the Hotel *Bellevue* where he is an interpreter. I agreed. It's a small but clean hotel. I took a large room with two beds because it's out-of-the-way and I can play [the piano] in it at will. I didn't sleep badly. This morning a doctor called on me, a handsome and likeable fellow. He investigated my

[2] *TLP6*, p. 50; *YDGC*, p. 130.
[3] *TLP6*, p. 50.
[4] *TLP6*, p. 60; *TPR*, p. 248.

complaint very thoroughly and gave instructions for taking the
waters and for baths. I've just been to drink my first glass.[5]

The lament was continued the next day, Tchaikovsky opening with a
quotation from Dante's *La divina commedia*:

Nessun dolor maggiore che ricordarsi del tempo felice nella miseria. The
melancholy that consumes me is the more terrible because those
three days I spent with you in Lyon are so clear in my memory. . . .
You know that even I am troubled by that intolerable condition of
the spirit which descends on me every time I am abroad by myself.
There is something unhealthy in this! Just imagine, yesterday I wept
ten times. . . . I got up at 5.30 with a headache, and at six I was already
at the baths. Just think, no other time could be found for me. . . . I've
obtained a piano for myself, but there's no music to be bought in all
Vichy.[6]

To Anatoly he was even fiercer: '. . . accursed, loathsome, revolting
Vichy! Here everything has conspired to make my stay intolerable . . .
the *bustle*, the crush for every glass of water at the spring, the way in
which it is fashionable to spend one's time, the complete absence of any
natural beauties, but most of all the *loneliness* – all this deeply poisons
each minute of my life. Such a *melancholy* has fallen upon me that I shall
scarcely be able to last out the entire course. . . . O accursed, accursed,
accursed Vichy!'[7] By the next day he had already tackled his doctor
about reducing the length of his treatment from the twenty-one days
originally planned. Being too embarrassed to give the real reason, he
declared that his affairs required his immediate presence in Russia.

His routine in Vichy was punctilious. First the early morning bath
and some glasses of mineral water, then (again to Modest) 'at eight I
drop in at a *café* and read the papers. At ten there's a long breakfast.
Alongside me there sits a thoroughly unpleasant Russian, and opposite
me a very nice fat man [another Russian] with whom I have become
good friends. . . . From breakfast to three I play, read, or wander
through the park and drop in at the *casino* which keeps [the periodical]
The Voice. At three I again drink the waters. At five another long *meal*.
Then I stroll, may go to the theatre, and promptly at ten go to bed.'[8]
Such highly regular routines had been Tchaikovsky's practice when
taking a rest in any place for an extended period, for it was one way of

[5] *TLP6*, pp. 51–2; *TPR*, p. 241.   [6] *TLP6*, p. 54; *TPR*, p. 242.
[7] *TLP6*, pp. 53–4; *TPR*, pp. 243–4; *TPB*, p. 109; *TZC1*, pp. 487–8 (partial).
[8] *TLP6*, pp. 57–8; *TPR*, p. 246.

coping with the tedium of having nothing purposeful with which to occupy oneself.

Modest realised his brother's depression at feeling no urge to compose, and took upon himself Balakirev's rôle, trying to stir the composer's creativity with a series of subjects for an orchestral piece:

> Wouldn't you like to do Hamlet? [he wrote on 16 July]. I think he could be organised delightfully into three pictures: 1. Elsinore and Hamlet before the appearance of his father's ghost; 2. Polonius (scherzando) and Ophelia (adagio); 3. Hamlet after the appearance of the ghost. His death and Fortinbras.... After Hamlet I considered Francesca, and she is really beginning to please me!... Then, if Iago worries you, why not do *the tale of Othello by himself*? Indeed, he does merit a symphonic tableau! As you see, Hamlet is the only new subject I've devised ... but if only you knew how much I wish you'd write music on *my* subject. And what do you say to Lermontov's Tamar (... the one who drowns her lovers)? She could be complemented by a variety of lovers, the first perhaps a poet, the second a knight, the third a youth.[9]

Modest's efforts had no effect on Tchaikovsky's current condition. So dormant was the composer within him that he alluded only briefly to his brother's suggestions in his reply. All he wanted was escape from Vichy, and his doctor had now approved his departure after eleven days, provided he bore away sufficient Vichy water to complete the prescribed length of the cure:

> You wouldn't believe the impatience with which I am waiting for the moment when I leave this most boring, but also beneficial Vichy [he wrote in his reply to Modest of 19 July]. I call it 'beneficial' because the waters have had an excellent effect upon me – at least, on my stomach.... Your doctor is quite right – I can't remain here because, having in front of me two and a half weeks to stay in this hateful place, my morale would be torn to pieces, and my doctor here assures me that if the cure is to be efficacious, absolute peace of mind is necessary. I now find myself in that state of mind, thanks to my bright idea of taking half my cure here, the other half in Lyon. It goes without saying that I'll go with you not only to Montpellier, but to Sète.... Thank you very much for your *programmes*. Of them *Hamlet* pleases me greatly, but it's devilishly difficult.[10]

[9] *TLP6*, pp. 59–60; *TPR*, pp. 698–9 (partial).
[10] *TLP6*, p. 59; *TZC1*, p. 488; *TPR*, p. 247.

Though they had no immediate effect, the ideas in Modest's letter were to bear some fruit. Tchaikovsky's interest later in the year in *Othello* (though as an opera subject) was short-lived, but after twelve years he was to embody Shakespeare's other tragic hero in a splendid fantasy overture. More important for the present, however, was Modest's idea that Francesca da Rimini might be the subject, not of an opera, but of an orchestral piece. This suggestion was to prompt Tchaikovsky's next major work, which he prefaced by lines from Dante beginning with the same words he had quoted to Modest soon after arriving in Vichy (though this time correctly set out):

.... Nessun maggior dolore,
Che ricordarsi del tempo felice
Nella miseria......

On 24 July Tchaikovsky was back in Lyon with Modest and Kolya. There remained a full fortnight before he had to be in Bayreuth. Klindworth had been pressurising him to attend the final *Ring* rehearsals, but Tchaikovsky had no inclination whatsoever to do so; without these he was going to have more than enough of Wagner's music for his taste. His trip to the south of France was already planned with Modest, and within forty-eight hours of his arrival in Lyon they had set out with Kolya and Sofya Ershova, governess to the latter, with whom both brothers had established a very cordial relationship. Together they journeyed by steamer down the Rhône to Avignon, where they spent a day before proceeding by train to Montpellier and installing themselves at Palavas-les-flots, a resort a few miles along the coast where they hoped to enjoy sea-bathing.

The journey from Lyon had been delightful, but their destination proved to be an unhappy choice. The bathing was poor, Palavas itself was unspeakably dreary (Tchaikovsky was later to confess that Vichy was paradise by comparison; the collective mood of Tchaikovsky and his companions may be gauged from the photograph following p. 192), and the local water made them all ill. Tchaikovsky, who was still imbibing regulation doses of Vichy water, was the least affected, and it fell to him to act as nursemaid to Kolya, a responsibility which, even allowing for Modest's characteristic ecstasy of expression on such matters, he clearly discharged with great care and affection.

All the untapped riches of parental feelings that were hidden in Pyotr Ilich's soul here had a chance to reveal themselves [Modest remembered]. Generally nervy, irritable moreover after his incarceration at Vichy, upset by the vestiges of the attack of depression that had overcome him while there, he was attentiveness, patience, gentleness itself in his handling of this deaf and dumb boy who was himself nervy, fidgety, able only with great difficulty to express himself to those around him. The mutual adoration of two friends, which had already before this established itself, became even stronger. I can truly say that this relationship with a boy who at that moment was entirely dependent upon him, this rôle as head of the family which for a short time had fallen to his lot, showed Pyotr Ilich a way out of the melancholy that was tormenting him, out of the 'loneliness' of his recent years.[11]

That there was a strong element of homosexual attraction in Tchaikovsky's feelings towards Kolya cannot be doubted; certainly the editors of the complete edition of the composer's letters felt there was, for they carefully expunged from them all Tchaikovsky's more impassioned expressions of feeling for the lad. In fact, Modest shared these emotions to a more critical degree, but Tchaikovsky himself had evidently managed to control his instincts, and one suspects that erotic drives were blended with a genuine element of paternal feeling and a longing for a family of his own. One cannot but wonder whether this little crisis at Palavas may not have been a factor of some significance in consolidating the incredible and fateful decision he was to announce within the next few weeks.

On 7 August Tchaikovsky bade farewell to his companions and set out for Paris. In the train he ate a vast quantity of soup, read the fifth canto of Dante's *Inferno*, 'and was inflamed with a wish to write a symphonic poem on *Francesca*'.[12] At last something seemed to be stirring in him, his health was mending well, and his spirits were, for the moment, good. He was delighted to be greeted as an old customer by the landlord and staff at the Hôtel de Hollande when he arrived in the French capital 24 hours later. A pleasant day was spent in relaxing, in shopping for clothes, and in choosing some presents for his valets, the Sofronov brothers. Though he does not mention it, he must have made one special purchase for himself: a piano score of Delibes' new ballet, *Sylvia*, which had been first performed in Paris only two months earlier. It captivated him instantly, and for some years was to be a great favourite of his, second only to that other masterpiece of French music, *Carmen*. His own *Swan Lake* was to suffer in his own estimation from comparison with it. So did Wagner's *Der Ring*. But if this Paris interlude had started delightfully, it ended painfully:

[11] *TZC*1, p. 489.
[12] *TLP*6, p. 62; *TZC*1, p. 490; *TPR*, p. 249; *YDGC*, p. 130; *DTC*, p. 366.

Tchaikovsky fell ill with terrible stomach-ache, rushed off to an apothecary for a strong laxative, took a mighty dose, passed a dreadful night, and spent the next day recovering. It was a Tchaikovsky far less buoyant than the one who had arrived in Paris who set out for Bayreuth on 10 August.

The whole musical world seemed to have congregated in this Bavarian town. From Russia alone there were Tchaikovsky's friends Nikolay Rubinstein, Laroche, Hubert, Albrecht, Klindworth, and Berthe Valzek, as well as Cui and Famintsïn. Tchaikovsky threw himself into the social hubbub with determination, and the letter he wrote to Modest on 14 August provides a vivid little sketch not only of part of his own brief but hectic passage through the town, but also of the conditions created by such an unnaturally large influx of people:

> I didn't arrive here until the eve of the performance, on Saturday, 12 August. I was greeted by Klindworth. I met a whole mass of people I knew and straightway fell into the maelstrom in which I am spinning all day like a madman. I met a whole mass of new people. I visited Liszt who received me with uncommon kindness. I visited Wagner who is now receiving no one, and so on. Of people whom you know, there are here: *Rubinstein*, with whom I'm staying and who arrived the same Saturday evening: *Laroche*, who's drunk from morning to night: *Cui*, whom I reconciled with Laroche, but only with the result that a couple of hours later[13] they quarrelled again, and so on. . . . Bayreuth is a tiny town in which several thousand people have now gathered, crowding into the accommodation, and with insufficient provision against hunger. Our quarters were booked a long time ago, and are very good. As for food, on the first evening I got supper with difficulty, and obtained dinner only as a result of happy coincidence. At least I'm not *bored*, though in no way can I say that I'm enjoying myself.[14]

This last sentence sums up admirably Tchaikovsky's state during his six days in this Bavarian town. He had come prepared not to enjoy the musical experience of the place, and the appearance of the new-opera house, where it was all to happen, did not please him. 'It must be confessed that it does not draw the observer's attention by the elegance of its contours, but simply by its colossal dimensions. It is more like a huge booth that might have been hurriedly put up for some industrial exhibition than a building which has to accommodate a mass of people

[13] 'the next day', according to Modest's citation of this letter.
[14] *TLP6*, pp. 63–4; *TZC1*, p. 490; *TPR*, p. 250; *TPB*, p. 111.

who have arrived from all the ends of the earth in search of artistic enjoyments. In that harmonious union of all the arts for which Wagner strives, architecture has been assigned too modest a place.'[15] The one thing about it that really impressed him was the stage lighting. The nutritional privations of Bayreuth were an unremitting source of discomfort. 'During the whole period of the first cycle of performances of Wagner's tetralogy, *food* was the prime concern of all, significantly pushing into the background interest in art. There was much more talk of beefsteaks, cutlets, and roast potatoes than of Wagner's music,' he reported further to his Russian readers,[16] with some evident satisfaction that there had been at least one grand failing in the festival arrangements that might moderate a little the adulation directed towards the composer for whose art alone this occasion had been designed.

Not having gained access to Wagner at the latter's sumptuous home, Wahnfried, his only opportunity to inspect the man was during the civic procession which set out for the railway station to greet Kaiser Wilhelm I on his arrival. 'I had to observe this meeting from the window of a neighbouring house,' he wrote, again for Russian consumption. 'There flashed past before my eyes several brilliant uniforms, then a procession of musicians from Wagner's theatre with their conductor, Hans Richter, at their head, then the tall, well-proportioned figure of the Abbé Liszt with his splendid, characteristic, grey-haired head which has so often fascinated me in his ubiquitous portraits – then, sitting in a very ornate carriage, a sprightly little old man with an aquiline nose and thin, supercilious lips – the characteristic trait of the initiator of this entire cosmopolitan artistic festival, Richard Wagner.'[17] Even when only glimpsing Wagner from an upstairs window, Tchaikovsky could not help disliking him.

Between 13 and 17 August Tchaikovsky was present at the first-ever *Ring* cycle. The performance should have been on four consecutive days, but the illness of one of the singers forced a 24-hour postponement of the last two music dramas, and Tchaikovsky, with Laroche, spent the free day on a carriage trip outside Bayreuth, both of them (so Laroche said) revelling in the silence. On the other days, Laroche added, Tchaikovsky only came to life when it was all over and he was confronted with supper and a large mug of beer. Knowing the views Tchaikovsky had already declared on the German master and his work, we might well wonder what could have possessed him to make the

[15] *TMKS*, p. 320.
[16] *TMKS*, p. 322; *TZC*1, p. 492.
[17] *TMKS*, p. 321; *TZC*1, p. 491.

journey. Curiosity, of course – for what musician of Tchaikovsky's generation was not fascinated by this most powerful musical personality of the post-Beethoven period, this inspired megalomaniac whose manœuvrings and sheer genius had now realised the dream of a personal musical capital such as no musician before (or since) had ever raised to serve his own art? In any case Tchaikovsky had fully perceived that Wagner had one supreme musical gift. In 1879 he was to look back sixteen years and reflect that only once in his life had he ever encountered the absolutely complete conductor. 'This was *Wagner* when he arrived in St Petersburg in 1863 to give concerts, conducting moreover several Beethoven symphonies. Whoever has not heard these symphonies as performed by Wagner has not fully appreciated them, or fully grasped all their unrivalled grandeur.'[18] And while Tchaikovsky might suspect, even loathe Wagner as a composer, only one irrevocably convinced of the worthlessness of Wagner's equally magisterial musical creations could have resisted an invitation such as Tchaikovsky had received in February to be present at the unveiling of this extraordinary achievement.

Tchaikovsky's journalistic reports were the price he had to pay for not expending his own resources on this part of his summer trip. As far as possible he avoided comment upon the works themselves. Only the last of his five articles is occupied at all with such matters, and it contains nothing that could in any way surprise after his earlier pronouncements on Wagner. The first article had appeared in the *Russian Gazette* in May, when Tchaikovsky had sketched the background to the whole Bayreuth enterprise. The next two merely outlined the plots of the four works, and were written at Palavas, appearing in the press during the very days when their author was in Bayreuth. Of the remaining two, the first is by far the more interesting. Ostensibly it is simply an account of his six days in the town, but its heavy emphasis upon the shortcomings and inconveniences in the festival's arrangements and facilities, its gleeful listing of the prominent European musicians who were *not* present ('Verdi, Gounod, Thomas, Brahms, Anton Rubinstein, Raff, Joachim, Bülow'), and so on, uncovers Tchaikovsky's resolve to diminish the grandiose image of this musical egoist and his art behind a heavy screen of trivia and even ridicule. In this article Tchaikovsky, who had now been within the courts of the temple, in the imminent presence of the priest (or godhead), who had experienced the full force of his musical creed and might, unwittingly disclosed as much of his personal antagonism to, even revulsion from

[18] *TPM*2, p. 57; *TLP*8, pp. 114–15.

Wagner's ideals and their embodiment as did any of his written notices on his music.

Far more candid and forthright than all the words he expended in the Russian press was Tchaikovsky's own brief account of his musical experiences at Bayreuth contained in two letters to Modest, the first an interim report after seeing *Das Rheingold*. 'As a stage presentation, this pleasantry excited my curiosity, and as a spectacular production it fascinated me. As music it is an unbelievable muddle in which, from time to time, unusually beautiful and striking details may be fleetingly glimpsed.'[19] On 20 August, six days later, and two days after leaving Wagner's new shrine, he summarised his final impressions. He had made one very gratifying discovery while he was there:

My recollection of Bayreuth remains oppressive, though much happened there that is very flattering to my artistic self-esteem. It seems that I am by no means as little known in Germany and other foreign countries as I had thought. The recollection is oppressive because the bustle all the time there was indescribable. Finally on Thursday it was all over, and with the last chords of *Götterdämmerung* I felt as though I'd been released from captivity. Perhaps *Nibelungen* is a very great work, but there's certainly never yet been anything more boring and prolix than this long-drawn-out affair. The piling-up of the most complex and recherché harmonies, the colourlessness of everything that's sung on stage, the endlessly long dialogues, the pitch darkness of the theatre [which made it impossible to follow the libretto], the lack of any interest or poetic quality in the subject – all this wearies the nerves to the last degree. And so this is what Wagner's reform has achieved! At one time they tried to make music give people pleasure – now they torture and tire them. Of course, there are some wonderful moments – but taken all in all, it's killingly boring! How many hundreds of thousands of times nicer is *Sylvia*![20]

The Bayreuth experience had confirmed all Tchaikovsky's earlier impressions and worst fears about Wagner's musical philosophy and the music that sprang forth under its banner. When he left the town he shook the dust from off his feet – though a few substantial particles still clung when he wrote his next major work which he was gestating while

[19] *TLP6*, pp. 63–4; *TZC1*, p. 490; *TTR*, p. 250; *YDGC*, p. 131 (partial); *TPR*, p. 111.
[20] *TLP6*, pp. 64–5; *TZC1*, p. 494; *TPR*, p. 251; *YDGC*, p. 131 (partial); *TPB*, pp. 111–12.

in Bayreuth, *Francesca da Rimini*. Modest was surely right in believing that there was a very real negative influence in his brother's experience – that it confirmed Tchaikovsky in what he would *not* do, especially convincing him that his operas yet unwritten should continue to adhere to the principles declared in those he had already composed. On his way from Paris he had stopped a night in Nuremberg, and he passed through that city yet again on leaving Bayreuth, pausing a day to finish his last Bayreuth despatch for the *Russian Gazette*, and to enjoy the sights. 'What a delight this Nuremberg is!' he exclaimed to Modest from Vienna, where he had arrived the next day.[21] Before leaving home he had planned, after Bayreuth, to visit some seaside resort for the rest of the summer, but as soon as he was abroad he had been overwhelmed by a longing to rush back to Russia immediately his Wagner obligation was discharged. Quitting Vienna on 21 August, he hastened to Verbovka in a highly tense condition. Three days later he was again with Sasha.

The fortnight he spent at Verbovka was by far the pleasantest part of the summer for him. Not only did he have his sister and her family: there were also his father, stepmother, Anatoly, and even Ippolit, who had now largely passed out of his life, but for whom he retained a strong affection. 'We are spending the time very, very nicely,' he reported to Modest, lamenting that the latter could not also be with them. 'Yesterday Ippolit arrived: tall, fat, thin-voiced, sentimental – but very sweet, and preserving still his ability to tell funny stories. I found Papa had grown *very* thin and aged. This is aggravated not a little by the condition of Lizaveta Mikhailovna, who is ill again. Sasha worries me a bit. She's become excessively wrapped up in curing ailments among the peasants. She busies herself with them from morning to evening.'[22]

Yet while so characteristically concerned with the well-being of members of his family, and despite the contentment he felt with Verbovka and his mode of living while he was there, he was himself torn within by tormenting thoughts that would not be stilled. He had confessed them to no one except Modest, nor would it have been in his nature to do so. The nearest he had come to revealing his secret was in the cries of 'loneliness' that occur more than once in his letters from abroad that summer, and in the morbid closeness he had felt to that little deaf-mute at Palavas. What he needed – and perhaps watching Sasha and her brood at Verbovka made him the more aware of it – was a family life. Yet how could this need be satisfied when he was as he

[21] *TLP6*, p. 65; *TPR*, pp. 251–2; *TPB*, p. 112.
[22] *TLP6*, p. 66; *TPR*, pp. 252–3.

was? It was surely thoughts such as this that were the real cause of his depressed state, and the summer would still have been miserable without Kondratyev's servants or the tedium of Vichy, without loathsome Palavas or the oppressive experience of Bayreuth. At Verbovka the crucial stage in this inner condition was reached, and his decision taken. 'I am now living through a very critical moment of my life,' he confided to Modest after a week with their sister. 'When an opportunity occurs I'll write to you about it in rather more detail, but meanwhile I'll just say: *I have decided to marry*. I cannot avoid this. I have to do it, and not just for my own sake, but also for *you*, and for Tolya, and for Sasha, and for all those I love. For *you* in particular. And you, Modya, need to think seriously of this.'[23] The immutable course towards disaster had now been set.

Tchaikovsky's last call of the summer was upon Vladimir Shilovsky at Usovo. He went there reluctantly, but he needed to collect the two thousand roubles he had requested from Shilovsky while he was in Lyon. Tchaikovsky had received a number of monetary gifts from this friend over the years, and in 1879, when Shilovsky revealed this to others, Tchaikovsky was highly embarrassed. Having spent a few days at Usovo, he returned to Moscow in mid-September, his muse still slumbering. 'I've still written nothing since my return – or almost nothing,' he wrote to Modest on 29 September.[24] Yet, astonishingly, within a week he had actually completed a new orchestral piece.

Tchaikovsky was in no way a political animal, as he had emphatically shown in that unfortunate incident that had occurred during a performance of *A Life for the Tsar* immediately after an assassination attempt on Alexandr II in April 1866. Nevertheless, he was at least a little stirred when, in June 1876, Montenegro and Serbia declared war on Turkey in consequence of Turkish massacres of Christians in the Balkans. Such atrocities against fellow-Slavs raised a colossal wave of sympathy in Russia, and Tchaikovsky had followed events with enough interest to allude to the struggle in one of his summer letters to Modest. Volunteers from Russia flooded to help defeat the Turks, and by September it seemed that Russia would be drawn into the conflict. Throughout the country the flood of sympathetic emotion towards the victims of Turkey continued to rise, and in this Tchaikovsky fully shared. 'The declaration of war is expected from hour to hour,' he wrote to Lev Davïdov on 24 September. '. . . It's terrible yet also gratifying

[23] *TPR*, p. 253; *TLP6*, p. 66; *TZC1*, p. 497. The last three sentences are included only in *TPR*.

[24] *TLP6*, p. 71; *TZC1*, p. 501; *TPR*, p. 256; *YDGC*, p. 132; *TPB*, p. 112.

that our beloved country is deciding at last to give confirmation of her worth.'[25]

Tchaikovsky's rare involvement in a contemporary event was suddenly heightened by a little incident that took place exactly a week after he wrote to Lev. 'Yesterday, at the home of a lady I know, I had to witness a heart-rending scene. Her son, a pleasant, intelligent young man, informed her in my presence that he was going to Serbia. Just imagine, she fell down in a faint and then, coming to herself, lay for a long while incapable of speech. I was terribly shaken by this scene,' he told Sasha.[26] It was under the immediate impression of this incident that Tchaikovsky responded to a request from Nikolay Rubinstein for a new piece that might be played in a special concert the RMS was planning in aid of the Slavonic Charity Committee's efforts both to equip Russian volunteers and to succour the victims of the war in the Balkans. Tchaikovsky reacted with remarkable vigour. All the torpor of the last five months was thrown off, and five days later, on 7 October, the Slavonic March (or, as it was first known, the Serbo-Russian March) was not only composed but scored.

According to Kashkin, Tchaikovsky, in his search for suitable materials for this topical work, 'got hold of some collections of Serbian songs but, to his distress, could not find in them a single tune that pleased him completely. However, despite this, he finally chose two, and wrote his march.'[27] In fact, Tchaikovsky drew from three Serbian tunes; the actual sources from which he took them are unknown. From one of his tunes he simply took a single central phrase (Ex. 120e), and in the first he appears to have followed his normal practice of modifying the original to 'improve' it for his requirements, squaring up the opening three bars into four (Ex. 120a and b), just as he was to do with the Russian folksong, 'Vo pole beryoza stoyala', in the finale of his Fourth Symphony (incidentally, the two tunes are clearly related), and then sacrificing a bar near the end.

The march that he built from these folk materials is a ternary structure, both of its component sections likewise exhibiting ternary organisation, with one folktune (Ex. 120a) forming the basis of the first section, the remaining two morsels (Ex. 120c and e) generating the flanks and centre respectively of the middle portion of the whole work. Before the first section returns to complete the ternary design, part of the Tsarist national anthem is heard, a full statement of it being held over to the patriotic peroration before the coda. Here it is combined

[25] *TLP6*, p. 70; *TZC1*, p. 499; *TPR*, p. 255; *YDGC*, p. 132.
[26] *TLP6*, p. 75; *TPR*, p. 259.
[27] *KVC*, p. 106.

Ex. 120

with a new tune of Tchaikovsky's own devising which seems to grow out of his own derivative from one of the folksongs (Ex. 120d). With the direct appeal of its borrowed melodies heightened by current events and presented with colourful and stirring accompaniments, with its extensive and unabashedly rousing dominant preparations, its tumultuous trumpeting of the Russian national anthem, and its blatantly noisy coda, the Slavonic March was calculatedly addressed to an audience that was only too ready to react to an emotional summons to its patriotic fervour. It was greeted with precisely such a response when it was first heard on 17 November. As one unnamed eyewitness recorded: 'The rumpus and roar that broke out in the hall after this [performance of the march] beggars description. The whole audience rose to its feet, many jumped up onto their seats: cries of *bravo* and *hurrah* were mingled together. The march had to be repeated, after which the same storm broke out afresh.... It was one of the most stirring moments of 1876. Many in the hall were weeping.'[28] Kashkin also vouched for its impact.

Tchaikovsky himself seems to have felt little personal pleasure in the occasion, for he knew the reception had nothing to do with the quality of his music. Only once, very briefly at the end of a letter to Sasha, did he ever mention the performance and its aftermath. His own judgement is implicit in what he wrote to Taneyev four weeks after the performance. 'Don't judge the March from its arrangement [for piano].

---

[28] *DTC*, p. 346; *TPR*, p. 700.

On the orchestra it proved to be effective.'[29] Its virtues, such as they were, lay in its dressing, not its substance.

Outwardly Tchaikovsky's first two months in Moscow that autumn were devoid of significant incident. Relations with Kondratyev remained uncomfortable after the upheaval at Nizy in June, but they began to be renewed in Moscow, and were soon sufficiently repaired for the two men to get drunk together. The fear (unjustified, as it turned out) that a Russian production of Rubinstein's opera, *The Maccabees*, might obstruct *Vakula*'s passage to the stage brought another bout of resentment such as he had confessed earlier in the year to Bülow. To balance this there was the gratification of being again approached by Rimsky-Korsakov, this time with a request for permission to use some of Tchaikovsky's own harmonisations in a collection of folksongs which Rimsky-Korsakov was compiling. Highly flattered, Tchaikovsky agreed.[30]

It was flattering, too, to be suddenly asked by the Vienna Philharmonic Society to play in one of its concerts, though Tchaikovsky was amused by the improbable rôle he was being expected to perform. The first major performance of one of his works in the Austrian capital occurred on 26 November and was not a success; conducted by Hans Richter, *Romeo and Juliet* was hissed, and Hanslick reviewed it very unfavourably. Fourteen days later the same work was played in Paris, to be greeted with no greater favour, though Taneyev, who was present and gave some detailed account of the event to the composer, blamed the conductor, Pasdeloup, for not understanding the piece. Nevertheless, some of the Parisian musical fraternity, including Saint-Saëns, had expressed approval of the work, and this encouraged Tchaikovsky to hope that a concert of his own music in the French capital might be timely. When he had been in Moscow a year earlier Saint-Saëns had suggested he should promote such an event; now Taneyev was instructed to approach Saint-Saëns for further counsel on the matter. Tchaikovsky was determined on one thing: if the concert did take place, he was going to attend rehearsals to see that the pieces were played properly – and he was even prepared himself to conduct if necessary. 'This will seem strange to you, but I'm able to decide upon this simply because it is *Paris* and not Moscow, where I'm too well known, and where the opinion that I'm not a conductor has got too firm a root,' he

[29] *TLP*6, p. 89; *TTP*, p. 11.
[30] Rimsky-Korsakov used two of Tchaikovsky's settings from T50RF: 'Na more utushka' (No. 23), which had been used in both *The Voyevoda* and the *Oprichnik*, and 'Sidel Vanya' (No. 47), which had formed the basis of the Andante cantabile in the First String Quartet.

added by way of explanation.[31] Finally financial obstacles proved insurmountable, however, and the concert was never given.

Yet all these matters, pleasant and unpleasant, were of small account compared to his new-found resolution to take by the throat the personal destiny nature had decreed for him, and make it submit to the force of his own will. The letters which he wrote to Modest in September and October are among those most mutilated by Soviet editors determined (or compelled) to suppress any direct reference to Tchaikovsky's homosexuality. Yet in the 1930s, when the Tchaikovsky–Nadezhda von Meck correspondence was published, such constraints were less severe, and the editorial notes to volume one of this great three-volume work incorporated invaluable extracts from letters the composer wrote to Modest – extracts not only suppressed by Modest himself in his published work, but also expunged from all but one Soviet edition of subsequent years. This exception is the collection of letters written up to 1879 by Tchaikovsky to members of his family, printed in 1940 but withdrawn before publication;[32] the text of this volume both confirms and supplements that of the Tchaikovsky–von Meck print. Unfortunately even in these fuller texts there are exasperating lacunae; yet from what Modest permitted to survive of his brother's literary remains (or, at least, from what got into print), there can no longer be any doubt that the 'vices' of which Tchaikovsky wrote were homosexual ones. Admittedly these letters contain only allusions; nor are they always coherent as documents, for the man who penned them was in a frantic state. Vladimir Volkoff has argued spiritedly against accepting too readily the homosexual interpretation, but without presenting a more convincing construction. On the other hand, V. Zhdanov and N. Zhegin, the editors of the Tchaikovsky–von Meck letters, were in no two minds about it. 'Tchaikovsky was homosexual,' they wrote bluntly, 'and in this lay, outwardly and inwardly, his greatest tragedy. He was tortured by his estrangement, feared publicity (and rumours had already circulated), and he sought a way out.'[33] On this matter let the documents speak for themselves (some of the quotations here and elsewhere are conflations from the first volume of the Tchaikovsky–von Meck correspondence, the official complete edition of the composer's letters and, most valuable of all, the suppressed edition of the composer's letters to his family, printed in 1940).

[31] *TLP*6, p. 90; *TZC*1, p. 515; *TTP*, p. 12.
[32] Only one copy of this edition is known to have been smuggled to the West, and the present writer has had free access to it.
[33] *TPM*1, p. 570.

It's now a month and a half since we parted [Tchaikovsky wrote to Modest on 22 September], but to me it seems that several centuries have passed since then. During this time I've thought much about myself, about you, and about our future.[34] As a result of all this ruminating I shall from today seriously prepare myself for entry into the union of a lawful marriage with whomsoever I may. I find that our *inclinations* are the greatest and most insuperable obstacle to happiness, and we must with all our strength struggle with our nature. I love you very much, I love *Kolya* very much, for your mutual good I hope very much you will not part – but it is a sine qua non for the stability of your relationships that you should not be *that* which you have been up to now. This is essential not for *qu'en dira-t-on*, but for your very self, your peace of mind. . . . You say that at your age it is difficult to overcome passions. To that I'll reply that at your age it is easier to direct your tastes elsewhere. Here your inclination to religion must, I think, be a firm support to you. As for myself, I shall do everything that's possible to get married during this very year, and if I don't have the courage for this, then I am in any case discarding for ever my habits, and I shall try to ensure that I'm no longer numbered among the company of [here there is a blank]. . . . I am thinking only of eradicating from myself my pernicious passions.[35]

A week later Modest had replied. His outright opposition to his brother's proposed marriage could have been predicted, and by now Tchaikovsky himself was openly revealing his antipathy to his intended state in a tone which recalls the airy unreality with which, years before, he had warned Sasha that she would have to prepare herself to provide domestic comforts for her world-weary brother. 'I cannot express to you that feeling of sweet peace, *almost* happiness, which I experience in my quiet and cosy little flat when I arrive home in the evening and take a book in my hand. At such moments I certainly hate as much as you do that beautiful, unknown woman who will force me to change my way of life and my associates. Have no fears for me. I do not intend to rush in this matter, and rest assured that if indeed I do involve myself with a woman [Modest has 'get married'], then I shall do it with great circumspection.'[36] Modest remained unconvinced.

[34] In *TPM*1 'about myself and my future': this source consistently suggests Tchaikovsky was writing solely about his own predicament.

[35] *TPR*, pp. 253–4; *TLP*6, p. 69; *TZC*1, pp. 498–9; *TPM*1, pp. 570–1 (all partial except *TPR*).

[36] *TPR*, pp. 255–6; *TLP*6, p. 71; *TZC*1, p. 501; *TPB*, p. 112 (partial); *TPM*1, p. 571 (partial).

Meanwhile Tchaikovsky wrote in much the same vein to Anatoly, who had visited Moscow for a week during which he had persuaded his brother to take a daily cold bath for the sake of his health. This had had a splendid effect upon Tchaikovsky's physical condition, but Anatoly had experienced no remission in his brother's nervous irritability. After the twin's departure Tchaikovsky was abjectly apologetic, and again voiced his own uncertainties on his intentions. 'I felt that I was *talking nonsense* when I told you that I had *fully* decided upon the abrupt *upheaval* in my life about which you know. In fact, I have not yet at all decided upon it. I only have *this* seriously in view, and I'm waiting for something which will make me act. . . . My flesh creeps when I reflect that I shall have to part with all this [his present secluded and quiet home life]. But parting is necessary. I repeat, I am serious in intending to *become a new man*, but I want to prepare myself for this only by degrees.'[37]

Meanwhile Modest had returned to the assault yet again, and this prompted from Tchaikovsky the most naked disclosure that is available to us of the nature of his condition and of its family and social consequences. Unfortunately published sources do not permit a complete reconstruction of this entire crucial letter:

Dear Modest,

I've lost your letter and I can't reply point by point to your arguments against marriage. I remember that many of them are unsound; many, on the other hand, coincide completely with my own thoughts. . . . You say that one should not give a damn for *qu'en dira-t-on*. This is true only up to a certain point. There are people who cannot despise me for my vices simply because they began to love me when they still didn't suspect that I was, in fact, a man with a lost reputation. For instance, this applies to *Sasha*. I know that she guesses *everything* and *forgives* everything. Many other people whom I love or respect regard me in the same way. Do you really believe that the consciousness *that they pity and forgive me* is not painful to me when, at bottom, I am guilty of nothing! And is it not a terrible thought that people who love me can sometimes *be ashamed* of me! But, you know, this has happened a hundred times, and it will happen a hundred times. In a word, I should like by marriage, or by a generally open liaison with a woman, to stop the mouths of various contemptible creatures whose opinion I do not in the least respect, but who could cause distress to people close to me. In any case, don't fear for me, dear Modya. The fulfilment of my plans is not nearly as close as you

[37] *TPR*, p. 257; *TLP*6, p. 72; *TZC*1, p. 502 (all partial except *TPR*).

think. My habits and tastes have become so hardened that it's impossible to discard them at once like an old glove. And besides, I am far from possessed of an iron character, and since my letters to you I have already some three times given way to the force of natural inclinations. Thus you are completely right in saying in your letter that, despite all one's vows, it is not possible to restrain oneself from one's weaknesses.

All the same, I am standing by my intentions, and you may be sure that, one way or another, I shall carry them through. But I shall not do this suddenly or hastily. In any case, I do not intend to take a *yoke* upon me. I shall only enter into a legal or an extra-marital union with a woman if I can fully guarantee my peace and freedom.[38]

Sasha also was horrified by her brother's decision, though not, it would appear, because she had yet perceived he was congenitally incapable of marriage, but because he was proposing to be so precipitate. Tchaikovsky did his best to quiet her fears, and to squash her suggestion that Sonya Peresleni, one of Lev's nieces, might be a suitable spouse. 'Please, my angel, don't worry about my proposed marriage. First, I have not the slightest intention of deciding upon this step in the immediate future, and in any case it will certainly not happen in the current year (that is, the academic year). But during these few months I simply want to accustom and prepare myself for matrimony which, for various reasons, I consider would be a very good thing for me. Rest assured that I shall not hurl myself into the maelstrom of an unfortunate marital union. Sonya Peresleni (who, by the way, would hardly marry me) I have finally struck off my list of candidates. I have had occasion to be convinced of the amazing *heartlessness* of this girl,' he wrote on 18 October.[39]

It was in this uncertain, tormented state that Tchaikovsky set about *Francesca da Rimini*, the orchestral piece upon which he had decided during the train journey from Palavas to Paris. In no work he had yet written had his personal condition been of such importance in determining the character of what issued from his creative faculties. Ironically, he himself thought that in *Francesca* might be found 'something new and fresher'[40] which he attributed to, of all things, his cold baths. He began the piece on 7 October, and in less than three weeks had completed composition. 'I have written it with love,' he informed Modest on 26 October, 'and the *love* [the central andante

[38] *TPR*, pp. 259–60; *TPM*1, p. 571; *TLP*6, pp. 75–6 (all partial).
[39] *TLP*6, pp. 78–9; *TPR*, p. 261; *TZC*1, p. 504 (partial).
[40] *TLP*6, p. 81; *TPR*, p. 263; *TZC*1, p. 505.

cantabile non troppo] seems to have come out respectably. As far as the whirlwinds are concerned, it would have been possible to make something corresponding more with *Doré*'s illustration, but it didn't come out as I wanted. On the other hand, a reliable judgment on this piece is inconceivable while it remains unscored and unperformed.'[41] Thus he was particularly anxious to hear it without delay, and seeing in a journal that three of his *Vakula* dances were to be played in a concert in St Petersburg on 2 December, he wrote forthwith to Nápravník, who was to conduct, asking him to substitute *Francesca da Rimini*, even though the concert was only a month away and the scoring operation scarcely begun. The St Petersburg RMS would not change the programme, however. *Francesca* was finally finished on 17 November, and the first performance took place at an RMS concert in Moscow on 9 March 1877, a second performance following nine days later, and yet a third after only five more days at a special RMS charity concert on 22 March. On all three occasions Nikolay Rubinstein conducted.

Francesca da Rimini was an immediate audience success, and Kashkin reviewed it enthusiastically, but there was more press comment after the first performance in St Petersburg, which took place under Nápravník on 23 March 1878. By this time Tchaikovsky was in western Europe, whither he had fled some five months earlier after the débâcle of his marriage. In consequence he had to rely upon Anatoly to report on the occasion. '*Francesca* had a great success,' the latter wrote on 30 March. 'The applause was endless ... Karl Yulevich [Davïdov] charged me to write to you that, in his opinion, *Francesca* is the greatest work of our time. Nápravník is also in raptures.'[42] From Taneyev, who was the work's dedicatee and who was also present at the performance, he received corroboration of Anatoly's excellent tidings, as well as a summary of informed opinion on the work:

> Cui likes the introduction most of all. The beginning of the narrative [the central section] pleases him little: [he thinks] it's like a Russian folksong, which is out-of-place here. All the following music of the narrative he finds superb, especially where the syncopations begin. Nápravník likes it very much, only he finds it too long; twenty-five minutes is a lot for a symphonic poem. I score-read *Francesca* to Laroche before the concert. He doesn't like its resemblance to Liszt; he finds that symphonic poems are not your genre. I think he only says this because he doesn't like *any* programme music. After the

[41] *TLP6*, p. 80; *TPR*, p. 262; *TZC1*, pp. 504–5, *YDGC*, p. 133; *DTC*, p. 367; *TPB*, p. 113.
[42] *DTC*, p. 368; *TPR*, p. 712.

concert I asked him whether he would praise or censure *Francesca*. He answered that he would incline to praise. [Rimsky-]Korsakov doesn't like the theme; everything taken as a whole pleases him very much. Davïdov finds *Francesca* not only the best of your works but of all contemporary music. Cui and others find that some bits are written under the influence of the *Nibelungen*.[43]

Tchaikovsky's reply to Taneyev, written from Clarens in Switzerland on 8 April, was tart about Cui's folksong remark, though it acknowledged the Wagner identification. 'That the first theme [of the middle section] is like a Russian folksong was not Cui's own idea. I told him that last year. If I hadn't said so, he wouldn't have noticed. The remark that I wrote under the influence of the *Nibelungen is very correct*. I myself felt this while I was at work. If I'm not mistaken, it's especially noticeable in the introduction. Isn't it odd that I should have submitted to the influence of a work of art that in general is extremely antipathetic to me?'[44]

Francesca da Rimini reached western Europe only five months later. At the performance in Berlin on 14 September under Benjamin Bilse it had to compete for attention with Brahms's Second Symphony, but the presence in the same programme of this recent major German piece at least ensured that Tchaikovsky's work was heard by a large number of Berlin's most important musicians and connoisseurs. Not surprisingly, the audience divided sharply on the relative merits of the two pieces, but Tchaikovsky's work received some praise from the press, and it was reported that even Joachim did not allow his natural partiality for Brahms's music to deafen him to the qualities of *Francesca*. Certainly it confirmed the admiration of Tchaikovsky's greatest German champion. Bülow was there, and wrote to Tchaikovsky that he took even more delight in *Francesca* than in *Romeo and Juliet*. Before the end of 1878 New York had heard *Francesca* too.

The printed score contained a brief prose explanation as preface to twenty-two lines from the fifth canto of Dante's *Inferno* in which is contained Francesca's pitiful tale. In the manuscript score, however, Tchaikovsky set out his own prose programme more fully and precisely:

Dante, accompanying the shade of Virgil, descends to the second circle of hell's abyss. The air here is filled with groans, wails, and cries of despair. In the sepulchral gloom a storm blows up and rages.

[43] *DTC*, p. 369; *TZC2*, p. 156; *TTP*, p. 31.
[44] *TLP7*, p. 201; *TZC2*, pp. 148–9; *DTC*, p. 369 (partial); *YDGC*, p. 179.

Furiously the hellish whirlwind races along, bearing in its wild whirling the spirits of mortals whose reason in life was clouded by amorous passion. From the countless human souls spinning there, Dante's attention is specially drawn to the two lovely shades of Francesca and Paolo spinning in each other's embrace. Shocked by the soul-searing sight of these two young shades, Dante summons them and asks them to relate the crime for which they have been prescribed so terrible a punishment. Dissolving in tears, the shade of Francesca tells her sad tale. She loved Paolo but was, against her will, given in marriage to the hateful brother of her beloved, the hunch-backed, deformed, jealous tyrant, Rimini. The bonds of a forced marriage could not drive from Francesca's heart her tender passion for Paolo. Once they were reading together the romance of Lancelot. 'We were alone,' Francesca narrated, 'and were reading without apprehension. More than once we blanched, and our confused glances met. But one instant destroyed us both. When, finally, the fortunate Lancelot gained the first kiss of love, he, from whom nothing will now separate me, kissed my trembling mouth, and the book that had revealed to us for the first time the secret of love fell from our hands.' At that moment Francesca's husband had entered unexpectedly and killed both her and Paolo with blows from his dagger. And, having said this, Francesca was again borne away in the embrace of her Paolo by the furiously and wildly raging whirlwind.[45]

Tchaikovsky himself vouched for the element of Wagner in *Francesca da Rimini*. Nevertheless, it seems clear from his letter to Taneyev that he felt this influence to be pervasive rather than one that could be readily identified in specific contexts – though he did himself believe, as we have seen, that the introduction had especially caught something from that source. Certainly the rapid five-note scale spanning a tritone in the bass instruments (see Ex. 122b) is ubiquitously found in *Der Ring*. Perhaps the work's broad time-scale (Nápravník had commented adversely upon its length) owes a little to the example of Wagner's monumentality, though its principles of organisation are very much Tchaikovsky's own. Some of the chromatic moments (such as, for instance, the progression between bars twenty-four and twenty-five of Ex. 124 below) sound like echoes from Wagner's world. Not only the music itself, but sometimes, too, the scoring; the low brass chording (Ex. 121) of the supertonic seventh which heralds the resurgence of the storm and whirlwind of the work's third and final section could easily

[45] *DTC*, p. 366.

Ex. 121

find a home in *Der Ring*. Though there is really nothing in *Francesca* that Tchaikovsky could not conceivably have written even if he had never been to Bayreuth, it is impossible to believe that the storm music, with its hectically piled sequences and wailing chromaticism, would have come out quite the way it did, had he not had the concentrated experience of Wagner's tetralogy, with its frequent orchestral eruptions of the elements.

Laroche thought he had spotted Liszt, and there would certainly be no cause for surprise if this descent into Dante's kingdom of the infernal should have turned Tchaikovsky's thoughts towards the Hungarian's earlier ventures into this world. Francesca herself had also occupied the centre of Liszt's own *Inferno* in the first movement of the Dante Symphony, but Tchaikovsky owed absolutely nothing to Liszt's portrayal except, perhaps, for the successive use of clarinet and strings to introduce this pathetic lady (though Liszt used a bass clarinet). In any case, Liszt's hell was musically too impoverished to have commanded much respect from Tchaikovsky. Whether the imposing *Après une lecture de Dante* from the *Années de pèlerinage* had any direct effect upon Tchaikovsky's musical conception is unknown, though it seems of some significance that both works employ a slow introduction, in the very first bars of which the tritone is the most prominent interval (Ex.

122), and both build what follows from two savagely contrasting types of musical invention, the one patently tempestuous, the other both tremulous and impassioned. Beyond these common features, however, the two works share nothing, for where Liszt, as his subtitle 'Fantasia quasi Sonata' suggests, cross-fertilises these two opposing musical worlds, Tchaikovsky maintains rigid segregation.

Ex. 122

In fact, there is more of Tchaikovsky's own symphonism in *Francesca da Rimini* than might at first be suspected. The E minor Allegro vivo, that so graphically conjures the storm and whirlwind, is not unlike a gigantic first subject based on the characteristic Tchaikovskyan pattern, two tonic statements of the basic material enclosing an extensive quasi-developmental centre, with Francesca's A minor music taking the rôle of a second subject (this symphonic analogy is the more persuasive if one looks ahead to the next symphony, the Fourth). Yet such expositional features are not Tchaikovsky's intention, for *Francesca* is simply a huge ternary structure with the storm music acting as flanks to the central matter of the heroine herself. Despite the suggestions of Tchaikovsky's manuscript, it is not Francesca's story but she herself that is the subject of the central section, for here the thematic rotations surely offer no suggestion of narrative. If *Romeo and Juliet* was a drama, and *The Tempest* a panorama, *Francesca da Rimini* was really a portrait set against a wild background. Thus there are none of the thematic conflicts of *Romeo*, nor the wide variety of *The Tempest*; instead each massive section is built from a limited store of thematic ideas which embody the character required of that section.

The work that Tchaikovsky generated from this high concentration upon a narrow range of materials has aroused very diverging critical opinions. To the approval from audience and press at the earliest performances, Balakirev years later added his enthusiastic endorsement. Certainly *Francesca* had all the qualities that would have appealed most strongly to Tchaikovsky's mentor of *Romeo and Juliet* days. Not only was its design lucid and reasonable, but its facture was the most polished Tchaikovsky had ever achieved. When Balakirev scanned *Francesca* from bar to bar, as was his practice, he could not but have admired the intricate yet precise chromatic embellishment of the basic harmony through which is conjured the swirls of the storm, or the lucid, fastidiously differentiated scoring of much of Francesca's music, or the sometimes striking textural support of the thematic material of this central section.

There were other virtues by which Balakirev might have set less store. The storm was markedly better than that of *The Tempest*, not relying for its musical substance upon an idea imported from another section and inserted into a collection of conventionally frenetic imagery to represent the turmoil of the elements, but instead growing from some very simple basic materials which easily proliferated into the chromatic turbulence through which Tchaikovsky could most aptly discharge the descriptive obligations of this section. Thus, as the winds stir after the infernal gloom so strikingly depicted in the opening andante lugubre, they extract a repeated shape from the heaving opening bass (Ex. 123a), and give birth to a new idea that is first embedded in the chromatic decoration (Ex. 123b) – an idea which only defines itself as a

Ex. 123

separate melodic fragment when the allegro vivace begins and the force of the tempest prepares to unleash itself (Ex. 123c); then, when the full fury of the winds is finally released, this melodic fragment in turn looks back to the gloomy opening bass which had been its original ancestor, and links with it to make a single and substantial melodic phrase (Ex. 123d). The sense of an organic melodic growth towards this point is admirable; if, as music, it has not been particularly rich, it has certainly not been simply a series of effects without musical cause. Admirable, too, is the progressive clarification of key from the tonal limbo of the opening to the unequivocal E minor stated at this tutti. Tchaikovsky's tonal scheme in *Francesca* is certainly not complex, but his control of spacious tonal areas is very assured. The chromatically hectic passage of the storm and whirlwind is the stronger for not raging in all tonal directions or in none, as *The Tempest* had tended to do, but for being directed into a straighter, more purposeful course centring on E minor. It is quite notable how much of *Francesca da Rimini* is grounded upon E, for even the A minor theme that is the foundation of the central section swiftly turns to E major and runs most of its course in that key (see Ex. 124). The more effective, therefore, is the gravitation in the second theme of this section to E flat major, a whole tritone removed from the point at which the section had begun, and a nice tonal complement to the interval that had dominated the work's opening. The contrasting syncopation of this theme adds a tremulous agitation to Francesca's misery – though in this section Tchaikovsky perhaps steers Dante's hell dangerously close to the world of *Swan Lake*. Even more commendable is the inventive syncopation of the tempest section, whose constant metrical dislocations within an unbroken $\frac{6}{8}$ (see, for instance, the last three bars of Ex. 123d) banish that stultifying rhythmic repetitiveness that had dogged Tchaikovsky's use of this time signature in some previous pieces.

On the melodic plane Francesca's main melody – for, despite the change of scoring on the last beat of bar seven, it is almost one long-breathed entity – is some thirty bars long (Ex. 124), organised in spans of ever-increasing breadth, each apparently new, yet with fresh

Ex. 124

configurations of notes twice turning back to contours of earlier shapes
(compare systems one and two of Ex. 124, and also the bars bracketed
⌐——x——⌐), thus fostering coherence in one of the broadest, most
widely-ranging, most magnificent, melodic statements Tchaikovsky
had ever conceived. Its pathos and passion are excellently complemented by the harmonic support, simply diatonic at first as the
clarinet sings the opening with pizzicato string support, warming and
declaring a fuller emotion when the arco strings and single horn take
over in bar seven, with chromatic lines (not Wagner-derived, but an
extension from Glinka's musical world) moving slowly between the
melody and the unbroken pedal E that provides the foundation. Then

finally, towards the end, the bass rises in firm measured steps (from here, for a few bars, a whiff of Wagner may be scented), fortifying the sadness before moving back to the pedal E as the violins shape out little cadential cells that dissolve into the accompaniment to the melody's next statement. This is first-rate Tchaikovsky. One must commend also the little upward-flashing scales that occur as appendages to the slender phrases of Francesca's second theme, and which swiftly take possession of the field to provide a deft, fleeting accompaniment as the main theme returns.

Francesca da Rimini has an abundance of excellent qualities – yet, despite them, Balakirev was wrong. It is certainly not Tchaikovsky's finest piece up to 1882, nor is it, perhaps, even one of his best compositions. As we have seen, this is certainly not for want of compositional skill, nor even really because it resonates with none of those deeper significances of a complex organic creation like *Romeo and Juliet*. Its real fault is excess. It is not merely that the storm is overladen with diminished sevenths (though there are fewer of these than some commentators' remarks would suggest); it is overburdened with repetitions and sequences, disproportionately furnished with preparations which studiedly rouse excited anticipation scarcely justified by what, if anything, issues from them. In the slow movements of his last two quartets Tchaikovsky had already used obsessive repetition of an emotionally charged phrase as a means of heightened expressive address, but the extravagance of these two movements is modest compared to that of *Francesca da Rimini*. The storm sounds inflated, pretending to a force and power beyond that which its musical embodiment possesses. Even more sadly is the portrayal of Francesca herself flawed, not simply by the overstatement of her theme, but above all by the grossly overblown conclusion that sets forth too brazenly her lovely, long-spun melody, bruising the refined image of this tormented lady whose griefs have been the more affecting because of her frailty. Himself possessed with feelings of sexual guilt, Tchaikovsky's identification with Francesca's shade has become so absolute, so complete that finally, as it were, her music becomes possessed with something of the agony that beset his own self. His own emotion overflows, and the whole canvas is indelibly stained.

Significantly, Tchaikovsky followed *Francesca da Rimini* with a work that had an elegant detachment quite new to his music. Between these two works came the first performances of *Vakula*. The composer had gone to St Petersburg some ten days ahead of the première on 6 December. While there his thoughts returned to another of Modest's summer suggestions, *Othello*, though now he was weighing it as an opera subject. Firmly parrying a suggestion from Vasily Avenarius that he should compose an opera on one of that writer's libretti, Tchaikovsky turned to Vladimir Stasov, who in 1873 had furnished him so fruitfully with a programme from Shakespeare's *The Tempest*, and asked that indefatigable source of musical schemes to draw up a scenario. Stasov agreed, but was doubtful about the suitability of the subject to Tchaikovsky's gifts, much to the irritation of the latter, who was tormented by a suspicion that Stasov would have considered Musorgsky to be equal to the challenge of *Othello*. In an attempt to deflect Tchaikovsky, Stasov put forward a programme for a substantial orchestral piece, *Ivan the Clown*, to be based upon elements derived from Russian folktales. But Tchaikovsky had no intention of abandoning a project that had so caught his imagination; trying to devise his own scenario for *Othello* had already cost him several sleepless nights, he informed Stasov on 23 December. The latter capitulated, designed a scenario, and received in return from a delighted Tchaikovsky a barrage of observations and suggestions which not only confirms how strongly the subject had gripped him, but also how clear-headed he could be in sifting the essential from the expendable in an opera plot, for all his proposals were aimed at pruning and clarifying Stasov's scheme. How long Tchaikovsky's enthusiasm remained at fever-heat we do not know. Two months later he was still pressing Stasov to send him the full scenario of Acts 2, 3 and 4, but already there is less urgency in his soliciting. Two further months, and he is confessing that he has done nothing. After this no more was heard of *Othello*.

That Tchaikovsky should have been able to compose his Rococo Variations at the very time when he was at the highest pitch of excitement over another creative proposal need cause no surprise, for this new piece was the most studied negation of self that he had yet composed. 'I'm writing some variations for solo cello and orchestra,' he wrote to Anatoly on 27 December,[46] thus providing the only snippet of information we possess about the composition of the work. It was dedicated to Tchaikovsky's colleague, Wilhelm Fitzenhagen, who had, presumably, commissioned it, and who gave it its first performance at an RMS concert in Moscow on 30 November 1877, with Nikolay Rubinstein conducting.

Tchaikovsky's obligation to the eighteenth century is explicitly declared in the title, and one need observe no more than the first half of the theme (Ex. 125a), with its graceful contours and well-mannered cadence in the dominant, to perceive from what period Tchaikovsky had taken his model. The orchestra used – double wind, two horns and

[46] *TLP6*, p. 95; *TPR*, p. 266; *DTC*, p. 471.

strings – is also a deliberate reflection of an eighteenth-century complement. Tchaikovsky had rarely been attracted to the variation design, and his purpose now was perhaps less to demonstrate his enthusiasm for the form than to avoid the structural complexities and

Ex. 125

dramatic issues that could not have been skirted, had he attempted to wed his borrowed manners to the concerto principle. In each variation he could, if he wished, simply retain the neat outlines and harmonic support of his decorous binary theme, embroidering them with tasteful ornamentation (as in the first two variations), or else he could ruminate upon the essence of the theme in a different melodic manner (as in the mildly Russian cantilena of the D minor variation, or in the valse triste that lurks within that in C major), expanding beyond the rigidly regular periods of the theme's phrase structure. Tchaikovsky biased heavily towards the former approach in which there lurked the serious danger that, even if there were sufficient inventive variety between the variations, such a formal procession of neatly symmetrical, self-contained packages could become stultifying. It is in avoiding this trap, more than in anything else, that Tchaikovsky showed that enterprising craftsmanship which he possessed in far greater measure than did any of his Russian contemporaries, for while there is scarcely a phrase within any variation whose relationship with its progenitor in the theme is not explicit, no two variations assemble their constituent phrases in quite the same way, nor build quite the same proportions (see Ex. 126). And, as an appendage to the binary theme itself, there is a codetta to which a quasi-cadential or linking extension is attached – an extension which Tchaikovsky could vary in length and direction, thus both gently modifying further the proportions of a variation, or providing a bridge passage to the next. This codetta material might even be mixed with the theme itself, as happens in the fourth variation (No. 5 in the original order).

If the original theme, chaste in outline and gracefully paced in its harmonies, masks the personality of its creator, a clear glimpse of the composer himself is provided in this codetta, with its richly detailed, pedal-supported chromaticism. His image may be equally discerned in the D minor variation, and even more in that in C major, by far the largest in the set, and the one which explores the regions farthest removed from the form and spirit of the original theme. In fact, there is a good deal more of Tchaikovsky himself in these variations than one might at first suspect from the apparent 'artificiality' of so much of the music's sound, for he had not simply resorted to ready-made solutions of long ago, and the more rococo stretches contain many details that no eighteenth-century composer would have written. If Tchaikovsky tried to select his materials and manners by tuning his ears to eighteenth-century criteria and tastes, those ears still remained his own. To put it another way; whereas the minuet in *Vakula*, or the *Faithful shepherdess* interlude he was to incorporate in *The Queen of Spades* are like studio pictures synthesised from snapshots, the variations resemble more a canvas painted from life with the artist experiencing fully his subject in circumstances which permit a far greater personal involvement in the final result.

While the refined craftsmanship and tasteful invention of this piece display much of that poise which Tchaikovsky so admired in the past musical world he has here annexed, the scheme of the variations as we know them is in fact far less immaculate than in Tchaikovsky's original design. Evidently from the beginning Tchaikovsky allowed Fitzenhagen much freedom in modifying the solo cello part (in the autograph score the greater part of this is actually in Fitzenhagen's hand), and the young cellist exercised his rôle as reviser with such vigour that

Jurgenson was moved to protest. 'Loathsome Fitzenhagen!' he fumed to Tchaikovsky in March 1878, while he was preparing the cello and piano version for publication. 'He is most importunate in wishing to alter your cello piece, to make it more suitable for the instrument, and he says you have given him full authority to do this. Good heavens! Tchaikovsky revu et corrigé par Fitzenhagen!'[47] Fitzenhagen, it seems, had assumed that he had some proprietary right to the work, for he had extended his revisionary activities far beyond the cello part, though precisely how far is impossible to determine on the available evidence. The one context he is known to have fundamentally rewritten – a few bars in the work's coda (Ex. 125b and c) – is arguably enriched by his intervention, but his complete reordering of the variations themselves, an operation which involved the actual excision of the final one, is in every way indefensible. Far from indifferent to his own personal success in performing the work, Fitzenhagen provided a clue to what had prompted this radical restructuring in a letter he wrote to the composer after playing the piece at the Wiesbaden Festival in June 1879. 'I produced a furore with your variations. I pleased so greatly that I was recalled three times, and after the Andante variation (D minor) there was stormy applause. Liszt said to me: "You carried me away! You played splendidly," and regarding your piece he observed: "Now there, at last, is real music!"'[48]

In Tchaikovsky's own original order the D minor variation was the third of eight, but doubtless Fitzenhagen, quickly perceiving its power to draw applause, had calculated that it might more effectively be placed later in the piece. Thus he exchanged it with Tchaikovsky's slow penultimate variation, the one in $\frac{3}{4}$ in C major. Since the Allegro vivace variation that followed upon that in D minor made a very effective contrast, Fitzenhagen retained this pairing but, in so doing, encountered a problem, for the eighth and last variation that now followed was of a very similar character. Tchaikovsky's improver did not flinch: this eighth variation had to go, the more so since it was perfectly easy to chop off the work's final thirty-two bars and tack them on to the Allegro vivace.

Just how seriously Tchaikovsky at first viewed Fitzenhagen's more radical changes is difficult to establish. After the appearance of the cello and piano version in 1878, he merely commented acidly to Jurgenson that Fitzenhagen, who had read the proofs, had done the job badly. Certainly, however, Tchaikovsky ultimately came to regret bitterly Fitzenhagen's licence, for the cellist, Anatoly Brandukov, recounted to one of his pupils what happened when the composer, evidently just before the full score was to be printed in 1889, reviewed once again his reviser's activities. 'On one of my visits to Pyotr Ilich I found him very upset, looking as though he was ill. When I asked: "What's the matter with you?" Pyotr Ilich, pointing to the writing table, said: "That idiot Fitzenhagen's been here. Look what he's done to my piece – he's altered everything!" When I asked what action he was going to take concerning this composition, Pyotr Ilich replied: "The devil take it! Let it stand as it is!" '[49]

And so Fitzenhagen's 1878 order was retained, and in that sequence the variations are still played to this day. Yet it is inexplicable that Tchaikovsky should ever have capitulated to these changes, for he had most carefully planned his original, the first five variations showing a progressive expansion and evolution of the theme's structure (Ex. 126), with the sixth briefly recalling the original phrases of the theme before the seventh, C major variation, new in metre and key, revealed a vast melodic sweep which provided the most substantial experience of the whole work. This was the real peak of the piece, after which the final (now excised) variation simply guided the listener back towards the world where it had all begun. Tchaikovsky's original score has now been published in the Soviet Union. Some enterprising Western publisher would do well to issue it, and Western cellists to discard Fitzenhagen's deplorably corrupt version.

To leave the impression that the central six months of 1876 had been entirely barren ones for Tchaikovsky is not quite accurate. Indeed, regularly, once a month, he had sat down to discharge the undertaking he had given the editor of the periodical, *Nouvelliste*, to provide a piano piece appropriate to the month of issue. As noted earlier, these twelve pieces, labelled collectively *The Seasons*, were to become Tchaikovsky's best-known piano work. Despite his characteristic concern that his client should be well satisfied, Tchaikovsky himself felt little interest in the work. As Kashkin recorded, he considered it 'of little significance, and so as not to miss any of the dates on which it had been agreed that the pieces should be delivered, he charged his servant to remind him, on a certain day of each month, of his commission. The servant carried out this instruction very punctiliously, and once a month on the agreed day said: "Pyotr Ilich, it's time to send off to St Petersburg" – and Pyotr Ilich wrote a piece at a single sitting and sent it off.'[50] It is not difficult to credit this account. *The Seasons* aspires to be no more than a set of salon pieces, tuneful and pretty, sometimes garnished with a mild picturesqueness prompted by the little poetic epigraph that Bernard selected to head each piece, at others breathing a light pathos that must

[49] *DTC*, p. 472.   [50] *KVC*, p. 105; *DTC*, p. 512 (partial).

Ex. 126

TCHAIKOVSKY'S ORDER	FITZENHAGEN'S ORDER (as printed)	STRUCTURE (ORIGINAL VERSION) (no account is taken of introductory bars except in the total of the final column) cad.=cadential; ext.= extension		NO. OF BARS (omitting final linking passages and introductory bars)
		THEME	CODETTA	
THEME	THEME	4+4 4+4 A1+A2 B+A1 *	6+2 bars C+link	22
VAR. I	VAR. I	4+4 4+4 A1+A2 B+A1	6+2 bars C+link	22
VAR. II	VAR. II	4+4 4+4+4 A1+A2 B+A1+A1	6+10 bars C+link +cadenza	26
VAR. III (D minor)	VAR. VI	4+8 4+6 A1+A1 extended B+D	4+8 bars C+cad. ext.	34
VAR. IV	VAR. VII	2+2 2+2 4+4+12 2+2 2+2+9 A1+A2 A1+A2 B+A2+ext. A1+A2 A1+A2+ext.		45
VAR. V	VAR. IV	4+6 4+6 4+6** 4+4 4+6 5+4 4+7 bars A1+A2 C+ext. A1+A2 B+B C+ext. A1+A1 C+link		51 [61]
VAR. VI	VAR. V	4+4+2 4+11 4+4 A1+A2+cadenza B+cadenza A1+A1	6+7 bars C+link	39
VAR. VII	VAR. III	8+8 8+14 8+18 A1+A2 B+E A1+A2 extended	6+9 bars C+link***	70
VAR. VIII		4+4 4+4 4+8 A1+A2 B+B A1+A1 extended	30 bars C extended into Coda	58

* The distinctive feature of A2 is that its cadence is other than in the tonic.

** This repetition of the first ten bars appears to have been abandoned by Tchaikovsky himself before he scored the variations. Fitzenhagen's interference in this variation seems to have been extensive.

*** These bars are written as the beginning of Variation VIII.

have prompted many a dewy-eyed response in many a drawing room. Bearing in mind the public at which these pieces were directed, one may sometimes be a little surprised by their technical demands, but nothing ever strains the listener's powers of musical response.

Yet one should not scoff too readily at *The Seasons*. Though, in their broad outlines at least, all are simply ternary in design, the dimensions of some are quite considerable. Tchaikovsky was never at a loss for an attractive opening idea, and his craft was always able to fill the musical space beyond this, even when – as in *May* – his idea has petered out and he only drifts for a few bars, with a mildly arresting harmonic shift to prime the listener's ear, before picking up his opening theme again. In his central sections his invention sometimes becomes undernourished, rather commonplace little phrases being repeated or extended sequentially; yet even when this has happened, tiny touches of harmonic spice may provide some compensating fare. At times Tchaikovsky's harmonic palette is surprisingly rich for pieces of such humble intent, notably in the very first, which is also the best of the set, with a middle section whose opening phrase sounds like an intimation of Tatyana's letter song (Ex. 127) – though the ensuing idea looks back more towards

Ex. 127

Schumann's world, echoes of which occasionally resonate elsewhere in these pieces. The coda nicely recalls the *Onegin* phrase of the middle section. There is much charm in the lark's plaintive twitterings in *March*, and the melody of *April*, for all its simplicity, displays admirably uncramped contours and a sufficiency of inventiveness that have deservedly made this lightly disguised waltz one of the most popular of the series. Another favourite is *June*, a barcarolle where, for once, the middle section is superior to the first, though the noisy diminished sevenths at the end are regrettable. Frequently in these pieces Tchaikovsky adds a little enrichment with a tenor melody that companions the main theme. He does this in the barcarolle: even more consistently he duets thus in the melancholy *October* so that this genuinely affecting piece, with its nicely dying conclusion, sounds almost as though it might have been fathered by the Pas d'action with violin and cello soli in Act 2 of *Swan Lake*. At the opposite expressive pole are the rumbustious hunting scene of *September* and the sparkling troika ride of *November*, an infectious piece whose merry jingling bells must have given boundless innocent pleasure (and posed not a few technical problems) to many of Russia's amateur pianists. It is yet another sure mark of Tchaikovsky's professionalism, his sheer competence as a composer, that he could discharge a lowly task such as this series of pieces so admirably.

For Tchaikovsky the last weeks of 1876 were notable for two new personal contacts. Modest stated that Tolstoy had been his brother's favourite author since his civil service days; now, at a Conservatoire soirée arranged by Nikolay Rubinstein[51] in honour of the great writer, Tchaikovsky found himself face to face at last with the man himself. For Tchaikovsky the circumstances of this first meeting could hardly have been more delightful, for on the programme was his own First String Quartet, of which the Andante cantabile reduced Tolstoy to tears. It was, Tchaikovsky recorded some ten years later, one of the most gratifying moments of his life. His interest stirred in this young composer of rapidly growing fame, Tolstoy called on Tchaikovsky several times, spending two whole evenings with him. Tchaikovsky was profoundly flattered by this attention. To show his appreciation of the deeply moving experience afforded him by Tchaikovsky's quartet, Tolstoy proposed to present a volume of his own work to each of the performers as well as to the composer himself. To the latter he also offered a further unexpected gift in return for the pieces by Tchaikovsky – the piano-duet arrangement of the First Symphony and the piano pieces, Op. 19 – which the composer had sent to Tolstoy when the latter had returned to his Yasnaya Polyana home.

> I am sending you, dear Pyotr Ilich, some songs [wrote Tolstoy]. I've looked through them again. In your hands they will be an amazing treasure – but, for God's sake, arrange them using the Mozart– Haydn manner and not the artificial, peremptory, outré Beethoven– Schumann–Berlioz fashion. How much there remained to talk to you about! I said nothing of what I wanted to say. There wasn't time! I was enjoying myself. . . . I haven't looked through your pieces, but when I do I shall, whether you need it or not, write you my verdicts –

---

[51] Modest asserted that his brother was the real instigator of this event because of the intense interest Tolstoy had expressed in his work.

and boldly, because I have grown fond of your talent. Goodbye: I give your hand a friendly squeeze.

Your L. Tolstoy[52]

It is worth quoting in full Tchaikovsky's own words of reply (the only letter he is known to have written to Tolstoy), partly for the unmistakable sincerity of their tribute to Tolstoy's eminence, and also because of the admirable frankness with which he, on his side, felt he should voice his verdict upon Tolstoy's musical offering, pointing out to the novelist that the gift was of less worth than he imagined:

Count! I am sincerely grateful to you for sending the songs. I must tell you frankly that they are noted down by an unskilful hand, and contain no more than vestiges of their former beauty. The chief imperfection is that they have been unnaturally and forcibly squeezed into a regularly measured rhythm. Only Russian dance songs have a rhythm with a regular and uniformly accented bar – and, you know, bïlinas can have nothing in common with the dance song. In addition, the majority of these songs have also, it appears, been forced into a festive D major, which again is contrary to the system of real Russian song, which nearly always has an undefined tonality, resembling most closely the old church modes. In general the songs that you've sent me are not susceptible to a proper and methodical treatment – that is, you couldn't make a collection out of them because for this a song must be written as closely as possible to the form in which the people sing it. This is uncommonly difficult to do and requires the finest musical sense and great musico-historical erudition. Except for Balakirev and, to some extent, Prokunin, I know of no man who is equal to this task. But your songs could serve as material, and even very good material, for symphonic exploitation, and I'll certainly use them one way or another.

How pleased I am that your evening at the Conservatoire has left you with such a pleasant memory! Our quartet players played *as never before* on that evening. From this fact you may conclude that the two ears of such a great creator as you can inspire an artist a hundred times more than the tens of thousands of ears of the public.

You are one of those writers who make one love not only their work but also themselves. It was evident that, in playing so *amazingly* well, they were striving because of one very beloved and treasured person. As for myself, I cannot tell you how happy and proud I was to see how my music could entrance and move you.

[52] *TZC*1, pp. 520–1; *TPM*1, pp. 572–3 (partial).

I will pass your message on to Rubinstein as soon as he arrives from St Petersburg. Except for Fitzenhagen, who doesn't read Russian, all the members of the quartet have read your works. I think they'll be very grateful to you if you send to each of them one or another of your works. As for me, may I ask you to give me *The Cossacks*, if not now, then on your next visit to Moscow, to which I shall look forward with the greatest impatience.

P. Tchaikovsky

If you send Rubinstein your portrait, don't forget about me![53]

Yet, strangely, the two men never met again. Modest believed that although Tchaikovsky did not deliberately avoid Tolstoy, he nevertheless felt relief that there were no further personal contacts, for the 'demi-god' (such Tchaikovsky himself had felt Tolstoy to be at this time) had proved to have much earthiness in him. He had revealed prosaic traits and even, in his view of Beethoven, a pettiness which Tchaikovsky felt unworthy in a writer of such majestic vision and such penetrating understanding of the depths of the human spirit. To meet the man brought disenchantment. 'He [my brother] himself told me that, in spite of all the pride and happiness he experienced at this acquaintance, his favourite Tolstoy works for a time lost their charm for him,' Modest noted.[54] It was easier to regain and retain veneration if, in future, Tolstoy were to exist solely in his creations. Not that the composer's reverence ever passed into uncritical adulation. Only eight months after meeting Tolstoy, he delivered to Modest a scathing verdict on part of the newly published *Anna Karenina*, though patently this was because the present circumstances in his own life made his sensibilities too raw to be able to bear this tale of the decay of a marriage and the destruction of the wife. Later, in 1882, he was to reverse this adverse verdict on the book 'which I have recently for the first time read with a delight bordering on fanaticism,' as he wrote.[55]

During the 1880s he was drawn more and more to the work of this colossus, while at the same time his liking for Turgenev cooled noticeably. 'I am eternally reading and re-reading him [Tolstoy], and I consider him the greatest of all living writers,' he wrote to the Grand Duke Konstantin Konstantinovich in 1889[56] – yet his last recorded comment on the master, on the farce *The Fruits of Enlightenment*, was that

[53] *TLP*6, pp. 100–1; *TZC*1, pp. 521–2; *TPM*1, p. 573 (last half only).
[54] *TZC*1, p. 523.
[55] *TLP*11, p. 56, *TPM*3, p. 616; *TZC*2, p. 519; *YDGC*, p. 266.
[56] *TLP*15a, p. 204; *TZC*3, p. 328; *YDGC*, p. 479.

it was an unworthy piece. Tchaikovsky's fullest and most considered estimate of this giant of literature, perhaps (as he himself recognised) the greatest Russian of his time, was that committed to his diary in 1886, by which time he had managed to push his image of Tolstoy some way back onto its pedestal. That he should, as so many since have done, deplore the radical shift of interest within Tolstoy's later work is further confirmation of what Tchaikovsky's own creations suggest, in their own particular way, about his attitudes to art's purpose – that its concern is with humanity, its aspirations and despairs, its joys and sorrows. As for literature itself, it should illumine and interpret mankind for us, making us more sensitive to ourselves and to the world around us; it should not be a vehicle for didacticism in which the image of human life is conditioned, distorted, even smothered to serve the advancement of some doctrine or dogma:

11 July 1886. When you read the autobiographies of our greatest men and women or memoirs about them, you are endlessly coming up against some feeling, impression, some general artistic sensitivity that you have more than once experienced yourself, and which you fully understand. But there is *one man* who is incomprehensible, unattainable, and alone in his inscrutable greatness. This is *Lev Tolstoy.* Occasionally (especially when I've been drinking) I become inwardly angry with him, almost hate him. Why, I think to myself, does this man who can, as no one ever before him, attune our spirit to the highest and most miraculously harmonious pitch: this writer who inherited as a gift a power greater than that bestowed upon any man before him to make us of meagre mind comprehend the most impenetrable alleys and recesses of our moral being – why does this man become addicted to *teaching,* to a *mania for sermonising and for the enlightenment* of our clouded or limited minds? Formerly one would receive an indelible impression from what seemed to be a simple and everyday scene which he had himself conjured. Between the lines you read a certain *higher* love toward man, a loftier *compassion* for his helplessness, his finiteness, and his insignificance. You would weep without knowing why ... because for a moment, through his mediation, *you had made contact* with the world of his ideal, of absolute goodness and humanity.... Now he annotates his texts, claims an exclusive monopoly in understanding questions of faith and *ethics* (or what-have-you). But a cold wind blows through all his current writing; you sense a *terror,* and you sense vaguely that he is also a *man* ... that is, a being who, when it comes to questions on our significance, on the meaning of existence, on God and religion, is just

as madly presumptuous and also just as insignificant as some
ephemeral insect that appears at noon on a warm July day and
which, by evening, no longer exists ...

Formerly Tolstoy was a demi-god – now he's a *priest*. But priests
are essentially teachers *not through the strength of their vocation but because
they have taken that rôle upon themselves*. But all the same I am resolved
not to pass judgement on his new activity. Who knows the man?
Perhaps it has to be thus, and I am simply unable to understand and
value properly the greatest of all artistic geniuses who has exchanged
the profession of a novelist for preaching.

13 July 1886. When I became acquainted with Lev Tolstoy I was
seized with fear and a feeling of awkwardness before him. It seemed
to me that this greatest student of human nature at one glance would
penetrate all the recesses of my soul. Before him, so it seemed to me, it
was quite impossible to hide successfully all the trash existing at the
bottom of my soul, and to exhibit only the palatable side. If he is
good, I thought (and such, of course, he *must be* and is), then
delicately, gently, like a doctor examining a wound and knowing all
the painful spots, he would avoid touching or irritating them, at the
same time making me feel that nothing is hidden from him: if he is not
especially compassionate, he would directly prod the centre of pain
with his finger. I was terribly afraid of both these things. But neither
happened. This man, in his writings the greatest student of the
human heart, proved in his intercourse with people to have a simple,
whole-hearted, sincere nature that manifested very little indeed of
that *omniscience* that I had feared. He did not avoid *probing*, but he did
not *cause* deliberate pain. It was apparent that he in no way saw in me
an *object* for his own investigations – but that he simply wanted to
chat about the music in which he was interested at the time. Incidentally, he liked to *denigrate* Beethoven, and straightway expressed
doubt about his genius. This particular trait is in no way a [worthy]
characteristic of great people; to bring down to one's own *incomprehen-
sion* a genius acknowledged by all is a characteristic of *limited people.*[57]

The other contact first made as 1876 drew to its close must have
seemed to Tchaikovsky a slight matter, unlikely to be maintained
except in the most casual fashion, and certainly of infinitely less
moment than his new dealings with Tolstoy. Among the graduates
from the Moscow Conservatoire in 1876 was a young violinist, Iosif
Kotek, who had also been a member of Tchaikovsky's class in musical

[57] *TD*, pp. 209–10; *TZCi*, pp. 519–20 (entry of 13 July only). ∎

theory. Gifted and likeable, Kotek had become a great admirer of Tchaikovsky's work, and a strong bond had developed between master and pupil. Then, also in 1876, a wealthy widow who had a house in Moscow approached Nikolay Rubinstein to help find a violinist who would read through violin and piano pieces with her. It was an ideal opening for a young musician, since the widow not only travelled a good deal but also had a very large family which occupied much of her time; thus the person appointed might both see something of the world at large and also find at his disposal a liberal amount of free time for perfecting further his playing. The salary, too, was generous. Kotek was not only highly talented, but impecunious. Rubinstein suggested the new graduate, and arrangements were concluded. The widow was already closely acquainted with some of Tchaikovsky's music and had been greatly attracted by it; now, with Kotek to fan the flames of enthusiasm, she decided upon a formal approach to the composer with a request that would provide her with more material for her sessions with Kotek. Would Tchaikovsky make violin and piano arrangements of some of his own music? The remuneration offered was very substantial. Kotek made the approach, the composer agreed, the commission was quickly discharged, and the finished work dispatched. A letter of thanks came swiftly:

Friday, 30 December 1876

Permit me to convey to you my sincerest gratitude for such a swift execution of my request. To tell you how much delight your compositions afford me I consider out of place because you have not been used to that kind of praise, and the worship of a being, in music as insignificant as I, might appear to you only ridiculous, and my enjoyment is so dear to me that I do not wish it to be ridiculed. Therefore I will only say, and I ask you to believe this literally, that with your music I live more lightly and more pleasantly.
    Accept my sincerest respect and sincerest devotion.

Nadezhda von Meck[58]

Tchaikovsky's reply, probably written the next day, was equally formal:

I am sincerely grateful for all the kind and flattering things you have been so good as to write to me. On my side I will say that, for a musician amid failures and obstacles of every kind, it is comforting to

[58] *TPM*1, p. 3; *TZC*2, p. 10; *TLP*6, p. 97 (partial).

think that there is a small minority of people, to which you also belong, who love our art so sincerely and warmly.

Sincerely devoted to you and esteeming you,

P. Tchaikovsky[59]

With these two brief notes began one of the most famed and extraordinary correspondences in the whole history of Western culture. There is no need to elaborate further upon it here, for the following pages will be filled with extracts from the letters exchanged by these two people, letters filled with a flood of feeling that could never have been foretold from the cool formality of these first exchanges. Suffice it to say that, as Tchaikovsky entered the most critical year of his life, this new contact with another solitary, restless soul could hardly have been more timely.

[59] *TPM*1, p. 3; *TLP*6, pp. 86–7; *TZC*2, pp. 10–11.

4

1877 – THE YEAR OF FATE

I: MARRIAGE

'THERE IS A saying: "A calm precedes the storm",' wrote Modest of the period his brother was now entering. '... In January and February 1877 ... Pyotr Ilich had the appearance of a man who accepted his situation with complete equanimity – a man whose spirits could not have been better, who desired nothing, sought nothing, and who exhibited a cheerfulness and good humour such as he had not known for a long time.'[1] Tchaikovsky's capacity for masking his personal anguish, even from himself, has already been observed in his letters to Sasha at the time when Vera Davïdova's yearnings for him were presenting an open challenge to his sexual nature. It was the same now. With his intent to marry declared, but with, as yet, no candidate for matrimonial partnership apparent, he could retreat into the illusion that his decision to follow a course of action that would override his sexual condition was the equivalent of actually solving that condition. This time, however, the problem was not to be skirted. 1877 was the most critical year of his life, and the man who had begun it with such outward equanimity was to emerge from it shattered, almost driven out of his wits. And if the effect upon the man was to be devastating, the consequences for his music were also profound.

Tchaikovsky's own apparent composure as 1877 began was matched by an equal evenness in the routine of his daily life. In addition, he found plenty of distractions from brooding on his own condition by caring for the needs of other members of the family, scraping together one hundred roubles to lend a cousin whose husband was financially embarrassed, modestly subsidising an aunt who was seeking some situation in Moscow, and providing also a full week's lodging for her son, his cousin Misha, despite the evident strain he found in having responsibility for the boy. Brother Anatoly was going through a period of depression, and this opened again the doors to that abundant fund of

[1] *TZC*1, pp. 525–6.

sympathy which Tchaikovsky had so liberally lavished upon his twin brothers in their years of adolescence. Most distracting of all, however, was his father's condition. Ilya Petrovich fell ill, so seriously that the family began to converge upon St Petersburg in anticipation of his death. It seems that Tchaikovsky himself paid a fleeting visit to see his father early in the year; certainly he was in the Russian capital in mid-February, by which time Ilya's health was mending. On this occasion Tchaikovsky passed a few pleasant days and was delighted to find that his father had also recovered his old spirits, though he was much distressed by the bursts of irritability Ilya was showing towards Tchaikovsky's stepmother. Outwardly Tchaikovsky seems at this time to have been particularly responsive to the needs and troubles of others. Nevertheless there was one thing which did give some indication of his true condition, though only later was this to be revealed to the outside world. Into the more tempestuous pages of his Fourth Symphony, upon which he was quietly embarking, he was projecting something of the stresses and strains that seethed beneath his self-possessed exterior.

Tchaikovsky certainly could not complain of lack of performances of his works. The première of *Swan Lake*, in Moscow, took place on 4 March 1877, and on the very same day his Second String Quartet was also heard in the city. Five days later came the first performance of *Francesca da Rimini*, and within a fortnight the work had been twice repeated. And only a very little earlier, on 25 February, Tchaikovsky had himself 'very clumsily, very nervously and uncertainly, but very successfully'[2] conducted his Slavonic March at a concert in the Bolshoy Theatre. It was nine years since his first nightmare experience of public conducting, and he was vastly relieved to have survived the ordeal so much better this time. 'I shall now generally seek opportunities to appear publicly conducting my own works,' he declared to Sasha. 'I've got to conquer my insane shyness, for if my plan for a foreign tour materialises, I shall have to be my own conductor.'[3] Evidently the collapse of his scheme for a concert of his own music in Paris had not destroyed his faith in his orchestral works' ability to make headway beyond the boundaries of Russia. In fact, it was to be another ten years before he began to conduct regularly. The sudden, unexpected gift of a fine grand piano from the St Petersburg firm of Becker was further proof of his growing stature in Russia's musical life.

But neither performances of his music nor prestigious gifts could touch his inner troubles. Nadezhda von Meck had written him a second letter – a brief note of thanks whose formal phraseology could not

[2] *TLP*6, p. 114; *YDGC*, p. 141; *TZC*1, p. 530; *TPR*, p. 275; *TPB*, p. 118.
[3] ibid.

smother the intensity of its almost passionate plea for the exchange of inner confidences. 'There is much, much that I would wish to write to you, when the opportunity occurs, of my imaginary relationship with you, but I am afraid of trespassing upon your so limited free time. I will say only that this relationship, however abstract it may be, is precious to me as the best, the highest of all feelings of which human nature is capable,' she wrote on 27 February.[4] Sensing the benefit for himself that lay hidden in this new association, Tchaikovsky responded swiftly and with matching warmth. 'I know you rather better than perhaps you think. If, one fine day, you would be so kind as to favour me with a written account of those many things you would wish to say, then I should be extremely grateful to you.'[5] Such an invitation broke down all Nadezhda von Meck's reserve. It now remained for the confession of love (for such, in its bizarre way, it was) to be made and received with equal fervour. Gone is the formality of expression; there is scarcely time even for a full-stop:

Your kind reply to my letter gave me a deep pleasure such as I have not felt for a long time, but you know the common characteristic of human nature: the more good you receive, the more you want, and though I promised you I would not resort to self-indulgence, I am beginning to doubt my own strength, for I am permitting myself to turn to you with a big request that may seem oddly disagreeable to you, though surely a person who lives as ascetically as I do will inevitably arrive at the conclusion that everything that people call social relationships, the rules of society, proprieties, and such-like, has become, as far as she is concerned, but a sound without meaning. I do not know fully your view on this matter, Pyotr Ilich, but from some of my observations of you, it seems to me that you least of all will condemn me for this; if I am mistaken, then I sincerely ask you to tell me openly and bluntly, and after that to turn down my request which is this: give me your photograph; I have got two of them, but I want to have one from you. I want to search out in your face those inspirations, those feelings under the influence of which you compose your music which carries a being into a world of sensations, expectations and desires that life can never satisfy.... The first of your works that I heard was *The Tempest*. I cannot describe the impression that it made on me; for several days I was as one delirious, and I could do nothing to free myself from this state. I must tell you that I cannot separate the musician from the man, and in

4 *TPM*1, p. 4; *TZC*2, p. 11.
5 *TLP*6, p. 113; *TPM*1, p. 5; *TZC*2, pp. 11–12.

him, the servant of such a high art, even more than in other people, I wish and expect to find those human qualities which I worship. My ideal man is certainly a musician, but in him talent must be equally matched by his human qualities; only then will he make a deep and complete impression.... I regard a musician–man as the highest creation of nature.... And so, as soon as I had recovered from the first impression of your work, I straightway wanted to know what sort of man had written such a piece. I began to seek out opportunities to discover as much as I could about you, never missed any occasion when I might hear something, paid attention to the opinion of the public, to individual judgements, to every remark – and on this I will tell you that often what they censured in you sent me into raptures – everyone has his own taste. Only the other day from a casual conversation I learned of one of your opinions which so delighted me, with which I felt such sympathy that, as it were, you immediately became close to me – or, at any rate, dear to me. It seems to me, you see, that it is not only relationships that make people close, but even more a similarity of opinion, equal capacities for feelings, and an identity of sympathies, so that it is possible to be close when one is far distant.

I am so interested to know everything about you that at almost any time I can tell where you are and, to a certain extent, what you are doing.... There was a time when I very much wanted to meet you. Now, however, the more I am enchanted by you, the more I fear acquaintance – I feel I would not be in a condition to begin talking with you – although if we should unexpectedly meet face to face anywhere, I could not behave towards you as to a stranger, and I would hold out my hand to you, though only to press yours – but I should not speak a word. Now I prefer to think of you from a distance, to hear you in your music and to feel myself at one with you in it.[6]

Nothing could more eloquently reveal the fantasy nature of this lonely, disturbed woman's 'love' for Tchaikovsky than this uncontained flow of words. Such unstemmed feelings roused Tchaikovsky to a response which, if less extravagant, is already notably uninhibited for a man usually as private as he. It also defines clearly that Tchaikovsky, on his part, was seeking the same kind of relationship as his new correspondent:

You are quite right, Nadezhda Filaretovna, in supposing that I am in

[6] *TPM*1, pp. 5–7; *TZC*2, pp. 12–13.

a condition to understand fully the peculiarities of your spiritual organism. I dare to think that you are not mistaken in believing me close to you as a person. Just as you have tried to listen to judgements made by the public on me, so I on my part have not missed an opportunity of learning details of you and your mode of living. I have always been interested in you as a person whose moral temper has many features in common with my own nature. There is certainly one trait that draws us together – that we both suffer from one and the same illness. That illness is misanthropy – but a misanthropy of a particular kind, at the root of which there is absolutely no hatred and contempt for people. People who suffer from this illness have no fear of that injury which can come from the machinations of someone who is close; instead they fear that disenchantment, that yearning for the ideal that follows upon every intimacy. There was a time when I was so oppressed by the yoke of this terror of people that I almost went out of my mind. . . . By now I have emerged sufficiently victorious from this struggle for life to have long ago ceased to be unbearable. I have been saved by work – work that is at the same time enjoyment. . . .

From what I have said above, you will easily understand that I am in no way surprised that, loving my music, you are not attempting to make the acquaintance of its author. You fear that you will not find in me those qualities with which your imagination, inclined to idealisation, has invested me. And you are quite right. I feel that, on closer acquaintance with me, you would not find that correspondence, that complete harmony between the musician and the man, of which you dream.[7]

The immediate fruit of this new contact was a series of small compositions and arrangements requested and handsomely rewarded by his new patroness. These took little time, however, and provided few distractions from work on the Fourth Symphony. Mariya Mamontova had asked him to harmonise some more children's songs as he had done for her in 1872. Tchaikovsky did a little work on this project, but then deferred completion (in fact, he had no sympathy for this chore, and the project was never finished). Nor did he let suggestions from Stasov for an opera on Alfred de Vigny's historical romance, *Cinq-Mars*, deflect him. The letter containing Stasov's proposed scenario was written on 2 April, the day after Tchaikovsky had left Moscow to spend Easter at Kamenka, and it was awaiting him when he arrived back home on 17 April. Having already cooled towards *Othello*, for which Stasov had

[7] *TLP6*, pp. 115–16; *TPM1*, pp. 8–9; *TZC2*, pp. 14–15.

only reluctantly prepared part of a scenario, Tchaikovsky was embarrassed that he felt he could not respond positively to this new proposition. Nevertheless, after pondering Stasov's work for a few days, he firmly declined it:

I'm definitely convinced that *The Cardinal* [as Stasov had re-titled de Vigny's piece] does not answer the demands of my musical make-up. It's very difficult for me to explain to you precisely what my spirit thirsts for. I need the sort of subject in which one dramatic motif predominates: for instance, *love* (maternal or sexual – it's all the same), *jealousy, ambition, patriotism,* and such-like. I would like a drama that is more intimate, more modest than this huge historical drama in which the noble self-sacrifice of Cinq-Mars, the craftiness of Richelieu, the weakness of the King, the empty-headedness of Marie, the martyrdom of Grandier, the devotion of the Abbot, the baseness of père Joseph constitute in aggregate a colossal drama that demands a colossal talent and, if presented as an opera, a huge theatre with a huge company, and so on.[8]

In any case Gounod had just written an opera on this same subject, and Tchaikovsky's admiration for that composer's craft made him hesitate to enter into competition with the Frenchman. ('Gounod is a first-class *master craftsman,* if not a first-class creative genius,' he added a little defiantly to Stasov,[9] knowing well the latter's aversion to the brand of opera that Gounod purveyed.) Tchaikovsky's own views on the type of opera he was seeking are significant: a subject with 'one dramatic motif ... for instance, *love* ... intimate' – in fact, just what Pushkin's prose-novel, *Eugene Onegin,* afforded. Within a month, with the composition of the Fourth Symphony at an advanced stage, Tchaikovsky had embarked on what was to be his finest opera.

The circumstances in which *Eugene Onegin* was composed are inextricably entwined with the whole strange and traumatic episode of Tchaikovsky's marriage. The principal facts of the affair can be easily summarised. His bride was a certain Antonina Ivanovna Milyukova. Her existence was unknown to him until May 1877. Some two months later, on 18 July, he married her; after only two and a half months of nominal conjugality, he fled to St Petersburg, and the 'marriage' was over. The most substantial account of the whole episode is Kashkin's, set down from Tchaikovsky's own words, but concealed by Kashkin until after Antonina's death in 1917, when he felt he might at last speak

[8] *TLP6*, pp. 118–19; *YDGC*, pp. 142–5.
[9] *TLP6*, p. 119.

openly of what his friend had confided to him many years before. Though the words that Kashkin put into Tchaikovsky's mouth cannot have been exactly those spoken by the composer, his record has the ring of authenticity, and it agrees substantially with what we may gather from letters extant from the time when the actual events were in progress (these letters include three from the aspiring bride to her chosen bridegroom). Needless to say, Modest is the most reluctant of informants, using extracts from his brother's own letters to record the facts leading up to the wedding only in so far as such an account was unavoidable, and eschewing personal comment as far as possible. On his brother's experiences after the ceremony Modest was utterly uncommunicative, though he did concur with Kashkin on the critical significance of the event for Tchaikovsky, confessing that this 'fateful day bore within itself the seeds of all that followed'.[10] He was at pains, however, to absolve Antonina from culpability in the break-up of the marriage.

If Tchaikovsky had begun 1877 in reasonable spirits, by May he was in a sorry state. Vladimir Shilovsky had just married, and this had naturally disrupted the close relationship between the two men. 'Life is terribly empty, boring and *trivial*,' he wrote gloomily in mid-May to Klimenko, who had attempted to enlist Tchaikovsky's help in finding a position in Moscow. 'I have been thinking much of *marriage*, or some other stable *union*.'[11] Now, without the slightest warning, he was confronted with a specific proposal. 'During the earlier or middle part of May 1877,' Tchaikovsky told Kashkin, 'I received a longish letter containing a declaration of love for me. The letter was signed by A. Milyukova, who told me she had started to love me some years earlier while she was a student at the Conservatoire.'[12] This Milyukova letter has disappeared,[13] as have all of Tchaikovsky's to her, but her second, penned on 16 May, is extant. Tchaikovsky's reply had clearly attempted to be gently evasive, and he had counselled his infatuated admirer not to let her emotions run away with her. Her response, though beginning dutifully enough, gave little hope that her ardour would cool:

> I see that it's now time that I began to master my feelings, as you yourself told to me in your first letter. Although I cannot now see you, I console myself with the thought that you are in the same city as I

[10] *TZC*1, p. 536.

[11] *TLP*6, p. 132; *TZC*1, p. 532 (with the marriage reference omitted).

[12] *KIVC*, pp. 118–19.

[13] This may, in fact, have been Antonina's second letter, an even earlier one having also been lost.

am, whereas in a month, maybe less, you will in all probability leave, and God knows whether I shall chance to see you, since I too do not intend to remain in Moscow. But wherever I may be, I shall not be able to forget you or lose my love for you. What I liked in you [when I first came to know you] I no longer find in any other man; indeed, in a word, I do not want to look at any other man after you. Meanwhile, a week ago I had to endure listening to the declaration of a man who had loved me almost from his student days, and who had remained true for five years. I found it distressing to hear him out.[14]

Having dispatched this relatively balanced letter, Miss Milyukova, before the day was out, sat down to begin another in which all the self-restraint to which Tchaikovsky had urged her is abandoned to the winds of gusting emotion:

I've been in the most agonising state for a whole week, Pyotr Ilich, not knowing whether to write to you or not. I see that my letters are already beginning to be wearisome to you. But will you really break off this correspondence with me, not having seen me even once? No, I am convinced you will not be so cruel. Do you, maybe, take me for a frivolous person or a gullible girl, and therefore place no trust in my letters? How can I prove to you that my words are genuine, and that ultimately I could not lie in such a matter? After your last letter I loved you twice as much again, and your shortcomings mean absolutely nothing to me.

Perhaps if you were a perfect being I would have remained completely cool towards you. I am dying of longing, and I burn with a desire to see you, to sit with you and talk with you, though I also fear that at first I shan't be in a state to utter a word. There is no failing that might cause me to fall out-of-love with you ...

Having today sent a man to deliver my letter to you, I was very surprised to learn that you had left Moscow, and longing descended upon me even more. I sit at home all day, pace the room from corner to corner like a crazy thing, thinking only of that moment when I shall see you. I shall be ready to throw myself on your neck, to smother you with kisses – but what right have I to do this? Maybe, indeed, you take this for effrontery on my part ...

I can assure you that I am a respectable and honourable woman in the full sense of the word, and I have nothing that I would wish to conceal from you. My first kiss will be given to you and to no one else in the world. Farewell, my dear one. Do not try to disillusion me

[14] *TPM*1, p. 569.

further about yourself, because you are only wasting your time. I cannot live without you, and so maybe soon I shall kill myself. So let me see you and kiss you so that I may remember that kiss in the other world. Farewell. Yours eternally, A.M. . . .

The day before yesterday my letter was already written, and only today am I sending it, for I assume that you have still not returned to Moscow. Again I implore you: come to me. If you knew how I suffer, then probably out of pity alone you would grant my request.[15]

Plagued by such wild declarations from this besotted, unbalanced woman, Tchaikovsky sought to discover more of his tormentor. Since she had disclosed that his Conservatoire colleague, Eduard Langer, had once taught her the piano, Tchaikovsky approached the latter secretly, who replied to Tchaikovsky's question about Antonina with, it seems, a single unflattering epithet. Yet nothing could now deter him, though he was quick to tell Antonina that his feelings for her contained no love. After all, he had only a matter of months before declared his irrevocable intention of marrying, and suddenly fate was presenting him with his chosen bride.

There was one deep cause for discomfort in this prospect, however: a marital bond could conflict with his new, intimately remote relationship with his 'beloved friend', Nadezhda von Meck. On 15 July, only three days before the wedding, he at last brought himself to confess to his new patroness the momentous step he was about to take. As far as the circumstances concerning Tchaikovsky's entry into matrimony are concerned, this letter is by far the fullest account to survive from the period during which the actual events were unfolding. Having briefly described Antonina's overtures and his own response, he then proceeded to outline what had followed upon the initial exchange of letters:

I will not begin to go into the details of this correspondence, but the result was that I agreed to her request that I should visit her in her own home. Why did I do this? It seemed to me now as though some force of fate was driving me to this girl. When we met, I again explained to her that I entertained nothing for her other than sympathy and gratitude for her love. But when I had parted from her, I began to think over all the thoughtlessness of my conduct. If I did not love her, if I did not wish to encourage her feelings, then why had I visited her, and what would be the consequence of all this? From the letter that followed upon this I concluded that if, having gone so far, I were suddenly to turn away from this girl, then I would

15 *TPM*1, pp. 569–70.

make her truly wretched, would drive her to a tragic end. Thus I was faced with difficult alternatives: either to preserve my own freedom at the price of this girl's death (*death* is not an empty word here; she does indeed love me to distraction), or *to marry*. I had to choose the latter course. My decision was supported by the fact that the sole dream of my 82-year-old father and all my relatives is that I should marry. And so, one beautiful evening, I went to my future wife, told her openly that *I did not love her* but that, whatever befell, I would be a staunch and grateful friend. I described to her in detail my character – my irritability, volatile temperament, my unsociability – finally, my circumstances. After this I asked her whether she wanted to be my wife. Of course her reply was in the affirmative. I cannot convey to you in words those terrible feelings I went through during the days that followed immediately upon that evening. It is understandable. Having lived 37 years with an innate aversion to marriage, it is very distressing to be drawn through force of circumstances into the position *of a bridegroom* who, moreover, is not in the least attracted to his bride. I must change my whole way of life; I must do my best for the well-being and peace of mind of this other person whose fate is joined with mine – all this is not very easy for a bachelor who has become inured to being self-centred. To enable me to change my outlook, to get myself accustomed to looking at my future calmly, I decided still to hold to my original plan, and still to go off to the country for a month. And so I did. The quiet mode of country life in a circle of very nice people and amid *delightful* natural surroundings had a very wholesome effect upon me. I decided that I would not evade my destiny, and that there was something fateful in my encounter with this girl. Besides, I know from experience how it often happens in life that what frightens and horrifies sometimes proves beneficial, and that, contrariwise, what you have striven after in the hope of bliss and happiness ends in disappointment. If it is to be, let it be!

Now I will tell you a little about my future wife. She is called *Antonina Ivanovna Milyukova*. She is 28 years old. She is fairly good-looking. Her reputation is above reproach. Because she loves to be independent, she supports herself, though she has a very loving mother. She is completely without means, and no more than moderately educated (she was taught at the Elizavetinsky Institute), but she seems to be very nice, and capable of making an irrevocable attachment.

In a day or two my marriage with her will take place. What will happen after that I do not know. . . . If I am marrying without love, it is because circumstances conspired to make it impossible for me to do otherwise.[16]

Of all Tchaikovsky's surviving letters this is perhaps the most terrible to read. The appalling determination with which this wretchedly unhappy man advanced to certain disaster would be almost bizarre, were it not so chilling. What is astonishing is that Tchaikovsky seems to have maintained an outward appearance of normality in his life. His professional work went on as before, and his inspiration to composition was flourishing. On 15 May he had finished sketching the first three movements of the Fourth Symphony, and within three days he had set out for a 48-hour visit to Konstantin Shilovsky on a family estate at Glebovo, near Moscow. Then, some five days after his return, on 25 May, he visited the singer, Elizaveta Lavrovskaya. The conversation turned to possible subjects for an opera. After her husband had suggested a series of choices as thoroughly inept as Modest's recent suggestion of Charles Nodier's *Ines de Las-Sierras*, Elizaveta suddenly suggested Pushkin's *Eugene Onegin*. 'The idea seemed to me wild, and I didn't reply,' Tchaikovsky wrote to Modest on 30 May. 'Afterwards, while dining *alone* at an inn, I recalled *Onegin*, fell to thinking about it, next began to find Lavrovskaya's idea a possibility, then was carried away by it, and by the end of the meal had made up my mind. Straightway I ran off to track down a *Pushkin*. I found one with difficulty, set off home, read it through with delight, and passed an utterly sleepless *night*, the result of which was the *scenario* of a delightful opera on Pushkin's *text*.'[17] On 27 May he sped for a second

[16] *TLP6*, pp. 144–7; *TPM1*, pp. 25–7; *TZC2*, pp. 20–1 (slightly shortened, including excision of last three sentences).

[17] *TLP6*, p. 135; *TPR*, p. 278; *TZC1*, p. 533; *TPB*, p. 120; *TPM1*, p. 568; *DTC*, p. 66; *YDGC*, p. 146 (partial and with text corrupted). Tchaikovsky's own account of how the scenario of *Onegin* came to be compiled is difficult to reconcile with Kashkin's. According to the latter, Tchaikovsky had got hold of some stage adaptation of Pushkin's *Onegin*, and then taken Kashkin to a restaurant. After they had dined, he had told Kashkin of the circumstances in which Lavrovskaya had suggested *Onegin* to him; he was now, he said, soliciting Kashkin's help in devising the scenario. There and then they set about it but, despite repeated attempts, had been quite unable to devise anything satisfactory. At midnight they had parted, and the next evening had returned to the restaurant to try again. At the end of this equally unsuccessful exercise, Tchaikovsky had exclaimed to Kashkin: 'Now I see it is impossible to make a real opera out of *Eugene Onegin*, but at the same time I have to tell you that I cannot *not* compose it; much is already prepared in my head'. [*KIVC*, p. 109] In the face of this evidence from Kashkin, who seems to have been an honest, if far from infallible biographer, it must be accepted that he did play some part in the early planning of the *Onegin* scenario. Kashkin did confirm that Konstantin Shilovsky had some hand in the libretto, and certainly wrote Triquet's couplets in French.

time to Glebovo for a two-day visit so that he might confer with
Konstantin Shilovsky on his scenario for this new project.

We will leave till later an account of Tchaikovsky's assiduous work
and rapid progress on *Eugene Onegin*. However, the new subject had a
coincidental but very real influence upon his rapidly developing
relationship with Antonina. Later Tchaikovsky told Kashkin that it
was the incident of Tatyana's letter to Onegin that had first attracted
him to this Pushkin masterpiece (in fact, he had long thought of
composing this as a separate vocal work), and he immediately applied
himself to composing this scene:

> Still lacking not only a libretto, but even any [final] general plan of
> the opera, I began to write the letter music, succumbing to an
> invincible spiritual need to do this, in the heat of which I not only
> forgot about Miss Milyukova, but even lost her letter[18] − or hid it so
> well that I could not find it, and only remembered it when, some time
> later, I received a second letter.
>
> Being completely immersed in composition, I so thoroughly
> identified myself with the image of Tatyana that she became for me
> like a living person, together with everything that surrounded her. I
> loved Tatyana, and was furiously indignant with Onegin who
> seemed to me a cold, heartless fop. Having received a second letter
> from Miss Milyukova, I was ashamed, and even became indignant
> with myself for my attitude towards her. In her second letter she
> complained bitterly that she had received no reply, adding that if her
> second letter suffered the same fate as her first, then the only thing
> that would remain for her was to put an end to herself.
>
> In my mind this all tied up with the idea of Tatyana, and it seemed
> to me that I myself had acted incomparably more basely than
> Onegin, and I became truly angry with myself for my heartless
> attitude towards this girl who was in love with me. Because the
> second letter also contained Miss Milyukova's address, I forthwith
> set out thither, and thus began our acquaintance.[19]

Tchaikovsky's first meeting with Antonina occurred on 1 June. After
a second encounter a day or two later, he made his proposal of marriage
and then, with the sketches of the Fourth Symphony now completed
and another Conservatoire session finished, on 10 June he set off for

[18] This is not quite consistent with what Tchaikovsky had told Nadezhda von Meck
(see above, pp. 140–1).
[19] *KIVC*, pp. 119–20.

Glebovo for an extended visit. Antonina was to make preparations for the wedding and for their future life together.

Now that the decision on his destiny had been made and acted upon, Tchaikovsky could concentrate more single-mindedly upon *Onegin*. The Shilovsky estate delighted him and the house had a good library. As Tchaikovsky's early collaborator on the opera, Shilovsky realised the importance of undisturbed peace for the creative process, and he put at Tchaikovsky's service working conditions that were as ideal as those the composer had enjoyed four years before when he had written *The Tempest* at Usovo, the estate of the other Shilovsky brother, Vladimir. 'You could not conceive a situation more favourable for composition than that which I am enjoying here,' he wrote to Modest on 21 June:

I have at my disposal an entire, separate, superbly furnished house. When I'm busy no one, not a single human soul except Alyosha [Sofronov, his servant], ever puts in an appearance and, most important of all – I have a piano whose sounds, moreover, don't reach anyone except Alyosha when I'm playing. [Tchaikovsky had already confessed to Sasha that he was in the habit of singing loudly when composing.] I get up at eight, have a bath, drink tea (alone), and then busy myself until breakfast. After breakfast I take a walk, and again work until dinner. After dinner I go for a lengthy stroll, and pass the evening at the big house. The company here consists of the master of the house and his wife, the two elderly Yazïkova maids, and me. There are hardly any guests – in a word, it's very peaceful and quiet here. The locality is delightful in the full sense of the word. However, what's terrible is the weather: it's so cold that there's a *daily* morning frost. Up to now there's not been a single warm summer day.

By virtue of all the above my work is going forward rapidly, and if nothing makes me budge from here before August, then I should certainly have managed to sketch the whole opera, and in the autumn should busy myself with the scoring. But I shall probably leave here in the middle of July. However, I don't think I shall get to Grankino [where Modest was currently staying with the Konradis]. I have to spend several days in Moscow with *Kotek*, then go to Sasha, where I hope to see you, and then go abroad, if only *for a bit*.[20]

Even without positive evidence to the contrary, it would be impossible to believe that Tchaikovsky's declaration of his intentions for the rest of the summer, in which it seems that Antonina had no part,

[20] *TLP6*, p. 141; *TPR*, pp. 281–2; *TPB*, p. 122; *TZC1*, pp. 535–6 (partial).

signified that he had not yet determined the season of his marriage. He had of course done so, and in the end he had to make public his intentions. Thus, on 5 July, nine days before he left Glebovo with two-thirds of the opera sketched, he wrote to Anatoly, revealing his plans, and asking him to be, with Kotek, the sole witness at the ceremony. With the note to Anatoly he enclosed a letter for his brother to hand over to Ilya Petrovich, in which he begged his father's blessing upon his imminent nuptials, though he urged his father still to say nothing to the other members of the family, except to his stepmother. Ilya's private response was touchingly immediate. Perhaps fearing that the Almighty might snatch away an 82-year-old before he could stretch out his hand for paper on which to reply, he straightway wrote across his son's brief, miserably embarrassed letter: 'Dear Pyotr, may the Lord God bless you!'

Next Nadezhda von Meck was told (in the letter of 15 July, quoted above). Only at the eleventh hour, when it was too late for them to exercise any dissuasion upon him, did Tchaikovsky inform the other members of the family. On the very eve of the wedding he wrote both to Modest, and to Lev and Sasha. The latter must have been stunned by the abruptness of the opening sentence of Tchaikovsky's letter to them, and the conclusion of the second must have induced an even greater horror. Nor, despite his profession of love for Antonina, can his sister and her husband have found any reassurance in anything that followed, while his distasteful reaction to the new relationship Antonina would acquire with the Davïdov children exposed all too clearly his actual repugnance towards his future wife:

Any day now will be celebrated my marriage with a young woman, *Antonina Ivanovna Milyukova*. While giving you this news, I shall for the moment refrain from describing my bride's qualities since, except that she is a thoroughly respectable girl and loves me very much, I still know very little about her. Only when we have lived together for some time will the facets of her character reveal themselves to me with complete clarity. . . . I shan't bring her to see you at Kamenka until I'm no longer shocked by the thought that my nieces will call her *auntie*. At the moment, although I love my bride, it still seems to me a little impertinent on her part to have become aunt to your children, whom I love more than any other children in the world.

I have spent a month not far from here in the country at the Shilovskys'. I needed to stay there, first to begin my opera, secondly to acclimatise myself to the thought that I'm getting married. The proof that I'm taking this important step not frivolously but with deliberation is shown by the fact that I spent this month very calmly and composed a whole two-thirds of the opera.[21]

Yet only two days before he had told Nadezhda von Meck that he would have written far more if it had not been for his agitated condition. There can be little doubt which was the truer report.

On 18 July the wedding took place. Tchaikovsky began the day by at last breaking the news in writing to Vladimir Shilovsky. Then he proceeded to the church of St George on the Malaya Nikitskaya Street, where he was married to Antonina. The officiating priest was Dmitri Razumovsky, who was also professor of the history of church music at the Conservatoire, and thus one of Tchaikovsky's colleagues. No other members of the family or friends were present except the witnesses, Anatoly and Kotek, for Tchaikovsky had not even told Kashkin or Albrecht about the wedding, or even about his intention to marry. Razumovsky, knowing Tchaikovsky well and realising the obvious strain such a ceremony would be for the composer, did his best to nurse him through the service. 'But, all the same, I remained a sort of bystander until the moment when Dmitri Vasilyevich [Razumovsky], at the conclusion of the ceremony, made Antonina Ivanovna and me kiss,' Tchaikovsky told Kashkin. 'Then a kind of pain gripped my heart, and I was suddenly seized with such emotion that, it seems, I wept. But I tried quickly to gain control of myself, and to assume an appearance of calm. However, Anatoly noticed my condition, for he began to say something reassuring to me.'[22]

That evening, after the wedding breakfast, Tchaikovsky and his new wife left for St Petersburg to visit his family. Such was the bridegroom's immediate and appalling dismay at his new predicament that within two days he was pouring out to Anatoly a full account of that bridal-night rail journey, though still deluding himself (as he was to do to the last) that all would come out all right in the end:

When the carriage started I was ready to cry out with choking sobs. Nevertheless I still had to occupy my wife with conversation as far as Klin in order that I might earn the right to lie down in my own armchair when it was dark, and remain alone by myself. At the second station after Khinok Meshchersky [one of Tchaikovsky's old friends from the School of Jurisprudence] burst into the carriage. When I saw him I felt that he simply had to take me away somewhere forthwith. This he did. Before beginning any sort of conversation

[21] *TLP6*, p. 148; *TPR*, pp. 285–6.
[22] *KIVC*, p. 123.

with him I had to give vent to a flood of tears. Meshchersky showed much tender sympathy, and did a lot to prop up my fallen spirit. When, after Klin, I returned to my wife, I was much calmer. Meshchersky arranged that we should be accommodated in a sleeping compartment, and after this I slept the sleep of the dead. The remainder of the journey after I woke up was not particularly awful.... Somewhere in the country near *Okulov* we were delayed about five hours because a goods train had been derailed, and in consequence we arrived in St Petersburg at three instead of ten. What I found most comforting of all was that my wife didn't comprehend or even perceive my ill-concealed anguish. Now and always she appears to be completely happy and contented. Elle n'est pas difficile. She is in agreement with everything and contented with everything.

We stayed at the Hotel Europa – very good, and even luxurious. I went off to have a bath, on the way called in at the telegraph office, and sent telegrams to you and Kotek.... We dined in our own room. In the evening we took a carriage to the islands. The weather was quite foul and it was drizzling. We sat through one part [of a concert?] and went home....

We had conversations which have still further clarified our relationship with each other. *She is positively agreeable to everything, and will never want more. All she needs is to cherish and care for me.* I have retained for myself complete freedom of action. After taking a good dose of valerian, and begging my upset wife not to be upset, I again slept the sleep of the dead. Sleep is a great benefactor. I feel the time is not far distant when I shall *finally* compose myself.

And what, indeed, is there to grieve for? Both you and I are very highly strung and both are capable of seeing things as blacker than they really are. I have guaranteed my freedom of action to such a degree that, as soon as my wife and I have got used to each other, she will not constrain me in anything. There's no point in deceiving myself. *She's a very limited person*, but this is even a good thing. An intelligent woman might instil fear of herself in me. I stand so far above this one, I am so superior to her that at least I shall never be frightened of her.

The weather today is abominable. All the same, this evening my wife and I are going to the Kamenno-Ostrovsky Theatre, and tomorrow I want to go to Pavlovsk....

All the best, play your violin, and don't worry about me. I know already that soon everything is going to be all right.[23]

[23] *TPR*, pp. 286–8; *TLP*6, pp. 151–2 (partial); *TPM*1, p. 571 (partial).

Tchaikovsky was perhaps too hard on Antonina in this letter, but his physical aversion to her could not but aggravate his reservations into open contempt. Later, when he could review the past with more objectivity, he told Kashkin that it was the lack of anything they held in common that horrified him during the days immediately following their marriage. He admitted that Antonina did all she could to be a good wife, but she had absolutely no interest in those things he held most dear, nor any capacity for responding to anything except the most trivial. Kashkin, who briefly taught Antonina the piano after her separation from Tchaikovsky, observed this extreme mundaneness; while she had a reasonable technique and an excellent ear, she showed absolutely no sign of any musical perception, nor any response to the music itself. The most shattering discovery made by her husband was that she did not know a single note of his music. Nor had she ever been to a concert of the RMS where she might not only have encountered his work, but would have been reasonably assured of catching at least a glimpse of the man she professed to have loved for years. And it was to this being that Tchaikovsky now found he had committed himself for the remainder of his earthly days. In his desperation he sought every opportunity not to be left alone with her. He invited to dinner Laroche, who was most charming to Antonina, and he escaped to Laroche's own home for part of the following day. Meeting a friend – even a relative – in the street, he could not bring himself to confess that the lady with him was his wife. Despite his attempt to reassure Anatoly (and himself) that all would finally be well, he found there was no remission in his anguish. All he was craving for was the break which Antonina had agreed to allow him during August and September. He introduced her to his father and stepmother:

Papa is enchanted by my wife, which was to be expected. Lizaveta Mikhailovna was very sweet and attentive, but several times I noted tears in her eyes. This perspicacious and dear stepmother must have guessed I was living through a critical moment of my life. I confess all this was painful to me – that is, Papa's display of affection and his endearments (the very opposite of my coldness towards my wife) and Lizaveta Mikhailovna's perspicacity. I am indeed living through a painful moment in my life [he continued this outpouring of 23 July to Anatoly]. However, I feel that little by little I shall grow accustomed to my new situation. It would be an intolerable sham if I were to deceive my wife in anything, but I have warned her that she can count only on my brotherly love.... Physically my wife has become *totally repugnant* to me.... Yesterday morning, while my wife was taking a bath, I went to mass at St Isaac's Cathedral. I felt a need to pray. When I returned, I learned with surprise that Rubinstein (Nikolay) had called on me; he's come for his brother's concert. He sat for half an hour, but didn't wait for me. My wife was enchanted by his courtesy.[24]

Worse was to follow; two days later, with the marriage only a week old, Anatoly received a further distress-filled bulletin: 'Tolichka, yesterday was perhaps the most painful day of all since 18 July. In the morning it seemed to me that my life was broken for ever, and I suffered a fit of despair. By three o'clock a lot of people had gathered at our place. Nikolay Rubinstein, his sister Sofya, Malozemova, Karl Davïdov, Ivanov, Bessel, Laroche. We dined together.' Yet again he thought that the worst might now be over, but the agony of what he had already gone through in so short a time could not be hidden. 'The crisis was *terrible, terrible, terrible*. If it had not been for my love for you and others close to me bearing me up in these *intolerable spiritual torments*, then it might have ended badly, i.e. with illness or madness.

Today we are going straight back to Moscow.'[25]

The expenses of the last week had left Tchaikovsky penniless, and immediately on his arrival in his home city he applied to Nadezhda von Meck for a loan. Then, after some days in Moscow, the bridal couple set off for a ritual visit to the bride's parental home. It proved as unpleasant as it was brief, and Tchaikovsky discovered that his new mother-in-law possessed none of those loving qualities in which he had been led to believe she abounded. 'Her [Antonina's] *family environment* I liked very little. I have now passed three days in the country at her mother's,' he wrote to Sasha on 1 August, the day of his return, 'and it convinced me that everything that does not completely please me in my wife stems from the fact that she belongs to a very weird family, where the mother was always at odds with the father and now, after his death, is not ashamed to revile him in every possible way, where this same mother *hates*!!! some of her own children, where the sisters exchange catty remarks with one another, where the only son quarrels with his mother and all his sisters, *and so on, and so on.*'

All the same, he still granted his wife those qualities of understanding and devotion with which he had repeatedly credited her in the letters he had written since his marriage. 'I already love my wife,' he concluded, clearly hoping to allay Sasha's fears before his imminent meeting with

[24] *TPR*, pp. 289–90; *TPM*1, pp. 571–2 (partial). No part of this letter is reproduced in *TLP*8.
[25] *TLP*6, p. 155.

her, 'but how immeasurably distant is this love from that which I entertain towards you, my brothers, Lev, your children!!! I shall spend only a few days with you, for I must travel to Essentuki to undergo treatment.'[26]

On 7 August, having finally decided to dispense with the services of Mikhail, the elder Sofronov brother, because he could no longer as a married man afford to retain two valets, and having profusely thanked Nadezhda von Meck for sending him a thousand roubles (four hundred of which he promptly placed in an envelope and lodged with Jurgenson in case Kotek had need of them), Tchaikovsky set out for his sister's home. 'I shall stop in Kiev for several hours specially to write you a long letter, and unbosom myself fully,' he wrote to his patroness. 'If I emerge victorious from my murderous spiritual struggle, then it is to you that I shall be indebted for this. To you, and only to you. A few more days, and *I swear to you* I should have gone out of my mind. Farewell, my best friend, my providence.'[27]

In Kiev, on 9 August, he wrote the promised letter. Despite the overt sentimentality of its references to Nadezhda von Meck (the 'dear, sweet friend, well known to you, who is now living at *Brailov*', one of the von Meck estates), and the frankly self-indulgent (though by now, desperately needed) release of feeling that swamps the rest, it remains a valuable document that both confirms and amplifies what he had confided to Anatoly during the last three weeks, and it is worth quoting extensively from it. Having briefly reminded Mrs von Meck of the events leading up to the wedding, Tchaikovsky unburdened himself on what had followed:

> As soon as the [marriage] ceremony was over, as soon as I found myself alone with my wife with the consciousness that it was now our fate to live with each other inseparably, I suddenly felt not only that she did not inspire me with even a simple feeling of friendship, but that she was *hateful* to me in the fullest sense of that word. It seemed to me that I, or at least the best, even the sole good part of the real *me* – that is, my musicality – had perished irrevocably. My future lot seemed to me a sort of pathetic vegetating, and a wearisome comedy, not to be borne. My wife was in no way guilty in my eyes: she had not invited herself into the bonds of matrimony. In consequence, to make her feel that I do not love her, that I look upon her as an intolerable encumbrance, would be both cruel and base. There remains pretence. But to pretend all one's life is the greatest of torments. And

[26] *TLP*6, p. 158; *TPR*, p. 291.
[27] *TLP*6, p. 160; *TPM*1, p. 31; *YDGC*, p. 149 (partial).

where in all this can one think of work? I fell into deep despair, the more horrifying because there was no one who could sustain me or give me hope. I began passionately, avidly longing for death. Death seemed to me the only way out, but there was no question of contemplating a violent end. You must understand that I am deeply attached to certain of my relatives – that is, to my sister, my two younger brothers, and to my father. I know that if I were to decide upon suicide and were to carry this idea into effect, I could not but strike a mortal blow at these relatives. There are also many other people, there are some dear friends, whose love and friendship bind me indissolubly to life. In addition, I have the weakness (if one can call this weakness) of loving life, of loving my work, of loving my future successes. Finally, I have not yet *said* all that I can and wish to say before the time comes for me to pass to eternity. And so death herself does not take me, I myself do not wish to go to her, nor can I: what remains? I forewarned my wife that I should travel the whole of August for my health which has, indeed, given way and requires drastic treatment. In this way my trip began to seem to me a sort of liberation, albeit only temporary, from a fearful captivity, and the thought that my day of departure was not so very distant began to give me courage. After spending a week in St Petersburg, we returned to Moscow. Here we found ourselves penniless because my wife had been misled by a certain *Mr Kudryavtsev*, who had undertaken to sell her piece of woodland [which Antonina had inherited on the death of her father], and who had then cheated her. At this point a new train of fears and torments began; uncomfortable lodgings, the necessity of establishing new quarters, the impossibility of carrying this through because of lack of money, the impossibility, for the very same reason, of me getting away – finally, the anguish and the most stupid life in Moscow without *work* (I could not work, both because I had not the energy for it, and because our lodgings were uncomfortable), without friends, without a single moment of repose. I do not know how I remained sane. Then we had to visit my wife's mother. Here my torments increased tenfold. Her mother and the whole family *entourage* I had entered are antipathetic to me. Their range of interests is narrow, their opinions are wild, they are almost always at daggers drawn with one another; during all this my wife (perhaps unfairly) became hourly more hateful to me. It is difficult for me to express to you, Nadezhda Filaretovna, the terrible pitch my moral torments reached. Before leaving for the country, in utter despair of finding the means of getting out of this frightful situation, and obdurately pursuing the idea of my journey, I turned to that dear, sweet friend, well known to you, who is now living at *Brailov*. I was sustained by the thought that she would come to my aid, by the certainty that she would free me from the murderous clutches of anguish and madness. But would my letter reach her? The supposition that it might not plunged me into horror.

We returned to Moscow. This killing life dragged on for several days more. I had two consolations: first, I drank a lot of wine, and this stupefied me and afforded me several moments of oblivion; secondly, I was gladdened by meetings with *Kotek*. I cannot tell you how much brotherly sympathy he has shown me. Except for you, he is the only person who knows everything that I am now writing to you. He is a good man in the truest sense of that word.

It is known that misfortunes never come singly. Completely unexpectedly I received news of the death of one of my closest friends, a certain *Adamov*. I was at school with him, we started work together; though our ways had parted completely, we maintained the most intimately friendly relations to the very end. He enjoyed all the blessings of life; he was a thoroughly healthy man, he had an excellent official position; he had married money, he was absolutely happy in his family life – and suddenly, death! This completely flattened me. At last, one beautiful evening, I receive a letter from Brailov. . . .

After this I suddenly took heart, spent three days in preparations for my departure and in giving instructions for our future accommodation, and then, on *Tuesday* at 1 p.m., I left. I do not know what the future holds – but now I feel as though I have come to my senses out of a horrifying, tormenting dream – or, rather, out of a horrifying long illness. Like a man recovering after a fever, I am still very weak. I find it difficult to connect my thoughts, it was very difficult for me to write even this letter – but, on the other hand, what a feeling of sweet peace, what an intoxicating feeling of freedom and solitude! Unless my knowledge of my organism deceives me, then very likely, when I have rested and calmed my nerves, when I have returned to Moscow and have found myself in my customary round of activities, I shall begin to look upon my wife quite differently. In fact she has many instincts which could subsequently combine to make me happy. She loves me sincerely, and wants nothing except that I should be calm and happy. I pity her greatly.

I have remained a day in Kiev. Tomorrow I go to my sister, and from there to the Caucasus. Forgive me, Nadezhda Filaretovna, that this letter is so incoherent, disjointed and gloomy. I know, however, that you will understand . . .

Nadezhda Filaretovna, if God gives me strength to survive this present frightful time, I will prove to you that my friend has not come to my aid in vain. I have not yet said a tenth part of what I want to say. My heart is full. It thirsts to pour itself out in music. Who knows, perhaps I shall leave behind me something really worthy of praise from a first-rate artist. I am bold enough to hope that this will happen.

Nadezhda Filaretovna, I bless you for all that you have done for me. Farewell, my best, my inestimable, dear friend.[28]

Though a trip to the Caucasus spa of Essentuki had long been Tchaikovsky's intention, it was not to materialise. Remembering the agonies of boredom and loneliness he had endured at Vichy the previous summer, he was easily persuaded by his family that he could as profitably imbibe the Essentuki waters in the Ukraine. Thus Kamenka claimed him for the rest of the summer break. During his month with Sasha he wrote for his 'providence' a series of bulletins on the state of his spirits, and on his thoughts and feelings. And if, through such outpourings, his lacerated emotions could gain comfort, he could also find, in scoring his Fourth Symphony, which he had already dedicated to his new 'best friend', a musical occupation which did not demand any conceptual activity of the sort of which he was still incapable. He was encouraged, too, by Modest's favourable opinion of this new symphony. All through the previous weeks his musical creativity had been completely stunned, and during his first days at Kamenka he still remained utterly incapable of work. Slowly, however, his faculties began to reawaken until, far from Antonina, he found he could begin to discover again in Pushkin's Tatyana a projection of that lovely, vulnerable femininity which he could never hope to find in the real world. At last his creative impulses stirred a little, and by the time he arrived back in Moscow he had sketched a little more of *Onegin*, and had scored the first scene of Act I.

Because he had both his twin brothers as company during his stay at Kamenka, there is a break in that flow of letters to them (especially to Anatoly) that had provided some vivid insights into the first three weeks of his marriage. To Nadezhda von Meck Tchaikovsky was always inclined to exaggerate and sometimes to gush, but to his brothers his declarations were normally less extravagant of words, more precise in description, and therefore more credible as evidence. After Anatoly had left Kamenka on 3 September the correspondence with that brother resumed, thus affording us some reasonably trust-

[28] *TLP*6, pp. 161–4; *TPM*1, pp. 32–5.

worthy account of Tchaikovsky's personal condition during this lull in his matrimonial affairs.

What is so striking is the degree to which he seems to have been able to immerse himself wholeheartedly and joyfully in the life-style of Sasha's home, almost as though he had forgotten that Antonina existed. He had developed a passion for hunting. Yet the very liveliness with which he now recounted to Anatoly the trivia of his day-to-day activities – numerous hunting expeditions, a visit to a neighbouring estate that Sasha and Lev were thinking of purchasing, attending mass at a nearby monastery, the festivities of his niece Tatyana's birthday, and so on – attests, perhaps, to the frantic determination with which he was living these current pleasures which might, for the moment, obliterate thoughts of Antonina. His stay should have been shorter, but constantly he put off his return to Moscow. Then, as departure became more inescapable, thoughts of Antonina again surged up in him. 'Ah, how little I love Antonina Ivanovna Tchaikovskaya!' he suddenly exclaimed in his letter to Anatoly of 14 September, in which he had been detailing some of the recent pleasures of Kamenka life. 'What profound indifference this woman instils in me! How little does the prospect of meeting her gratify me! She doesn't, however, excite horror in me, just ennui,' he added, perhaps trying to convince himself that his reactions to her might have become less violent by the time of their next meeting.[29]

Finally on 19 September he bade farewell to Sasha and her family. In Kiev, where he delayed three nights, he had his last taste of freedom – a taste he indulged to the full. He saw Verdi's *La traviata* at the opera, visited St Sofya's Cathedral, and made a round of a multitude of other sights. Also in Kiev he received a letter from Antonina which told of her impatience for his return. On 23 September he was again in Moscow.

'My wife met me,' he recorded for Anatoly the next day. 'She, poor thing, has suffered many painful moments in arranging our flat pending my arrival.... I am completely satisfied with the arrangements of the flat; it's very elegant, nice, and not without luxury.... Naturally you want to know what I now feel. Tolya, allow me to pass over this in silence. I'm distressed: that's all I'll say. But, of course, this was inevitable after that abundance of happiness I experienced at Kamenka. I know that I'll still have to have patience for a bit, and then calm, contentment and – who knows – perhaps even happiness will come bit by bit.'[30]

[29] *TLP6*, p. 172; *TPR*, p. 293; *TPM1*, p. 573.
[30] *TLP6*, pp. 176–7; *TPR*, p. 296; *TPM1*, p. 573 (partial); *TZC2*, p. 29 (first three sentences only).

That same day, 24 September, began the new Conservatoire term. Kashkin remembered Tchaikovsky's determined efforts to mask his true condition. 'He had an exaggeratedly free-and-easy and cheerful appearance, but this smacked of affectation. Pyotr Ilich was quite incapable of dissimulation, and the more he tried, the more obvious became his dissembling. Noticing his nervous agitation, we all handled him very carefully, asked no questions, and waited for when he would introduce us to his wife.'[31] It seems almost incredible that, though his courtship and marriage had both taken place in Moscow, Tchaikovsky had succeeded in concealing Antonina from his friends, and they only heard of her existence after the wedding. Albrecht was the sole one to have any recollection of her, and he could only dimly remember her as someone with whom he had had administrative dealings on her entry to, and departure from the Conservatoire. Perhaps because Albrecht felt he knew Antonina a little, or else because Tchaikovsky had asked him to do so, the former helped Antonina with preparing her new home while Tchaikovsky was in the Ukraine. However, Kashkin, like most of Tchaikovsky's other friends, first met Antonina at the dinner which Jurgenson arranged at his own home soon after Tchaikovsky's return:

In general she made a favourable impression both in her outward appearance and in her modest manner of behaviour. I engaged in some conversation with her, and couldn't help noticing that all the while Tchaikovsky himself scarcely left us. Antonina Ivanovna seemed either to be shy or to be having difficulty in finding words, and from time to time, when there were involuntary pauses, Pyotr Ilich chimed in after her, or completed what she had been saying. However, our conversation was so trivial that I would not have paid attention to Pyotr Ilich's intervention, had the latter not been over-persistent every time his wife engaged in conversation with anyone. Such solicitude was not quite natural and, as it were, bore witness to a fear that Antonina Ivanovna would perhaps find it difficult to carry on a conversation in the proper tone. In general our new acquaintance produced an impression which, though favourable, was rather colourless. On one of the following days, when some of us had gathered in the director's office at the Conservatoire during a break in our commitments, Nikolay Rubinstein, recalling the evening at Jurgenson's and talking of Antonina Ivanovna, observed: 'You know, she's pretty, and she behaves nicely, but yet she's not particularly winning; it's as though she's not a real person, but some sort of confection.' For all its vagueness, such a characterisation was

[31] *KIVC*, p. 110; *YDGC*, p. 151.

nevertheless appropriate, for Antonina Ivanovna really did give the impression of being someone 'not real'.[32]

She must surely have been very ill-at-ease at the Jurgensons', for at home Tchaikovsky had found her incorrigibly garrulous, her three favourite topics being the shortcomings of members of her own family, her life at boarding school, and the succession of men who she said had been attracted to her: these were mostly generals, the nephews of noted bankers, famous artists, and even members of the imperial family.

The débâcle of Tchaikovsky's marriage approached with a swiftness that would have appeared frightful, had it not been so inevitable and such a blessed release. For many of those who were at Jurgenson's that evening, this first meeting with Antonina also proved to be the last. Though Tchaikovsky continued, as always, to be punctilious in attending to his duties at the Conservatoire, he disappeared as soon as his personal commitments were completed, and his friends found communication with him an increasingly trying matter. The only record of the last dying days of his married life is contained in the account he gave to Kashkin many years later. So desperate did he become that he concluded death was the only way out of his position. He was still against suicide because of the effect this might have on his family. Some more natural way had to be found, and he went so far as to make one pathetic attempt to engineer his own end. He disclosed this to Kashkin during the course of an account of his personal condition after his return to Moscow:

Although not more than a week had passed since my return from my sister's, I had already lost all ability to cope with the burden of my situation, and from time to time, so it seemed to me, my consciousness became clouded. During the day I still tried to work at home, but in the evenings it became intolerable. Not daring to go off to a friend or even to the theatre, I set off each evening for a walk, and for several hours wandered aimlessly through the distant, out-of-the-way streets of Moscow. The weather had become gloomy, cold, and at night there was a slight frost. On one such night I came to the deserted bank of the River Moscow, and there came into my head the thought that it would be possible to kill myself by contracting a chill. To this end, unseen in the darkness, I entered the water almost up to my waist, and stayed there until I could endure no longer the bodily ache produced by the cold. I came out of the water with a firm conviction that either from pneumonia or some respiratory illness I

[32] *KIVC*, pp. 110–11; *YDGC*, p. 151 (partial).

should die. At home I told how I had taken part in a nocturnal fishing expedition, and had fallen into the water by accident. However, my health showed itself to be so sound that the icy bath had no consequence for me.[33]

By now the need to escape from his wife had become absolute. Realising that nature would not intervene to deliver him, Tchaikovsky resorted to a more direct remedy. He telegraphed Anatoly in St Petersburg, imploring him to send a telegram over Nápravník's name, requiring his presence in St Petersburg. Anatoly responded immediately, and on 6 October Tchaikovsky hastily scribbled a couple of notes to Albrecht, informing him that his immediate attendance was required in St Petersburg in connection with the revival of *Vakula* for the next operatic season; he would be back in Moscow the next Tuesday. He did not return.

When he arrived in St Petersburg on 7 October he had passed beyond the final limits of endurance. Anatoly met him at the station, and could scarcely recognise him, so marked was his brother by the emotional havoc of the last fourteen days. He carried him off straightway to the Hotel Dagmar, where Tchaikovsky's nerves gave way. When the attack had passed, he fell into the long and deep sleep of sheer exhaustion. A psychiatrist declared that his only hope was a complete change of scenery, and that there could be no question of his ever living with his wife again, or even of his seeing her. Anatoly hurried to Moscow, set in order his brother's affairs as best he could, and sought a meeting with Antonina to explain the situation. Nikolay Rubinstein, fearing that Anatoly would not be outspoken enough in telling Antonina the truth about her husband's state and the psychiatrist's pronouncement, accompanied him.

Antonina invited the two men in, ordered tea, listened calmly while Rubinstein told her everything with a bluntness that made Anatoly go hot and cold, declared that she would agree to everything for the sake of 'Peti', and offered the two men tea. Having played his part, Rubinstein left Anatoly to discuss more personal family matters. What followed dumbfounded Anatoly, as he told Kashkin. 'Antonina Ivanovna accompanied him [Rubinstein] to the entrance hall and, returning with her face beaming, said to Anatoly Ilich: "I certainly never expected that Rubinstein would take tea at my home today!"'[34] Shocked by this evidence of extraordinary insensitivity on Antonina's part, Anatoly left the flat and returned quickly to St Petersburg. Then, on 13 October, he

[33] *KIVC*, p. 145; *TPM*1, pp. 573–4; *YDGC*, p. 152 (partial).
[34] *KIVC*, p. 113; *YDGC*, pp. 152–3.

bore his brother away for a prolonged stay in Western Europe. Tchaikovsky's marriage, still less than three months old, was over. So, too, was his period of residence in Moscow.

The documents that have been quoted in this chapter tell the story of this nightmare incident in Tchaikovsky's life with a terrible eloquence. That Tchaikovsky should ever have precipitated himself into such a situation seems incomprehensible; the fact that he did so is proof enough of the strength of those implacable forces within him that were driving him on. After this experience he could never revert to his former condition. If his recent emotional turmoils had been no more than the consequence of responding violently to a train of uncomfortable but transitory circumstances that had by chance cropped up in his day-to-day existence, then a few weeks or months might have sufficed to bring him back to his former state. However, he had merely separated from Antonina. Divorce would be a protracted and tiresome process under any circumstances, and Antonina was actively to inflict more suffering upon him before he was finally rid of her. Far worse: the conclusion was now inescapable that fate had sealed his condition, that he could never be as other men, that not only did he have to resign himself finally to this, but that all the world also knew it.

5

1877 — THE YEAR OF FATE
II: FOURTH SYMPHONY AND *EUGENE ONEGIN*

THE TWO WORKS whose creation was in progress while the events of the last chapter were running their course are among the finest of Tchaikovsky's compositions, and we have already observed the profound importance of the opera *Eugene Onegin* in consolidating his personal destiny. The Fourth Symphony, however, was begun some months before ever Antonina had intruded into his existence, and while there can be no doubt that his emotional state vis-à-vis his sexual condition accounts for much that is agonised and agitated in the expressive world of this symphony, it is more his relationship with Nadezhda von Meck than with Antonina Milyukova which is implicated in this particular piece. Certainly Tchaikovsky felt that his new friend would, of all people, be able to understand it. 'I am now absorbed in a symphony which I began to compose as far back as the winter, and which I very much want to dedicate to you because I think you will find in it echoes of your innermost thoughts and feelings,' he wrote on 13 May.[1] Though his emotional condition was making composition difficult, he could report to his patroness two days later that the sketches of the first three movements were complete, and that he had embarked on the finale. This likewise was finished in outline by 8 June, when he next wrote to her. The form of the dedication had not yet been settled, however:

'I have finished my symphony – that is, in sketch form. I shall score it at the end of the summer. I have heard, Nadezhda Filaretovna, that you have never agreed to pieces being dedicated to you. You have made an exception of me, for which I am extremely grateful to you. But if having your name on the title page of the symphony is disagreeable to you, then, if you wish, we can manage without it. Let you and I alone know to whom the symphony is dedicated.'[2] Such utter anonymity did

[1] *TLP6*, p. 126; *TPM1*, p. 15; *TZC2*, pp. 17–18; *DTC*, p. 373.
[2] *TLP6*, p. 140; *TPM1*, p. 22; *DTC*, p. 373.

not appeal to the lady, however, and her reply resolved the matter with a direct challenge to the degree of Tchaikovsky's devotion to her.

> Permit me to ask you one question, namely: do you consider me your friend [she wrote on 8 July]? Because of my liking for you, my opinion of you, my concern for you, and my boundless desire that everything should be for your good, I have grounds for calling myself your friend. But because *you* have never yet once called me by that name, I do not know whether *you* acknowledge me as your friend, and regard me as such. If, in answer to my question, you can say *yes*, then it would be extremely agreeable to me if you would set down on your symphony that you dedicate it *to your friend*, mentioning no name.[3]

Such an appeal demanded an unreserved response. To leave no vestige of doubt about his unqualified acceptance of Nadezhda von Meck into that intimate category, Tchaikovsky wrote across his manuscript: 'Dedicated to my best friend'.

As the narrative of the preceding chapter has shown, his relationship with Antonina and the competing creative claims of *Eugene Onegin* conspired to delay the completion of the symphony. On 24 September, the day after his return to Moscow and Antonina from his month with Sasha in the Ukraine, he reported that he had been scoring the first movement, but it seems that much of the task still remained to be done. When he fled from Moscow and his wife, he left behind what he had written of the symphony, having scribbled an instruction that, in the event of his death, the manuscript was to be entrusted to his patroness. On 28 October, still alive and now staying at Clarens in Switzerland, he wrote to his servant, Alexey Sofronov, asking that the manuscript should be sent to him. He was optimistic that he could finish the work before the end of the year, but it was mid-December before he was able to resume work. When he did at last settle down to it, he quickly found himself taking increasing pride in the new symphony. 'There's no doubt that it's the best I've composed,' he wrote to Modest from Venice on 18 December, three days after restarting, 'but it's not coming easily, especially the first movement.'[4] His love for his work was inflaming his zeal, however. 'I am not only occupying myself assiduously with scoring *our* symphony: I am utterly engrossed in it,' he wrote to its dedicatee three days later. 'None of my previous orchestral works ever cost me such labour, yet I have never yet felt such a love for one of my

---

[3] *TPM*1, p. 24; *DTC*, p. 373 (partial).
[4] *TLP*6, p. 293; *TPR*, p. 326; *TPB*, p. 129; *DTC*, p. 374; *YDGC*, p. 159.

own pieces.'[5] Two more days, and the first movement was at last finished. 'I'm composing this symphony with a full awareness that it's a composition *out of the ordinary*, and far more perfect in form than anything I've written before,' he enthused to Anatoly the next day (24 December).[6] With such unremitting application the piece was swiftly brought to completion. Within twenty-four hours the second movement was done, and on 27 December the scherzo was completed. The finale took longer, and the operation of scoring was interrupted by the composer's migration from Venice to Sanremo. There, on 7 January 1878, the last note was committed to paper.

Tchaikovsky wasted no time in sending the score off to Rubinstein in Moscow, for the latter had agreed to conduct it before the end of the season. The alacrity with which he set about arranging the first performance exceeded all Tchaikovsky's hopes, and on 22 February, less than seven weeks after Tchaikovsky had completed the work, Rubinstein included it in an RMS concert. Now that it had been performed, Tchaikovsky was impatient to hear his friends' critical verdicts, but they appeared reluctant to comment. After a month of such silence a perplexed and badly hurt composer could restrain himself no longer. His bitter reproaches instantly stirred Taneyev to reply with a commendable honesty that won Tchaikovsky's respect, though it can scarcely have brought unalloyed joy to his heart:

> Although there are some superb bits in it, it pleased me less than other works such as *Francesca*. I will enumerate frankly everything in it that I don't like. The first movement is disproportionately long when compared with the others. It has the appearance of a symphonic poem to which three movements have been appended fortuitously to make up a symphony. The trumpet fanfares which constitute the introduction, and which afterwards appear from time to time, the changes of tempo in the second subject, all make you think this is programme music. Nevertheless, I like the movement very much.

Taneyev had reservations about the rhythmic repetitiveness in part of this movement, and also about the central theme of the following Andantino, though he judged this as a whole to be

> ... exceedingly nice.... The scherzo is marvellous, and sounds

---

[5] *TLP*6, p. 290; *TPM*1, pp. 115–16; *TZC*2, p. 62; *DTC*, p. 374; *YDGC*, p. 160.
[6] *TLP*6, p. 301; *TZC*2, p. 66; *TPR*, p. 333; *TPB*, p. 131; *DTC*, p. 374.

excellent; I don't like the trio which is like a dance out of a ballet.

Nikolay Grigoryevich (Rubinstein] likes the finale best of all. I can't agree with this. Knowing how you treated 'The Crane' ['Zhuravel' in the finale of the Second Symphony], knowing what you are able to make out of a Russian theme, I think your variations on 'Vo polye beryozinka stoyala' too slight and insufficiently interesting.

One of this symphony's failings with which I shall never be able to reconcile myself is that in each movement there is something that recalls ballet music: the middle of the Andante, the trio of the scherzo, the march-like bit in the finale . . .

That's my *honest* opinion of this symphony. Perhaps I've expressed myself too bluntly, but you won't be angry with me for this.[7]

Taneyev was right. Tchaikovsky could not take offence at such transparent honesty, and in his reply he expressed his gratitude for Taneyev's forthrightness. As an initial impression of the new symphony, this assessment by Tchaikovsky's former pupil showed a good deal of perception, though Taneyev's identification of a ballet music idiom in the symphony – a criticism that has been echoed by other commentators – did sting Tchaikovsky into a substantial reply. This letter is an important one, for in it Tchaikovsky disclosed much about his views of what a symphony should be, and since he was talking to a fellow-professional, his words are purged of that exaggeration which so often tainted his communications with Nadezhda von Meck:

I simply do not understand what it is that you call ballet music, and why you cannot reconcile yourself to it. Do you understand as ballet music every cheerful tune that has a dance rhythm? If that's the case, you must also be unable to reconcile yourself to the majority of Beethoven's symphonies in which you encounter such things at every step. . . . I simply do not understand how in the term *ballet music* there can be anything *censorious*. . . . I can only suppose, therefore, that the *ballet-like* bits of my symphony that displease you do so not because they are *ballet-like*, but because they're bad. Maybe you are quite right, but all the same I do not comprehend why a dance tune may not appear occasionally in a symphony, even if only when it has a deliberate shade of vulgar coarse humour. Again, I'll cite Beethoven, who resorted to this effect more than once. . . . As for your observation that my symphony is programmatic, I completely agree. The only thing I don't understand is why you consider this a defect. I fear

[7] *TTP*, pp. 31–2; *DTC*, p. 379.

the very opposite situation – i.e. I should not wish symphonic works to come from my pen which express nothing, and which consist of empty playing with chords, rhythms, and modulations. Of course my symphony is programmatic, but this programme is such that it cannot be formulated in words. . . . Ought not a symphony – that is, the most lyrical of all musical forms – to be such a work? Should it not express everything for which there are no words, but which the soul wishes to express, and which requires to be expressed? . . . Please don't think that I aspire to paint before you a depth of feeling and a grandeur of thought that cannot be easily understood in words. I was not trying to express any new thought. In essence my symphony imitates Beethoven's Fifth; that is, I was not imitating its musical thoughts, but the fundamental idea. Do you think there is a programme in the Fifth Symphony? Not only is there a programme, but in this instance there cannot be any question about its efforts to express itself. My symphony rests upon a foundation that is nearly the same, and if you haven't understood me, it follows only that I am not a Beethoven, a fact which I have never doubted. I'll add, moreover, that there is not a note in this symphony (that is, in mine) which I did not feel deeply, and which did not serve as an echo of sincere impulses within my soul. The exception is perhaps the middle of the first movement, in which there are contrivances, seams, glueings together – in a word, *artificiality*.[8]

This letter is also invaluable as a qualification to the explicit programme which Tchaikovsky had confided to Nadezhda von Meck some weeks earlier, and which has been often quoted. Here Tchaikovsky appears flatly to contradict what he was to declare to Taneyev (his memory for his own themes is not always infallible):

In *our* symphony there *is* a programme – i.e. it is possible to express in words what it is trying to say, and to you, and only to you, I am able and willing to explain the meaning both of the whole and of the separate movements. Of course I can do this only in a general way.

The introduction is the *seed* of the whole symphony, undoubtedly the main idea:

[Ex. 128a]

[8] *TLP*7, pp. 200–1; *TTP*, pp. 33–4; *TZC*2, pp. 147–8; *DTC*, pp. 279–81; *YDGC*, p. 179 (final portion only).

This is *fate*, this is that fateful force which prevents the impulse to happiness from attaining its goal, which jealously ensures that peace and happiness shall not be complete and unclouded, which hangs above your head like the sword of Damocles, and unwaveringly, constantly poisons the soul. It is invincible, and you will never overcome it. You can only reconcile yourself to it, and languish fruitlessly:

[Ex. 128b]

The cheerless and hopeless feeling grows yet stronger and more burning. Is it not better to turn away from reality and submerge yourself in day-dreams?

[Ex. 128c]

O joy! There appears, at the very least, a sweet and gentle day-dream. Some blissful, radiant human image hurries by and beckons you away:

[Ex. 128d]

How good this is! How distant now sounds the obsessive first theme of the allegro. Day-dreams little by little envelop the soul completely. Everything gloomy, joyless is forgotten. There she is, there she is – happiness!

No! These were day-dreams, and *fate* wakes you from them:

[Ex. 128e]

Thus all life is an unbroken alternation of hard reality with swiftly passing dreams and visions of happiness.... No haven exists.... Drift upon that sea until it engulfs and submerges you in its depths. That, roughly, is the programme of the first movement.

The symphony's second movement expresses another phase of depression. This is that melancholy feeling which comes in the evening when, weary from your labour, you are sitting alone, you take a book – but it falls from your hand. There comes a whole host of memories. It is both sad that so much is now *past and gone*, yet pleasant to recall your youth. You both regret the past, yet do not wish to begin your life again. Life has wearied you. It is pleasant to rest and look around. You remembered much. There were happy moments when the young blood boiled, and life was satisfying. There were also painful moments, irreparable losses. All this is now somewhere far distant. It's both sad, yet somehow sweet to immerse yourself in the past.

The third movement expresses no definite feeling. It is made up of capricious arabesques, of the elusive images which rush past in the imagination when you have drunk a little wine and experience the first stage of intoxication. Your spirit is neither cheerful nor yet sad. You think of nothing; you give free rein to your imagination – and for some reason it began to paint strange pictures. Among these you suddenly recalled a picture of drunken peasants and a street song.... Next, somewhere in the distance, a military procession passed. This [movement is made up of] these completely disjointed images which rush past in your head when you have fallen asleep. They have nothing in common with reality; they are strange, wild, and disjointed.

The fourth movement. If within yourself you find no reasons for joy, look at others. Go among the people. Observe how they can enjoy themselves, surrendering themselves wholeheartedly to joyful feelings. A picture of festive merriment of the people. Hardly have you managed to forget yourself and to be carried away by the spectacle of others' joys, than irrepressible *fate* again appears and reminds you of yourself. But others do not care about you. They have not even turned around, they have not glanced at you, and they have not noticed that you are solitary and sad. O, how they are enjoying themselves, how happy they are that all their feelings are simple and direct! You have only yourself to blame; do not say that everything in this world is sad. There are simple but strong joys. Rejoice in others' rejoicing. To live is still possible![9]

Perusing this programme, the reader cannot but have reservations about accepting it precisely as it stands; equally, despite Tchaikovsky's denial to Taneyev of the existence of any sort of literary programme, it would be foolish to reject this declaration to Nadezhda von Meck as nothing more than the post factum romanticising of an excited mind. Yet the postscript to Tchaikovsky's letter makes it abundantly clear that the work was not written *to* this programme, which was simply Tchaikovsky's attempt to find a verbal definition for the expressive experiences which the symphony embodied:

Just now, as I was about to place this letter in its envelope, I re-read it and was horrified by the vagueness and inadequacy of the programme which I am sending you. For the first time in my life I have had to put into words and phrases musical thoughts and musical images. I have not succeeded in saying this as I ought. I was terribly

[9] *TLP*7, pp. 125–7; *TPM*1, pp. 217–19; *TZC*2, pp. 118–20; *DTC*, pp. 376–8; *YDGC*, pp. 172–4. It is interesting to compare Tchaikovsky's account of his fourth movement with the passage in the recently serialised *Anna Karenina* where Tolstoy described Levin's feelings as he watched some peasant women. 'The singing women approached Levin, and it seemed to him as though a thunder-cloud of merriment were coming towards him. . . . Everything began to move and sway to the rhythm of this wild, gay song, with its cries, whistles and hiatuses. Levin grew envious of this wholesome merriment, and wanted to participate in this expression of the joy of living. But he could do nothing, and had to lie, gaze and listen. When the peasants with their song were out of sight and earshot, Levin was engulfed by a heavy sense of melancholy for his loneliness, his physical idleness, for his alienation from this world.' I am grateful to Miriam Phillips for drawing my attention to this passage.

depressed last winter when I was composing this symphony, and it
serves as a true echo of what I was going through at that time. But it
is merely *an echo*. How can it be translated into clear and defined
verbal forms? I am not able to, I do not know how to. Also I have
already forgotten much. There have remained general recollections
of the strength, the horror of the feelings I experienced.[10]

This is surely confirmation enough that the Fourth Symphony is a
true piece of emotional autobiography even though its successive
musical events may not chart Tchaikovsky's experiences in every part
with the precise delineation of the programme just quoted.

One fact is inescapable: whatever credence or disbelief the listener
may possess concerning · the work's extramusical content, he will
certainly realise abruptly, if he comes upon it after tracing his way
through Tchaikovsky's earlier music, that here are some quite new
elements which require him to widen his channels of receptivity. The
forceful introductory theme of the first movement, for instance,
operates subsequently with expressive results quite different from those
of the similarly sited Friar Laurence theme in *Romeo and Juliet*, or the
first folksong in the Second Symphony. Both these ideas had also
penetrated into the sonata structures which had followed their initial
appearances, the former with explicit dramatic intent. Yet none of the
friar's thematic interventions had possessed anything like the violence
with which the introductory theme of the Fourth Symphony (see Ex.
129b) intrudes into later events, whether it is savagely hammering at
the first movement's main material, as in the climax of the develop
ment, or intruding peremptorily to sweep aside other ideas, as it does
before both the development and the coda of this same movement, or
when it suddenly resurges towards the end of the finale. That this
theme really does symbolize fate, as Tchaikovsky would have
Nadezhda von Meck believe, is wholly credible. Likewise the hesitant
waltz theme of the first subject (see Ex. 128b), by mating an almost
limitless capacity to extend into new melodic shapes with a seemingly
total incapacity to escape from the confines of a narrow range of
metrical matrices, convincingly begets a sense of frustration – in this
instance an inability to escape the workings of an implacable fate. True,
the content ascribed to the middle movements carries little conviction,
but we should not dismiss too lightly Tchaikovsky's verbal account of
the finale, remembering his recent encounter with Tolstoy, and his
admiration for *The Cossacks*, that portrayal of 'natural' men and women

[10] *TPM*1, pp. 217–18; *TLP*7, p. 128; *TZC*2, p. 120.

whose freedom from the pressures and constraints of sophisticated society enabled them to engage much more readily in the basic joys and satisfactions of life.

The origins of Tchaikovsky's motto theme are an interesting subject for speculation. Was this remorseless invention an unconscious expansion of the terse main motif in the first movement of Beethoven's Fifth Symphony, or could it have been compounded from recollections of Tchaikovsky's Bayreuth experience of not so many months before? Certainly this would be completely consistent with Tchaikovsky's well established practice of constructing new melodic expanses from protoshapes already firmly lodged in his mind (see, for instance, the first movement of the First Piano Concerto). The central section of Tchaikovsky's motto theme could have been born from a union of the forge motif (ex. 129a) and the initial phrase of Siegfried's horn call (Ex. 129c), sometimes likewise heard unaccompanied. And if the opening

Ex. 129

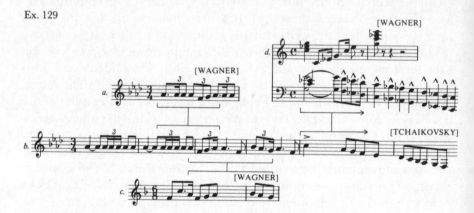

monotone rhythm might just conceivably be a faint remembrance of Hunding's horn call which signalled his approach as the agent of Siegmund's destruction in *Die Walküre*, there can be no doubt about the similarity between the descending scale which closes Tchaikovsky's theme and the motif, variously described as the 'spear' or 'treaty', so ubiquitous in *Der Ring*, particularly since this powerful conception in Wagner's tetralogy is usually blazed forth in lusty brass scoring (as in Ex. 129d, where it declares Siegmund's fate as he succumbs to Hunding's spear). The descending scale was to become the embodiment of fate in a number of Tchaikovsky's works, from this symphony's companion creation *Eugene Onegin* (though a matchingly ominous scale has already been heard in *Francesca da Rimini*, also a few bars after the beginning (see Ex. 122b, bars 7–8)), to his last masterpiece, the Sixth

Symphony. It would certainly have been symbolically apt that an element in Tchaikovsky's work signifying a baleful force should have insinuated itself from the music of a composer whom Tchaikovsky saw as the leading assailant upon those values he most cherished.

But beyond this the Fourth Symphony owes nothing to Wagner except, perhaps, the epic scale of certain slabs of the opening Moderato con anima. This is the most daring symphonic movement Tchaikovsky had yet composed. Proportions are changed, expositional and developmental elements are reshuffled, the key scheme is unprecedented, and the coda function is revised. To begin with, the exposition is remarkable not only, as we shall see, for its unexpected thematic and tonal organisation, but also because of its scale within the whole movement. Tchaikovsky's definition of the symphony as 'the most lyrical of all musical forms' was a clear declaration that for him a symphony should spring primarily from melodic impulses. In the development there could be no avoiding what was, to Tchaikovsky, a calculated and cerebral process; hence his admission that this part of the movement was filled with 'artificiality'. The exposition, however, could accommodate a more purely melodic continuum, and it was perfectly natural that he should feel driven to enlarge this section to permit his strongest natural gifts the maximum room in which to exercise themselves.

The result of these considerations is a radical redistribution of the proportions of the movement (see Ex. 130), with the exposition, which was certainly Tchaikovsky's most original to date, occupying something like one-half of the entire piece. Yet, original as it is, some of its most apparently novel features are simply drastic extensions of practices already well rooted in Tchaikovsky's earlier symphonic works: for instance, the behaviour of the introductory theme in the main body of the movement, as we have already noted. We have observed in earlier works – most notably in the First Piano Concerto – a process of thematic synthesis whereby quite fresh melodies are generated through the apparently intuitive redistribution of certain basic thematic particles. It has already been suggested that the motto theme may have grown thus; certainly within the main body of this movement the process is applied with self-conscious deliberation to produce what is, in effect, a whole third subject. And this clear emergence of the three-subject exposition is, in its turn, only a consolidation of the explicit three-stage exposition of the Third Symphony. Here, by disentangling the last two themes and allocating each its own key, Tchaikovsky had at last complemented tonally his long-standing predilection for three themes in his exposition. In the

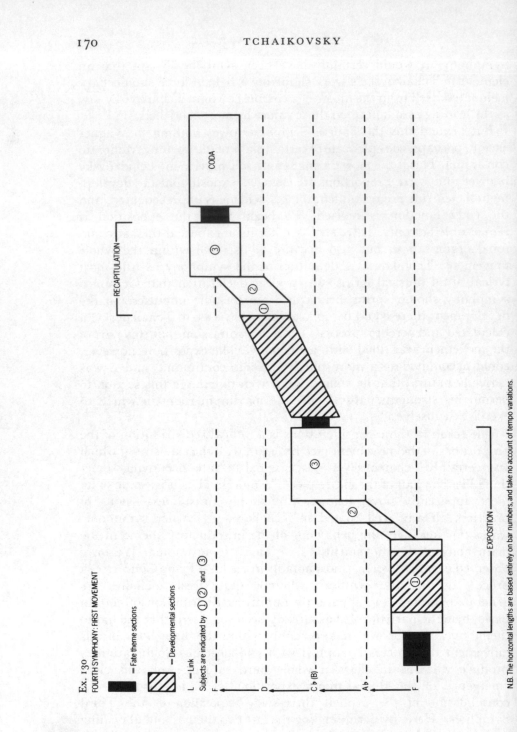

Ex. 130

FOURTH SYMPHONY: FIRST MOVEMENT

■ = Fate theme sections

▨ = Developmental sections

L = Link

Subjects are indicated by ① ② and ③

N.B. The horizontal lengths are based entirely on bar numbers, and take no account of tempo variations.

Third Symphony there had been nothing unusual in the trinity of keys; in this new work the three subjects are exposed in a most unconventional three-key succession which is simply the first stage in a highly unorthodox tonal scheme embracing the whole movement. So, too, the first subject follows a pattern familiar from earlier Tchaikovsky sonata schemes, for its flanks are two slabs of identical tonic-centred music enclosing a quasi-developmental centre. In this instance, however, the middle portion is so expanded that there is no longer any question of the tonic restatement of the opening sounding simply like a tutti reinforcement of the opening proposition, for this mini-development (or, perhaps, one should say 'continuous extension') of the first subject has already moved the experience forward by significantly enlarging upon the expressive potentialities within this melancholy waltz theme, and by setting out on a tonal expedition which has reached as far as a firm A minor. In fact, this first subject is only marginally shorter than the later official development (77 against 82 bars).

The link to the second subject is, as might be expected, short and unabashedly functional, and the new tune which enters in A flat minor on the clarinet (see Ex. 128c) is a slight, tripping invention which is quickly counterpointed by a second theme which first stirs among the violas, then emerges fully in the cellos, and which quickly directs the music's course towards C flat (written B). If the listener, hearing the first sounds of the charming clarinet tune, fears that the steam is already going out of the movement, he is quickly disabused. As well as being a subject in its own right, it quickly turns out to have a transitional and prophetic function, for it both manoeuvres towards the key of the impending third thematic element and also, by its scoring, brings progressively to the fore the new cello theme in preparation for the moment when this tune is ready to usurp the place of the clarinet theme and introduce the third subject (see Ex. 128d). Nevertheless, although this third subject substantially widens the expressive horizons, it is thematically retrospective, being entirely an inspired amalgam of thematic material already heard – the tripping anacrusis to the clarinet melody, a couple of bars of the rocking cello theme (this theme is itself extracted from the contour of the fate theme (Ex. 131b and c)), and two further bars derived from the opening of the first subject. This new composite idea is unfolded at some length over persistent tonic-dominant timpani strokes before the exposition is rounded off by a substantial codetta based mainly upon the rhythmic figures of the first subject. The precipitate entry of the fate theme (see Ex. 129b) fortifies the listener's awareness of being within a sonata experience of a very unusual kind.

Ex. 131

The development, which brings a sudden lull in the aggressiveness which has taken possession of the movement, returns to a world which has already been probed in the extensive thematic excursion within the first subject. However, whereas that section had occupied itself solely with self-examination, the development proper is to be thematically acquisitive. It has three distinct stages, the first displaying an almost obsessive preoccupation with the rhythmic world of the first subject in a manner which raises a suspicion that the corresponding section of Beethoven's Seventh Symphony was in Tchaikovsky's mind at this moment; the second stage enlarges this world with a new sustained theme which has been germinating during the first stage and which now grows in the strings, while the third stage is marked off by the sudden intervention of the fate theme from the work's opening. Throughout the entire development the first subject elements have remained ever-present; now, abruptly, the fate theme retreats and the first subject in its original form is thundered out by the full orchestra. The key is D minor – yet this thematic statement, despite the 'wrong' key and the absence of any significant preliminary signals that a crucial juncture in the structure has been reached, turns out to be the recapitulation.

It is now that Tchaikovsky's tonal strategy begins to clarify. Whereas the classical composer had constructed his sonata movements upon a frame with three fundamental points of tonal rest (the tonic key at the opening and again at the recapitulation, with (normally) the dominant or relative major at the end of the exposition), Tchaikovsky has grounded this movement upon five tonal foundations, each a minor third higher than the one preceding (F, A flat, C flat/B, D, F). Three of these keys have been absorbed by the exposition, while the fourth has now been reached at the beginning of the recapitulation. The apparent problem is that there are two more subjects, but only one more key. Tchaikovsky's solution was as simple as it was, in a way, inevitable. To have opened the recapitulation by reiterating the full first subject as it had been unfolded in the exposition would have been prolix, and even more wearisome after its ubiquitous rôle in the development. Instead Tchaikovsky cut it to the minimum and passed straight to the second subject, still maintaining D minor. Thus a substantial weight is given to this new key-point; at the same time, by repeating this second subject exactly as it had appeared in the exposition, Tchaikovsky ensured that the thematic composite which is the third subject would arrive in F.

This reduction of length in the post-exposition part of the movement may have eased some of Tchaikovsky's problems, but it had also created another major one. Compression has meant loss of weight, and since the recapitulation has merely summarised the exposition without shedding any new light upon its material, there is a grave danger that the latter stages of this movement may sound almost dismissive. This imposes a new responsibility upon the coda and Tchaikovsky completely reversed its normal rôle by making it not a section which formally rounds off an experience which has already run its full course, but a new and crucial stage in that experience. The irruption of the fate theme as the recapitulation closes is an abrupt warning that the movement is not to proceed straight to its end. What actually ensues is the movement's biggest single surprise, for this theme, which has stamped its mark upon some of the other material in the movement (compare, for example, the bracketed portion x in Ex. 131c with Ex. 131a and b), while itself apparently remaining immutable, now displays a chameleon-like capacity to change its character, swiftly subsiding to yield a solemn, soothing tune (see Ex. 131d) which is the most placid incident in the whole movement. Yet beneath this briefly stable surface the first subject element persists as accompaniment, and this serene tune in its turn abruptly annexes the rhythmic character of the first subject (see Ex. 131e) and, with fragments of the revitalised fate theme again breaking out beneath, leads to the final statement of that first subject which has dominated everything, now set at last in the tonic key

This movement by itself would suffice to establish Tchaikovsky as a major innovatory mind, and not until the first movement of his last symphony did he produce another symphonic conception of comparable boldness. The sheer force of the music matches that of *Francesca da Rimini*, but by marshalling his wide range of expressive elements to produce a more varied and complex experience, he has mitigated the sense of overstatement that had marred the earlier work. After such a colossal utterance, respite is essential. Already in the slow movement of the Second Symphony and in the second and fourth movements of the Third, Tchaikovsky had shown an inclination to place less momentous matters in the central part of the symphonic experience, and the trend reaches fulfilment in this new piece, for both the middle movements might reasonably, in this context, have been labelled intermezzi. Both are ternary structures, the first a receptacle for some charming lyrical ideas, the second an opportunity for Tchaikovsky to parade his flair for light, fanciful invention. The extensive thematic repetitions against differing backgrounds in the slow movement disclose again Tchaikovsky's heritage from Glinka, especially in the central section which, *Kamarinskaya*-like, does little more than reiterate the simplest of two-bar fragments with constant reharmonisation. Tchaikovsky was particularly pleased with his notion for the 'new instrumental effect' in the scherzo. 'First the strings play by themselves entirely pizzicato; in the trio the woodwind enter and also play by themselves; they are replaced by the brass section, again playing alone; at the end of the scherzo all three groups answer one another in short phrases. I think this sound effect will be interesting,' he had written enthusiastically to the symphony's dedicatee in August 1877.[11] It is no surprise that this movement scored the most immediate success with the first audiences – nor that Taneyev should have readily associated the musical world of the trio with ballet.

With the passage of these two faultlessly assured movements the ear is refreshed and the nerves rested in preparation for a resumption of more weighty matters in the finale. In the same way that the opening theme of the scherzo seems to have borrowed its initial contour from the main theme of the preceding Andantino (and even more from the central section of that movement), so the final Allegro con fuoco takes the opening notes of the scherzo, now presenting them in a forceful tutti. Remembering how Tchaikovsky had confessed his debt to the programmatic intent (as he saw it) of Beethoven's Fifth Symphony, we may note that he chose to reintroduce his fate theme just prior to the last appearance of the movement's first theme, just as Beethoven had done with the scherzo theme in his finale. Yet the basic forms of the two movements are quite different. Beethoven's is a clear sonata structure,

[11] *TLP*6, p. 168; *TPM*1, pp. 40–1; *DTC*, p. 374; *TZC*2, p. 26 (partial).

Tchaikovsky's a less clear rondo. This is another instance of an apparent confusion between the sequence of thematic events and the tonal behaviour. The thematic distribution suggests the simplest of simple rondos; the tonal behaviour, especially in the second episode, undermines this. The brief two-stage introduction presents successively the two elements that are to provide the substance of what follows, the second of these ideas (the Russian folksong whose phrases Tchaikovsky gratuitously squares up to two-bar lengths by inserting a minim rest after each phrase (see Ex. 132) endeavouring to pull the music into A minor, but without complete success, thanks to the persisting dominant pedal which asserts F major. When the first collection of ideas has been paraded in its entirety exclusively in the tonic, there is an abrupt shift to the subdominant (B flat minor, the key of the slow movement), and the folksong enters (Ex. 132b; Ex. 132a, from Balakirev's Overture on three Russian Themes, uses the tune

Ex. 132

more correctly) to be treated to a series of changing backgrounds. B flat
minor is rigorously preserved for about half of this episode; subsequently new variations radically alter the theme, treating it more
motivically and contrapuntally, and exploring other keys before
leading back to a full and exact restatement of the first section, once
again in the tonic. At its conclusion, exactly as before, the folksong
re-enters, now in the relative minor, and somewhat modified. This time
the tonal excursions begin earlier, and successive variations seem to
grow within an ever more hectic developmental situation. Suddenly the
fate theme bursts forth; then, after a dominant preparation to restore
the tonic, the F major section resumes, this time changing course to pair
itself with the Russian folktune, just as it had done in the introduction.
A short whirlwind coda follows.

    This account of the finale's events is enough in itself to show that the
movement has nothing of the complexity or audacity of the first
movement. It lacks even the scope and ambition of the last movement
of the Second Symphony, Tchaikovsky's most successful symphonic
finale to date. There is no significant interaction between the various
materials, no striking new ideas introduced to add enrichment, or to
stir Tchaikovsky's mind to inventive thematic engagements. The
folksong variations are pleasant, even at times resourceful, but
Taneyev was indubitably right to rate them below those which
Tchaikovsky had so dazzlingly devised for 'The Crane' in the Second
Symphony. Nor does the sudden intrusion of the fate theme carry much
conviction, for none of the other music seems in any way to relate to the
emotional world this theme represents (which may be some confirmation that Tchaikovsky really *did* see its rôle here as purely programmatic, and that his explanation of the last movement was, in fact,
authentic). It is a rather sad end to a symphony which had begun so
magnificently. Not until his very last completed work, the Sixth
Symphony of 1893, was Tchaikovsky to find a solution of the finale
problem that was as successful as it was original.

    If, without Tchaikovsky's programme, we could do no more than
speculate on the close engagement between his own existence and the
musical expression of the Fourth Symphony, there are no such doubts
about *Eugene Onegin*. The birth process of the opera is altogether more
liberally documented from the very first moment when a casual
observation by Elizaveta Lavrovskaya implanted in Tchaikovsky's
mind the idea which fertilised his creativity. Within two days he was at
the Shilovsky estate of Glebovo to consult with Konstantin on the
libretto. Many of those to whom he confided his choice of subject
shared the reservations which he had himself felt when Pushkin's verse

novel had first been suggested to him. 'This opera will, of course, have no powerful dramatic movement but, on the other hand, the human side of it will be interesting – and, moreover, what a wealth of poetry there is in all this! What is the scene of Tatyana with her nurse worth by itself!' he wrote to Nadezhda von Meck.[12] One of those with the strongest doubts was Modest. 'Maybe my opera won't be theatrical,' Tchaikovsky had retorted on 21 June from Glebovo, where he had now been for some ten days after the end of the Conservatoire term, 'maybe there will be little action in it – but I'm in love with the image of Tatyana. I'm enchanted by Pushkin's verses, and I'm setting them to music because I'm being drawn to do this. I've been utterly immersed in composing the opera ... I've already written all the second scene of Act I (Tatyana with her nurse), and I'm very satisfied with what's come out. The greater part of the first scene is also already written.'[13] Six days later he could report to Anatoly, who was as sceptical as his twin about the wisdom of Pyotr's choice, that all three scenes of the first act were composed. As we have already seen, when he left Glebovo on 14 July, he had completed two-thirds of the work.

From the beginning Tchaikovsky recognised that *Onegin* would be a very unusual species of opera, unlikely to enjoy the kind of broad success for which he might have hoped if he had chosen a more conventional operatic subject. Yet such was its particular closeness to his own heart, so precious and personal had the subject become to him, that at this stage he scarcely cared about its wider fortunes. After Glebovo he did little work on it for some months. Though Modest believed that all the remainder of the opera, save the duel scene, was sketched at Kamenka in August and September, it seems more probable that Tchaikovsky did scarcely more than score the first scene. By the time that he was preparing to leave Sasha's home for Moscow and his last days of married life, he could look back with some objectivity on what he had already composed of the work.

Its content is very artless [he wrote to Nadezhda von Meck on 11 September]. There are no scenic effects, its music is devoid of brilliance and high-flown effectiveness. But I think that a *select* few, hearing this music, will perhaps be touched by those feelings which excited me while I was writing it. By this I do not wish to say that my music is so good that it is inaccessible to the *contemptible general public*. I simply do not understand how it is possible to write deliberately for the general public or for the select few In my view you need to write

[12] *TLP*6, p. 140; *TPM*1, p. 22; *DTC*, p. 67.
[13] *TLP*6, p. 141; *TPR*, pp. 281–2; *TPB*, p. 122; *DTC*, p. 67.

in obedience to your own spontaneous inclination, in no way thinking of pleasing this or that part of humanity. Thus I wrote *Onegin* without pretending to other, outside aims. Yet *Onegin* has come out in such a way that it will not be *interesting* theatrically. Therefore those whose first requirement of an opera is *theatrical action* will be dissatisfied with it [*Onegin*]. However, those who are capable of searching within an opera for the musical reproduction of ordinary, simple, universal sensations far removed from high tragedy and theatricality can (*I hope*) find ultimate satisfaction in my opera. In a word, it is written sincerely, and I am placing all my hopes on this sincerity.

If I made a mistake in choosing this subject, i.e. if my opera does not enter the repertoire, it will distress me little.[14]

It seems that Tchaikovsky did no more work on *Onegin* until after his separation from Antonina. On 29 October, from Clarens, he wrote to Modest that he had resumed scoring the work, and within three days Act I was complete. Now that much of the opera was either done or well advanced, Tchaikovsky was impatiently looking ahead to its production, if only for the 'select few'. This time he was not in Russia to foster his work's fortunes nor, in view of all that had happened, was he wishing to return home in the foreseeable future. Through Rubinstein's persuasions the Conservatoire had just agreed to continue the payment of part of Tchaikovsky's salary for the next session, thus rendering his return unnecessary. Perhaps feeling that the new opera would not commend itself very strongly to the musical establishment of the Imperial opera houses, and being himself firmly convinced that they would be unable to perform it as he required, he now turned to Rubinstein. Upon no other man did Tchaikovsky feel he could place such reliance in the performance of his music, and if Rubinstein did not control an opera company, he did have the forces of the Conservatoire at his command.

With this in mind, Tchaikovsky now made a surprising proposal. 'Is it possible to mount a public performance of Act I and the first scene of Act 2?' he asked Rubinstein on 1 November.[15] To do this would require neither large forces nor a big stage, he added encouragingly, and the evening could be completed by some other work. It is difficult to understand how Tchaikovsky could ever have countenanced such a truncated performance, let alone have encouraged it, except that

[14] *TLP6*, pp. 170–1; *TPM1*, pp. 44–5; *TZC2*, pp. 27–8; *DTC*, p. 68.
[15] *TLP6*, p. 193; *TZC2*, p. 33; *DTC*, p. 68; *YDGC*, p. 154.

it would provide some sort of setting in which his Tatyana and the music she had so persuasively drawn from him might be swiftly brought to life.[16] A week later he was urging Rubinstein even more insistently. He had now despatched Act 1 to Moscow. 'O how glad I shall be if this music pleases you!' he exclaimed. 'Pay particular attention to the scene of *Tatyana with her nurse*, and also to Lensky's *arioso* at the end of the first scene. I think that the first number, in which two girls off-stage sing a sentimental duet and two old women on stage chatter against this music, is not without some piquancy of sound. . . . I should be happy to the bottom of my heart if you should find it possible to put on these four scenes at a performance at the Conservatoire.'[17] A fortnight later he was bombarding Rubinstein with suggestions for casting. Above all, he was desperate to know whether Rubinstein and Albrecht liked Act 1.

When at last these two colleagues replied, it was to express warm approval of the music, but also to discourage him from hoping for a performance at the Conservatoire. Tchaikovsky was not to be deterred. Never would he give *Onegin* to either of the Imperial opera houses with their routine, their convention, untalented producers, and so on. What he needed was not stars but good average singers who could act, a staging that was not elaborate but faithful to the 1820s in which *Onegin* was set, a chorus who behaved like real people and not as a flock of sheep, and the collaboration and direction of his real friends and colleagues. The Conservatoire singers would not be ideal, he conceded, but if he waited for such paragons to appear, he would wait for ever. As he also expressed it to Nadezhda von Meck:

> Where shall I find a *Tatyana* – the one whom Pushkin imagined and whom I have tried to embody in music? Where will be that artist able even to approach a little the ideal of Onegin, of that cold dandy filled to the core with worldly *bon ton*? From where shall I be able to get a Lensky, an eighteen-year-old youth with thick curls, with the impetuous and individual ways of a young poet à la Schiller? How Pushkin's delightful picture will be cheapened when it is transferred to the stage with its routine, with its muddle-headed traditions, its

---

[16] For all his passionate involvement in Tatyana's letter scene, Tchaikovsky could not tolerate it being given separately, as sometimes happens today, because it had no proper ending. When he heard that it had been twice performed in concerts ahead of the opera's première, he was very angry. It is the more strange, therefore, that he should advocate the performance of four scenes where dramatic sense is equally incomplete.

[17] *TLP*6, p. 206; *TZC*2, p. 38; *DTC*, pp. 68–9 (partial); *YDGC*, p. 155 (partial).

veterans of both sexes who, like Alexandrova, Komissarzhevsky and
tutti quanti, shamelessly take on the rôles of sixteen-year-old girls and
beardless youths![18]

If the Conservatoire could not mount these four scenes this session,
he was quite prepared to be patient until the next session. Finally
Tchaikovsky won, though he did have to wait for more than a year. In
December 1878 they were performed at a dress rehearsal at the
Moscow Conservatoire,[19] and three months later, on 29 March 1879,
Tchaikovsky's colleagues and the Conservatoire's students gave the
première of the complete opera.[20]

But this is leaping ahead. At the beginning of November 1877, when
Tchaikovsky had first proposed to Rubinstein a performance of the
opening four scenes of *Onegin*, the last of these was not even scored. How
much of the rest remained to be composed is uncertain. When he wrote
to Rubinstein with casting suggestions on 21 November, it seems that
he had not quite completed Act 3, though Gremin's aria, with which
Tchaikovsky was well satisfied, was certainly done. The scoring of the
first scene of Act 2 was finished on 28 November. Now that
Tchaikovsky had completed the first four scenes and could send them
off to Rubinstein, he rested from his work on *Onegin*. From the middle of
December until early January he was engrossed with the completion of
the Fourth Symphony; then, on 14 January 1878, he announced to
Anatoly that he had that very day passed on to scoring the third act of
the opera, for as yet the second scene of Act 2, the duel scene, had not
been fully composed. Act 3 was finally done on 25 January. Three days
later Tchaikovsky took himself off into the hills outside Sanremo, found
a secluded spot, and completed the composition of the duel scene. On
29 January, he set about writing the Introduction. A further three days
of intensive labour, and on 1 February, *Eugene Onegin* was finished.

Tchaikovsky's impatience to have *Onegin* performed was equalled by
his urgent wish to see the opera published. Two years earlier Jurgenson
had made him an advance against his next opera, but Tchaikovsky now
refused to consider that with *Onegin* he had discharged this particular
debt. Recognising that the novel intimacy of this new work was unlikely

[18] *TLP6*, p. 309; *TPM1*, p. 124; *TZC2*, p. 65; *YDGC*, p. 161 (partial).

[19] The planned performance (for Nikolay Rubinstein's name-day) had to be
cancelled because of the illness of one of the singers.

[20] The very first complete run-through of *Onegin* (a concert performance in costume,
with piano accompaniment) seems, in fact, to have taken place in St Petersburg earlier
in March at the home of Yuliya Abaza, a singer. Anatoly Tchaikovsky informed his
brother of the event, but though the composer expressed interest, he declined to hasten
his return from Western Europe to attend.

to make it a good commercial proposition, he at first declined any remuneration from his publisher friend. His one request concerned the designation of the work. He did not wish it to be described as an opera; instead, it was to be subtitled 'Lyrical scenes in three acts'.

The boundless enthusiasm which Tchaikovsky's friends developed for *Onegin* was to give him the deepest satisfaction. By the time of its first performance Tchaikovsky had resigned his professorship at the Conservatoire and had left Russia, but he determined to return specially for the première of the complete work. Arriving back in Moscow the day before the performance, he went straight to the dress rehearsal at the Maly Theatre. A chorus of forty-eight Conservatoire singers had been mustered, and all but six of the thirty-two strong orchestra were students. The scenery was partly borrowed from the Imperial theatres, but had been adapted and supplemented by Karl Waltz. Through the generosity of the RMS the costumes had been specially made. Tchaikovsky had some reservations about the soloists, but was delighted by the chorus and orchestra, and by the production. Above all, the genuine and unanimous warmth of his friends towards *Onegin* moved him profoundly. After Act 1 Taneyev, who had earlier been among those who had reproached Tchaikovsky for its dearth of theatrical effectiveness, could express his admiration only through tears.

The performance next day was far less enjoyable for the composer. Anton Rubinstein appeared in Moscow, but maintained an inexorable silence about the work; in fact, he disliked it. Nikolay Rubinstein had insisted that Tchaikovsky should acknowledge all applause, and his misery was increased by being summoned on to the stage before the performance to receive a congratulatory wreath from the members of the entire Conservatoire, to loud and unanimous applause. These ovations were repeated by the capacity audience after each scene. Yet Tchaikovsky sensed that these plaudits were more for him personally than for the work.

Modest attributed the cool reception of what was happening on the stage to several factors, including the novelty of the subject for a Russian opera, and the fact that his brother was using a much-loved classic of Russian literature, and was obviously having both to modify it drastically and to supplement Pushkin's text with alien stanzas. More than once that evening, said Modest, he heard the word 'blasphemy' muttered in the Maly Theatre. In addition all the soloists were inexperienced students, patently nervous. Only Triquet's Couplets, Gremin's aria, and the first two choruses drew really warm applause, and to set against these triumphs there were some really bad moments on stage, especially during the couples' quartet in the first scene in which the singers got hopelessly lost and then attempted to redeem the situation by re-entering in a variety of keys. It is not surprising that Nikolay Rubinstein was initially in a bad temper at the supper after the performance, though everybody's mood seems to have improved once Anton had left. There were speeches, and again Tchaikovsky had to reply. At four o'clock in the morning he returned home with a bad headache, decamping to St Petersburg by the mail train to avoid having to travel with Anton Rubinstein.

The press, however, was in general favourably inclined towards *Onegin*. Laroche was in raptures, while the critic, Osip Levenson, writing in Tchaikovsky's old journal, the *Russian Gazette*, predicted that, despite its lack of dramatic life, it would become one of the most popular operas in the Russian repertoire. The designer, Karl Waltz (quoted by Kashkin), recorded that Nikolay Rubinstein was of a similar mind to Levenson, and at the supper after the first performance brushed aside all the composer's protestations about the work's technical deficiencies, its intimacy, and so on, and insisted that it ought to be done at the Bolshoy. Waltz added that it was through Rubinstein's persistence that two years later, on 23 January 1881, *Eugene Onegin* was heard for the first time in that theatre.

Tchaikovsky had treated subjects of strong dramatic intent in both *The Voyevoda* and *The Oprichnik*, but that which he had chosen for his fourth surviving opera was different from these in one crucial respect: it was a literary masterpiece. Here was no melodrama basing its appeal upon fabricated situations of heightened drama, peopled by characters whose rôle was to be little more than the begetters of histrionic tempests. Pushkin had set about *Eugene Onegin* in 1823, intending to write a satirical work on the lines of Byron's *Don Juan*, but during the eight years it took to complete, it became a novel in verse set in contemporary Russian society, embodying much of Pushkin's own self and experience, and parading a gallery of living characters, from the engagement of whose personalities flows the events of the tale, whether these be romantic, humorous, pathos-filled, or even verging on tragedy. As satire on that Russian society which Pushkin himself knew so well, *Onegin* is merciless, but as the novel unfolds the strain of lyricism is fortified. Pushkin's cynical eye could gaze with compassion, and the pathos of Onegin's predicament can finally win some sympathy from the reader, however strongly he may censure the havoc Pushkin's hero has wreaked upon the lives he has encountered along the way. Onegin, too, is a victim of the world into which he was born.

Neither in its poetic form, nor in its abundant discursiveness did

Eugene Onegin offer easy material to the composer; it is no wonder that Tchaikovsky first thought the idea of making an opera from it wild. Reading Pushkin, one is dazzled by the sheer range and variety of the poet's vision – by its irony, its parody, its satire, sentiment, its unsentimental humanity. Yet Tchaikovsky's ultimate insistence on the description 'lyrical scenes' for his version of the story defined clearly the quality he recognised as predominant in the version he had created. He had no use for Pushkin's asides, submerging himself solely in the emotional worlds of Pushkin's characters, in some cases touching only lightly on their inner feelings, but in others identifying to a degree which drew from him some of the most expressively pointed music he ever wrote. Just how quick he was to perceive how *he* could treat *Onegin* is clear from the scenario he devised during the night following that visit to Elizaveta Lavrovskaya, when the singer had first suggested the subject to him. He outlined this scenario to Modest in a letter on 30 May:

Act 1, Scene 1.   When the curtain rises the old lady, Mrs Larina, and the nurse are making preserves and recalling old times. Duet for the old people. Singing is heard from the house. It is *Tatyana and Olga*, accompanied by a harp, singing a duet to words by Zhukovsky. Peasants appear *bringing in the last sheaf*: they sing and dance. Suddenly a boy servant announces: *Guests*! Commotion. Evgeny and Lensky enter. Ceremony of introduction and offering of refreshment (bilberry wine). Evgeny communicates his impressions to Lensky, and the women exchange theirs: quintet *à la Mozart*. The old women go off to prepare supper. The young people remain to stroll in pairs. They alternate (as in [Gounod's] *Faust*). Tatyana is shy at first, then falls in love.
Scene 2.   Scene with the nurse, and Tatyana's letter.
Scene 3.   Scene of Onegin's talk with Tatyana.
Act 2, Scene 1.   Tatyana's name-day. A ball. Scene of Lensky's jealousy. He insults Onegin and challenges him to a duel. General horror.
Scene 2.   The aria Lensky sings before his death, and the duel with pistols.
Act 3, Scene 1.   Moscow. An Assembly Ball. Tanya's meeting with a whole string of aunts and cousins. They sing as a chorus. Appearance of the general. He falls in love with Tatyana. She tells him her story, and agrees to marry him.
Scene 2.   In St Petersburg. Tatyana awaits Onegin. He appears. Big duet. After his declaration Tatyana yields to the feeling of love for

Evgeny, and wrestles with herself. Onegin implores her. Her husband appears. Duty triumphs. Onegin flees in despair.[21]

This first draft of the scenario is very close to that which Tchaikovsky eventually adopted. A few adjustments of detail were made in the first scene. The nurse left before the men entered, and Mrs Larina very soon afterwards; in consequence there was no offering of refreshment, and the quintet became a quartet solely for the young people. The one really major change, however, was reserved for the last act. Tatyana's precipitate acceptance of the general so soon after meeting him was implausible; in any case, she never fell in love at all, and Pushkin drew a veil over the progress of the general's courtship of his young and merely acquiescent bride. On the other hand, the opera's last scene was incomprehensible unless some account had already been given of the drastic effect upon Onegin of meeting Tatyana again. Thus Tchaikovsky turned Act 3, Scene 1 into a different ballroom occasion. Tatyana is already married to Prince Gremin (the name acquired in the opera by Pushkin's anonymous general), and the new ball becomes the occasion on which Onegin first sees Tatyana after his duel with Lensky, and where he falls in love with her.

When the work was first performed at the Moscow Conservatoire in March 1879 the original scenario of the final scene was still retained. In the definitive published version Tchaikovsky dispensed with the entry of the husband, and concluded with Tatyana's rejection of Onegin, who then cried out in despair, and rushed away. The music, however, remained unaltered, for no more was required than the modification of some of Tatyana's lines. In the end Tchaikovsky also altered Onegin's final words. One other change was made at a much later stage. In 1885 Vsevolozhsky, the director of the Imperial Theatres, requested Tchaikovsky to compose the écossaise which appears in the middle and again at the end of the St Petersburg ballroom scene. Its first appearance involved the shedding of some twenty-eight bars of chorus, and its second the excision of the concluding eleven orchestral bars.

For the non-Russian audience *Onegin*, like Musorgsky's *Boris Godunov*, presents something of a problem. Tchaikovsky, like Musorgsky, knew that he was dealing with one of the most famed pieces of native literature; thus his Russian audience would have no problem of plot comprehension if he abbreviated the original. Equally, if he dwelt only upon certain sides of a character, there was little risk of misconstruction by his compatriots, who would already possess a fuller, more rounded

[21] *TLP6*, p. 135; *TZC1*, pp. 533–4; *TZC2*, pp. 203–4; *TPR*, pp. 278–9; *DTC*, pp. 65–6; *TPB*, p. 120.

conception of that character from Pushkin's own text. This is something the Western listener does not normally enjoy, and so the following synopsis of the plot of Tchaikovsky's opera incorporates a very brief summary of what he excluded from his scenario both between the scenes and – still more important – before ever the curtain has risen (such matters are printed in italics).[22]

Onegin epitomises Russian society youth of the 1820s. Educated into the decadent mores of that society, his personality and gifts win him easy success in it, and he indulges in its amusements and elegant dissipations until satiety brings boredom. His father has squandered the family wealth; now only the timely death of an uncle with a rural estate restores Onegin's fortunes. He has already tried to find a new purpose in life by writing and reading, but without success. Thus he decides to try the country way of life as an avenue to personal fulfilment. But boredom instantly returns, and only in the company of his young neighbour, Vladimir Lensky, does he find any kind of satisfaction. Lensky is an eighteen-year-old just returned from the University of Göttingen. He is something of a poet and idealist, untarnished by the tawdry, corrupt ways of that high society which has already soiled and bored Onegin. He has long been betrothed to Olga Larina, younger daughter of a family in the neighbourhood. Olga is a simple extrovert; by contrast her elder sister, Tatyana, is a more private individual, a solitary with a passion for novels. One evening Lensky introduces Onegin to the Larins.

ACT 1, SCENE 1. *The garden of the Larins' country house.*
Mrs Larina sits listening to the singing of her daughters, Tatyana and Olga, from within the house. The nurse, Filipevna, is helping her to make preserves. The two women gossip, recalling Mrs Larina's unwilling betrothal to her husband, now dead. A group of peasants is heard singing offstage. The peasants enter carrying a ceremonial sheaf, and greet Mrs Larina. She asks them to sing a merry song, and they perform a choral dance for her. While the peasants are dancing, Olga and Tatyana come out of the house. Olga comments upon Tatyana's constant propensity to dream. She herself is the very opposite: 'I'm carefree and playful. Everyone calls me a child!' she observes cheerfully. Mrs Larina orders the peasants to be given wine, and they and the nurse leave the stage. Before this the nurse had asked Tatyana whether she is ill, and Olga now draws their mother's attention to her sister's pallor. Tatyana herself attributes this to the agitating effect of the romantic novel she is reading. Suddenly the nurse rushes in to announce that Lensky is coming and that Onegin is with him. Tatyana would rush away, but her mother detains her.

The two men enter, and Lensky introduces Onegin. Mrs Larina receives them, and then leaves to see to domestic matters. The young people sing a brief quartet in which Onegin compares Olga unfavourably with Tatyana, while the latter declares that she sees in Onegin the one who is predestined for her.

[22] Since the libretto of the opera is readily available in translation, it seems unnecessary to identify the precise location of each portion of the action as in the case of libretti for the earlier Tchaikovsky operas.

The four young people pair off. Olga and Lensky chatter happily while Onegin engages Tatyana in conversation, commenting upon the limitations of the world within which she lives. Tatyana admits that she reads and dreams much, and Onegin recalls that he, too, was once like that. They retire, leaving Lensky to continue pouring out his delight and happiness in Olga. Mrs Larina and the nurse re-enter to invite the guests into the house. They notice that Tatyana and Onegin are missing. The nurse is sent to find them, but the couple promptly emerge, Onegin still talking, and Tatyana now clearly besotted with him. The nurse perceives her condition, and goes off, shaking her head thoughtfully.

ACT I, SCENE 2. *Tatyana's room.*
Tatyana, in a white nightdress, is sitting pensively before her mirror. The nurse is with her. Tatyana cannot sleep, and she asks Filipevna to tell her about her past. 'Were you ever in love then?' she asks. 'In our time we never heard of love,' replies the nurse and, in response to Tatyana's request, she tells of her own arranged marriage. Suddenly she notices that Tatyana is not listening. 'Ah Nanny, I'm suffering, I'm miserable!' blurts out Tatyana. The nurse thinks she must be ill, but Tatyana confides that she is in love. As she dismisses the nurse, she asks for pen and paper. Left alone, Tatyana gives vent to her feelings of excitement, and then sits down to write her confession of love to Onegin. She tears up her first attempt, but then settles down assiduously, pausing from time to time to read over what she has written, or to reflect. As she finishes dawn is breaking. She draws back the curtains, and a shepherd's pipe is heard. The nurse enters to rouse her. Tatyana has thoughts only for the letter, however, and she begs the nurse to send her grandson with it. At first she cannot bring herself to name the person to whom it is to be directed. 'Can't you guess, Nanny?' she exclaims, but the nurse remains uncomprehending. 'To Onegin!' finally cries Tatyana. The nurse, with some hesitation, at length leaves with the letter, and Tatyana once more sinks into thought.

ACT I, SCENE 3. *Another part of the garden of the Larins' country house.*
A women's chorus is heard singing offstage. Tatyana enters precipitately; Onegin is coming, and she is in a state of miserable agitation. When he arrives he straightway addresses her 'quietly and with a certain coldness'. His matter-of-fact response appals Tatyana. Having detailed the various reasons why he would not marry her, he ends by enjoining her to learn self-control. Tatyana experiences the deepest sense of humiliation. As the offstage women's chorus is heard again, Onegin offers her his arm, and mechanically she takes it. They go out.

Onegin pays no further visits to the Larins until Lensky persuades him to attend the celebration of Tatyana's name-day. Meanwhile Tatyana in a nightmare has a premonition of trouble between Lensky and Onegin.

ACT 2, SCENE 1. *A well-lit room in the Larins' house.*
A dance for Tatyana's name-day is in progress. Among the guests are a number of military men. Onegin is dancing with Tatyana, and Lensky with

Olga. The other guests pay particular attention to the former pair, and sour comments are made about Onegin by some of the mammas. Onegin, bored by the whole occasion and annoyed with Lensky for bringing him, decides to have his revenge on his friend by flirting with Olga. He asks her to dance the waltz with him, to Lensky's distress. When the waltz is over Lensky reproaches Olga bitterly, but she pretends to shrug it off as a trifling matter, and deliberately tries to make him jealous. Seeing Monsieur Triquet preparing to sing his couplets, she cuts short Lensky's complaints. Triquet performs his offering in praise of Tatyana, who is thoroughly embarrassed at this public tribute, especially when, at the conclusion, Triquet kneels and presents the copy to her. The dancing resumes with a mazurka. At first the company commander dances with Tatyana while Onegin sits with Olga, Lensky standing behind them. Onegin dances briefly with Olga, leads her back to her seat, then pretends he has only just noticed Lensky, and asks him why he is not dancing. An exchange of words ensues, Lensky becoming more heated until the other guests begin to notice. 'Onegin, you are no longer my friend! . . . I despise you!' he finally cries. By this time the two men are the centre of attention, and Onegin attempts to calm Lensky, but to no avail; the latter 'demands satisfaction'. Mrs Larina is appalled that such an incident should have happened 'in our house', and Lensky leads off a huge ensemble by reflecting on the past happiness he has enjoyed at the Larins'. At the end of this the two men confront each other yet again, and Lensky hurls the ultimate insult. 'You are a dishonourable seducer!' he shouts. 'Be silent – or I'll kill you!' rejoins Onegin. Mrs Larina, Olga and some of the guests restrain Lensky, but Onegin hurls himself at his opponent. The guests separate them, and Tatyana bursts into tears. Finally Lensky turns to Olga: 'Farewell for ever!' he shouts, and rushes out. Olga falls in a faint.

The next morning Lensky confirms his challenge to Onegin through his second, Zaretsky. Onegin, now regretful of his behaviour at the party, nevertheless accepts.

Visiting Olga that same day, Lensky finds her again affectionate as though the previous night's events had never transpired. He tells her nothing of the duel and, returning home, sits down to write his last verses.

ACT 2, SCENE 2. *Early morning on a river bank with a watermill.*
Lensky and Zaretsky are awaiting the arrival of Onegin, who is already late. While Zaretsky talks to the miller, Lensky sings of his lost happiness, muses upon the fate that hangs over him, and reaffirms his love and longing for Olga. Finally Onegin arrives, bringing his valet, Guillot, as his second. Zaretsky, who is a stickler for observing the proper formalities in a duel, is affronted at this impropriety. While Zaretsky and Guillot discuss the arrangements, Lensky and Onegin each ponder the fateful situation in which they are now both imprisoned. The seconds load the pistols and pace out the proper distance. Zaretsky claps three times, and the opponents take four paces towards each other. Onegin raises his pistol and fires. Lensky falls. Zaretsky and Onegin rush to him, and Lensky is pronounced dead. Onegin, horrified, buries his face in his hands.

Onegin leaves the area. Olga's grief is short-lived; she marries a lancer and also departs,

188 TCHAIKOVSKY

leaving Tatyana alone. On a long walk one evening the latter comes upon Onegin's house. She visits it, and asks the housekeeper's permission to return and read in Onegin's library. Through his choice of books and his annotations in them, she begins to understand something of the sort of man Onegin is. Disenchantment ensues: 'Is he no more than a parody?' she asks herself.

Mrs Larina decides to take a reluctant Tatyana to Moscow for the winter in the hope of finding a husband for her. Paraded in the social marriage market, she is paired off with a stout general. Meanwhile Onegin, tormented by his rôle in the Lensky affair, has been travelling. Finally he arrives in St Petersburg where Tatyana, now some two years married, is already a noted and respected beauty, and sees her at a ball.

ACT 3, SCENE 1. *A side-hall in a sumptuous mansion in St Petersburg.*
A grand polonaise is in progress. Onegin is standing watching. He is bored by the occasion, and is still tormented by the affair of the duel. An écossaise follows, and the choir announces that Princess Gremina is coming. Tatyana enters with her husband. Onegin recognises her with amazement, and as her husband leaves her side to speak with Onegin, Tatyana enquires who the stranger is. On being told, she endeavours to hide her agitation. The Prince discloses to Onegin that Tatyana has been his wife for some two years, and Onegin reveals that he already knows Tatyana. The Prince sings of his love for Tatyana. He then introduces Onegin to his wife. Tatyana cuts short the interview by pleading fatigue, and she and her husband depart. Left alone, Onegin confesses aloud his love for her, and goes out hurriedly as the écossaise is resumed.

It is now Onegin's turn to write confessing his love. He receives no answer and writes twice more. Finally he bursts in on Tatyana at her home.

ACT 3, SCENE 2. *The drawing room in Prince Gremin's house.*
Tatyana enters holding a letter. She is terribly agitated by Onegin's return, and weeps. Onegin appears at the door, looks at her for a while, and then rushes forward and falls on his knees before her. She gazes at him and signals him to rise. She recalls the time when he had come to reject her. Onegin confesses how mistaken he had been, but she continues to dwell on it. Is he now pursuing her because of her new social rank and wealth, she asks bitterly? Onegin makes more protestations of his love, and Tatyana tearfully reflects upon how close happiness had once been; now, however, her fate is decided, for she is married, and will remain faithful. She orders him to leave, but then confesses she still loves him. He embraces her, but she quickly tears herself from his arms, declaring again that she will remain faithful to her husband. Finally, in great distress when he embraces her again, she bids him farewell for ever. With a cry of despair, Onegin flees.

It was clearly Tchaikovsky's precise perception of the kind of opera he wished to write that made him dispense early with the services of Konstantin Shilovsky, whom he had originally intended to use as his librettist. Instead he did most of the job himself, Shilovsky merely providing the verses (in both Russian and French) for Triquet's couplets, and perhaps contributing something to the definitive form of the scenario. As far as possible Tchaikovsky used Pushkin's own stanzas, carving and trimming them, even altering words where he deemed this necessary, and converting reported into direct speech. There is hardly anything in the whole letter scene that is not taken intact from Pushkin, and Tchaikovsky had to invent only five brief passages – the nurse's opening words and her goodnight, Tatyana's exclamations as she tears up her first attempt to write, the brief reflective recitative that follows upon her first successful burst of writing, and her words after she draws back the curtains before the nurse returns. Nearly as large a proportion of the ensuing scene, where Onegin rejects Tatyana's avowal, was transferred from the original. True, a good deal of Tatyana's outburst came from Tchaikovsky's pen, but Onegin's words are entirely from Pushkin, as is the text of the women's chorus which, with such irony, opens and closes the scene (the composer himself took special pride in this chorus). So, too, Tchaikovsky compounded the final scene of the opera very largely by interleaving Tatyana's bitterly reproachful farewell to Onegin with portions of the first letter he had written to her, though Tatyana's brief opening soliloquy and the last stretch (from the allegro moderato) are entirely Tchaikovsky's own. Most of the duel scene is out of Pushkin, the verses Lensky wrote during the previous night affording nearly all his aria of farewell. But in the remaining three scenes Tchaikovsky was compelled to be much more his own librettist. Admittedly in the St Petersburg ballroom scene a good deal of Onegin's part, both at the beginning and the end, is from the original, as is his brief exchange with Gremin. But Gremin's aria is not, nor is any of what follows until Onegin is left alone. In the first scene the only sizeable borrowings are in Lensky's arioso, the quartet for the couples, and the opening movement in which the girls do not sing a lyric by Zhukovsky, as had been Tchaikovsky's first intention, but two stanzas from an early poem by Pushkin himself, while the old women's gossipings are mostly derived from four of Pushkin's stanzas which Tchaikovsky shuffled between the two of them. For the rest, only a couple of lines in Tatyana's first conversation with Onegin, and the latter's words in the last section of the scene are from Pushkin. And Tchaikovsky wrote the entire big dance scene at the Larins', except for Onegin's words in the first part of the finale, and the text Shilovsky provided for Triquet.

Onegin bears constant witness to Tchaikovsky's acute perception of how the problems of dramatic organisation might best be solved. The continuity of plot that is possible with the written word could not be preserved if that plot were reduced to a few stage scenes. What

Tchaikovsky had to do was, as it were, to part the curtains on the continuum of time to permit us to see certain crucial stages in Pushkin's narrative. Put another way, his scenario is like a strip cartoon in seven pictures, demanding of the spectator some ability to leap comprehendingly across considerable stretches of intervening, unrecorded action. And Tchaikovsky recognised that, even before the plot of *Onegin* began to bound from incident to incident, there were certain bases that had to be established. For instance, at the root of *Onegin* is not simply an encounter between two people, but the collision of two worlds as represented by those people – on the one hand by Onegin himself, bred in the elegant, decadent society of the Russian metropolis, on the other by Tatyana, a child of a rural community with its simple, provincial tastes, its naturalness and innocence. Thus there is no question that the opening numbers of the first scene (the sentimental duet against which the old women chat, and the two folk-choruses that follow) are merely decorative. The former makes a memorably novel beginning, its relaxed informality, even more than the colour and life of the splendid but stiffer folk-choruses which follow, catching the leisureliness of the Larins' unsophisticated lives into which Onegin is to bring such devastation.

The latter makes his entrance, but not before we have had a chance to divine something of the personalities of the two girls who are to be the main representatives of this world. And here Tchaikovsky again showed perception in his choice of dramatic priorities, for it was not Tatyana but Olga whom he placed first at the centre of the stage. After all, we are bound to learn much about Tatyana – she cannot but reveal her heart to us in the next scene – but future events are to provide few natural opportunities for Olga to define herself, and the aria Tchaikovsky now affords her is patent self-declaration. Olga is a straightforward, cheerful being ('in essence very insipid' was Tchaikovsky's own description[23]) for whom day-dreaming and nocturnal musings have no attraction, and who lightly mocks, with a twist to the minor and a touch of exaggerated harmony, the propensity of such as her sister to sigh their souls out on twilit balconies (Ex. 133). Her melodic world is that of her betrothed, Lensky, but without his passion or commitment. It is significant that her aria makes prominent use of a phrase which descends through four adjacent notes (the first bar of Ex. 134 is only the culmination of a whole trail of such phrases) – a move towards, yet no more than a partial exposition of the 'fate embraced' motif which is to play so prominent a rôle in the music of Lensky and Tatyana. Olga is as gregarious as Tatyana is recluse, easily estab-

[23] *TLP*7, p. 69; *TTP*, p. 28; *DTC*, p. 74.

Ex. 133

[I am not capable of languid melancholy; I don't like dreaming in silence, or sighing, sighing, sighing my heart out on a balcony in the dark night]

lishing superficial social relationships of the kind Tatyana shuns, yet quite incapable of the sort of deep and abiding love such as her sister conceives for Onegin. Take the climactic phrase of Tatyana's letter monologue (see Ex. 139a), in which the love-sick girl agonises over Onegin's future rôle in her life, and place beside it the four bars (**Ex. 134**) where Olga joyfully sings of her certainty of good fortune and stability ahead, and the gulf between the two sisters is apparent, for

Ex. 134

[Life will always, always be kind to me, and I shall always remain the same]

Olga's phrase, while being in fact an embryo of Tatyana's, is yet as carefree and slight as Tatyana's is momentous and steeped in intense feeling.

Of the remaining two tableaux scenes the country dance at the Larins' shows a particularly careful dramatic planning. Again there is no question here, any more than there had been with the opening quartet and folk-choruses of the opera's first scene, that the generous slabs of dance music which occupy much of the scene are there simply to pad out substantial tracts of musical space with pleasant substance until a point of significant drama is reached; nor are they there merely to satisfy the expectations of a Russian audience for a substantial ballet element. These dances have the profoundly dramatic rôle of affording ironic contrast with the early stages of the growing Lensky/Onegin quarrel until that quarrel explodes in a way which transforms the chorus/dancers into horrified spectators of what has developed. The whole scene is symmetrically organised with the passage of maximum relaxation (Triquet's rococo-styled couplets) in the centre, and not preceding the dances, as in Pushkin. These couplets are then flanked by two large dance movements which incorporate foreground engagements between Lensky and Onegin. Between the initial waltz and the couplets there is more dialogue for Lensky and Olga, while the lengthy

Modest Tchaikovsky, Nikolay Kondratyev, Anatoly
Tchaikovsky, the composer (1875)

A holiday group (1876): the composer, Kolya Konradi, Sofya
Ershova, Modest Tchaikovsky (standing)

Nadezhda von
Meck

Vittorio,
a Florentine
street singer

Tchaikovsky (1875): 'To Nikolay Andreyevich
Rimsky-Korsakov in sincere affection: P. Tchaikovsky.
Moscow, 18 May 1875.'

Tchaikovsky in 1877

Tchaikovsky and his wife (1877)

Iosif Kotek and Tchaikovsky (1877)

Sergey Taneyev

In Sanremo (1878): Kolya Konradi, Modest Tchaikovsky,
Alexey Sofronov, the composer

instrumental opening of the following mazurka offers an opportunity for a further pantomimic elaboration of the Olga/Lensky/Onegin situation. As the finale is approached, background and foreground merge for a corporate amplification of the passions and emotions which have grown during the preceding portion of the scene. Finally the last two twists in the main action (Lensky's ultimate abuse of Onegin, and his distraught farewell to Olga) bring down the curtain at a point of maximum tension.

In the more intimate scenes for which Pushkin's own text provided much ready-made verbal substance, the greatest single problem of musical organisation was posed by Tatyana's letter monologue. For Tchaikovsky there could be no question of through-composing this extensive soliloquy as Musorgsky might have done, had he ever attempted it. Instead he divided the setting of the letter itself into three distinct sections, the first two ternary in design, seated in D minor and C major respectively, while the third grounds itself upon D flat, thus returning to the key in which Tatyana had given rein to her excitement before sitting down to write. But if the clear periodic structure and the internal thematic organisation of the constituent parts disclose explicitly Western structural attitudes, the broad tonal design does not, for it has nothing whatever to do with the hierarchy of relationships that was the foundation of normal Western tonal practice, employing instead semitonal shifts (either side of D flat) of a sort to which Russian composers sometimes showed especial favour. This is quite certainly the finest scene in all Tchaikovsky's operas. The melodic world is never far from that of the sentimental romance, but this is perfectly appropriate for this young, naïve girl whose feelings, though intense, have not been tempered by experience. Yet music that springs from such ingenuousness and innocence can have a peculiar power to awaken, if not our deepest, then some of our most tenderly sensitive responses, and the first two pages of the final D flat section are among the most affecting in all Tchaikovsky's music. Gerald Abraham commented upon the remarkable way in which Tchaikovsky contrived to fuse emotional expression with a sense of the physical activity in which Tatyana has been engaging in the preceding portion of the scene; he went on to observe how 'the dual quality of the music also touches a new level in a horn phrase of melting warmth [see Ex. 139a] which contains the purest essence of Tchaikovskyan melody, while the harmony of the second bar touches the very nerve centre of Russian romantic harmony (the flattened sixth)'.[24] The contour of this same horn phrase generates the opening notes of the next section (see

[24] G. Abraham: *Slavonic and romantic music* (London, 1968), p. 146.

Ex. 138a), while bars two to four of this same example yield the motif which dominates so much of the earlier part of the opera. Here, within these two examples, we have the three primary thematic germs of the whole opera, as we shall see.

The association in *Onegin* between key and the personalities or dramatic forces of the tale is a direct bequest from Tchaikovsky's most recent stage work, the ballet *Swan Lake*. In the opera there could be nothing like the systematic opposing of sharp and flat keys such as Tchaikovsky had employed in *Swan Lake*, for there was no such neat polarity of good and evil. In *Onegin* more significance is attached to the particular flavour of certain keys than to relationships between them, though Tchaikovsky did use tonal juxtapositions to underline emotional disharmony between characters (as in the altercation between Olga and Lensky after the waltz in Act 2, Scene 1).

Most explicit of all his tonal associations is that between E minor and painful, even doomed love. The key first occurs when Tatyana speaks of the unhappy lovers in the novel she has been reading, and it is E minor that announces the entry into her life of the being who is to bring her so much grief of heart (though the instant Onegin enters, the key switches to G major, for the unhappiness he bears with him still lies in the future). When Lensky quarrels with Onegin at Tatyana's name-day party, the dispute develops against a background of E minor. It is the key of Lensky's farewell aria in the duel scene and of Tatyana's first heartbroken words in the last scene – and it is in E minor that the opera ends. By contrast E major may reveal happiness in love, as in Lensky's amorous chatter with Olga and his ecstatically happy arioso in the first scene, or when the love theme rises in the orchestra after Tatyana is first left alone in the second scene before her letter monologue. E major emerges quite suddenly towards the end of the St Petersburg ballroom scene when Onegin, watching Tatyana leave, gazes with swelling and joyful emotion after the woman he had once rejected. And it was with brutal irony that Tchaikovsky set the disastrous end of Tatyana's name-day party in E major.

Of other keys, D minor seems to be particularly associated with agitation or disaster in love (the opening of the letter monologue itself, Tatyana's distracted utterances before Onegin's entry in the third scene, the end of the duel scene), while B flat seems to be the special key of the Larins' world – though Tatyana favours G minor. The whole of the opening stretch of the opera centres on two flats, and B flat returns when Mrs Larina and the nurse re-enter. When Onegin addresses Tatyana in the third scene, he chooses B flat as though he were ostentatiously trying to talk in the tone of her world. It is worth noting, too, that at the end of the St Petersburg ballroom scene, when Onegin with unwitting irony declares his love for Tatyana through exactly the same music as she had once confessed her passion for him, B flat again resurges as he is willy-nilly drawn into emotional subjugation to a member of that Larins' world he had once so deeply despised.

Yet Tatyana herself has a very special realm – D flat. The key occurs on only five occasions in the whole opera, and it provides the tonal centre of Tatyana's love for Onegin, first appearing as she deliriously declares her resolve to join her destiny, come what may, with her 'fateful tempter', then returning when, more calmly yet with an almost unbearable emotional intensity, she reflects upon the rôle which he may play in her life. This second moment (see Ex. 139a) provides one of the most crucial thematic inventions of the whole opera, and this melodic outline is to be a subtle ally to D flat on that key's two remaining occurrences, first in the quiet waltz (see Ex. 139l) which begins as Tatyana enters (and later leaves) the St Petersburg ballroom with her husband, here gently embodying the slumbering yet persisting love which Onegin is about to reawaken, and then in the last scene where it uncovers something of the agony which lies beneath Tatyana's firm and final banishment of her beloved (see Ex. 142). The rich thematic significances of *Onegin* are a matter to which we shall give close attention later.

After Tchaikovsky's most recent opera, *Vakula the Smith*, of three years earlier, *Onegin* represents a radical shift, not in the nature of the musical apparatus, but in the actual style of the music which fills the arias, recitatives, and choruses. There is some legacy from the national idiom that had dominated in *Vakula* (most explicitly heard in the two folk-choruses of the first scene and in the women's offstage chorus of Scene 3, less forcefully in the music of the old peasant nurse), but the more elevated social regions inhabited by the characters of the new opera drew Tchaikovsky naturally towards the cultural world of the drawing room and salon. As in *Vakula*, the explicit reminiscence theme is not of great importance, though Tchaikovsky showed himself a master, even more than in the earlier opera, of the technique of long-range recall for emotional and dramatic ends. The only theme in *Onegin* to be associated explicitly with a particular character (as distinct from a character's emotions) is the five-bar phrase which accompanies the nurse, an ingenuous thematic label with a slightly folky cachet upon it which sets this old peasant woman clearly apart from the other personalities of the opera (Ex. 135a, concluding five bars of the orchestral part). Likewise there is only one substantial theme which explicitly represents one of the main factors within the human drama.

Ex. 135

[I'm bored; let's talk about the past.

About what, Tanya? . . .]

[Another!   No, ...]

Admittedly Mrs Larina possesses a little phrase of resignation, first heard at the beginning of the opera (Ex. 136a) as she reflects upon how life has shown her that God-given habit becomes the substitute for happiness, and recurring as she observes to Tatyana how she discovered that the romantic heroes who had once so excited her in novels were nothing but fanciful inventions (Ex. 136b). But this phrase possesses none of the significance that attaches itself to the theme of her elder daughter's love. This is heard five times during the second scene, intruding suddenly as Tatyana blurts out to her nurse that she is racked

Ex. 136

a. Larina

Pri - vïch - ka svï - she nam da - na

[Habit is given to us from above]

b. Larina

Vsyo e - to vï - mï-sel. Proshli go-da,

[All this is fantasy. The years pass,]

by inner torment (Ex. 137), returning a page later more calmly as she confesses that love is the cause of her distress, unfolding itself for a third time when, left alone by her nurse, she can for a moment indulge in the emotion which engulfs her before she sits down to write the letter. It

Ex. 137

Tatyana

Akh, nya nya, nya-nya, ya stra-da-yu, ya to-sku-yu, mne toshno,

[Ah, nanny, nanny, I'm suffering, I'm miserable, I'm wretched, my dear; I'm ready to cry, to sob!]

mi - la - ya mo - ya; ya pla - - - - - kat, ya rï - dat go-to-va!

enters yet again when, the letter done, she draws back the curtains and reflects upon the calm of the world outside, so different from her own inner turmoil, and finally swells up in greatly extended form to provide a coda to the whole scene as she ponders that overpowering feeling which has driven her to make her precipitate confession to Onegin. Crushed by Onegin's rejection, the theme is banished until, in the glittering ballroom of St Petersburg, Tatyana again comes face to face with Onegin; the gentle but firm resurgence of this love theme on a solo clarinet as Gremin reintroduces his wife to her old tormentor, thus awakening old emotions, is one of the most haunting moments of the whole opera.[25]

Yet, of the recurrent thematic elements in *Onegin*, this love theme is not the most important, even if it is the most obvious. Throughout *Onegin* Tchaikovsky scattered smaller thematic particles as agents of musical and stylistic integration, just as he had done in *Vakula* (see Vol. I, Ex. 89). One is the four-note motif *c* in bars three and four of Ex. 139a, a cell already nascent in the opening duet (see Ex. 138c). With its accent shifted it provides the opening contour for Olga's aria (see Ex. 133), thus affording an audible bond between the two sisters. Later in the first scene it infiltrates the end of the young couples' quartet, similarly entering the coda of Lensky's arioso. In the next scene Tatyana turns to it as she asks her nurse to recount her past (see Ex. 135a), and it persists in the little orchestral link to the beginning of the nurse's narration, also impressing itself upon the end of the oboe theme which introduces the letter monologue itself; this is only the first of a whole succession of quiet allusions to the motif before it reaches its most memorable manifestation in Ex. 139a (before the C major section it even inverts itself (see Ex. 135b)). It nudges itself into the introduction to the duel scene, and into Lensky's farewell aria which this introduction foretells (especially into the coda). Gremin's aria twice exhibits it (in the codetta to the first section, and at the very heart of the central one), and it progressively infects the final scene, emerging fully in Tatyana's broad phrase of dismissal (see Ex. 142) which distantly echoes the climactic phrase of the letter monologue, also in D flat (Ex. 139a).

Far more portentous dramatically, however, are the two other motifs we have already observed in Exx. 138a and 139a. Yarustovsky made a very pertinent point when he observed that, whereas Musorgsky tended to link particular themes with personalities or groups of people in his operas, Tchaikovsky's main thematic material in his mature

[25] It seems possible that Tchaikovsky intended us to hear an echo of the orchestral melody accompanying the first words ('How happy I am!') of Lensky's Act 1 arioso when the same, now heartbroken Lensky leads off the finale to Act 2, Scene 1 ('In your house!').

operas is always associated with emotions. Tatyana's love theme is a patent instance of this; equally so, if less explicitly, are these two other motifs, though they are connected more with the force that produces much of the emotional swell of the opera than with the emotions themselves. One of these thematic particles is associated solely with Tatyana, the other with her male counterpart also, the equally unfortunate Lensky. Patently for Tchaikovsky these motifs (and here we come to the dramatic heart of the opera) represented fate just as surely as had the opening theme of the Fourth Symphony.[26] Now, however, fate operates more insidiously, for it lurks within the very being of his characters, and functions as an integral part of their inner lives. Thus there could be no question of Tchaikovsky treating it as he had the supernatural in *Vakula* which, being an external power, might be represented through separate materials and procedures which could engage with the musical world of the ordinary mortals. Nor could he represent it, as in the Fourth Symphony, by a remorseless theme set apart from the other thematic materials except for moments of implacable conflict with them. Instead he embodied it in smaller, more malleable units that might be absorbed into the characters' own musical worlds.

A number of commentators have observed the similarity of the first of these units to the 'fate motif' in that opera which had recently so impressed Tchaikovsky: Bizet's *Carmen*, and the text to which it occurs in Tatyana's letter monologue (for this, being the first part of the opera to be composed, was the context in which this motif was born) is some confirmation that this resemblance was not fortuitous (see Ex. 138a). As a nucleus for thematic generation it proved admirable, for its constituent intervals might readily be modified without destroying its identity. Likewise the fundamental chromaticism of its original form not only permitted, but was a positive incitement to the use of a richly varied harmonic support. The distribution of the motif in the opera suggests that it represents 'fate in prospect'. More specifically, it is Tatyana's destiny as she envisaged it in her imagination – a destiny that Onegin is to fulfil. This is her inner obsession and, as such, the motif monopolises the exquisite short orchestral prelude, generating on the first page (Ex. 138b) a succession of sighing phrases which, successively striving to be born in an ever higher world of freedom and light, are always fated to be drawn down and firmly pinioned in an

[26] Yarustovsky, in comparing Tchaikovsky's libretto for *Onegin* with Pushkin's original, observed cogently how Tchaikovsky had brought a deliberate element of fate into the opera through his supplementations, the words he gave Tatyana while writing the letter: 'Alas, I have no power to control my spirit. Let what must happen to me happen!' for example.

Ex. 138

a.

No tak i bït! Sud - bu mo - yu ot -

[But, so be it! Henceforth I entrust my fate to you!]

- nï - ne ya te - be vru - cha - - - yu!

b. **Andante con moto**

c.

Andante con moto

Tatyana

Slï - kha - li   vï?   slï - kha - li   vï?_____   tog - da svi -

[Have you heard the simple, melancholy sound of the reed pipe?]

- re - li zvuk u - nï - ly i pros - toy

d. **Andante**

immutable cadence on D. In the first scene it haunts Tatyana's melodic
world. Singing a sentimental duet with her sister, she is unable to
suppress it, and it infiltrates her vocal part at the duet's climax (Ex.
138c). After the harvesters have left it accompanies the first words she
sings (Ex. 138d – orchestral part only given), and it resurges in the same
form a little later as her thoughts turn to the plight of the lovers in the
novel she is so voraciously reading. Agitatedly in semiquavers, the
motif flutters in the orchestral passage that announces the entry of
Onegin into her life, and it companions her brief rejoinders in the
ensuing conversation with him. And, in the form in which it had
occurred in the centre of the prelude, it rounds off the scene as the nurse
perceives what we all by now know – that Tatyana's fate is to be
identified with Onegin. Throughout the whole opening section of the
next scene, the very touching and intimate exchange between Tatyana
and her nurse, it stalks through the orchestral part, on two occasions
appearing within the extended context of Ex. 138d, and yet again in the
same form as Tatyana makes her first abortive attempt to write. Yet
once Tatyana prepares to commit herself, the motif recedes, only twice
occurring briefly in the letter monologue (Ex. 138a sets out the second
and more crucial of these),[27] and once in the very last scene of the opera,
when the married woman's thoughts fly back to her childhood, for it is
now superseded not only by the love theme, but by the six-note motif in
the first three bars of Ex. 139a.

The characteristic of the second motif is a step-wise descent from the
mediant to the dominant. If the first motif had functioned as a nucleus
for the generation of larger thematic organisms, this second six-note
motif acts as a contour upon which wide variations may be made,
sometimes spreading itself over several bars, and even insinuating its
shape into dance tunes that are the accompaniment to critical incidents
in Tatyana's or Lensky's lives. Lensky shared Tatyana's fresh,
innocent view of love, and for both this second motif served to
symbolize 'fate embraced'. Lensky's destiny with Olga is already

[27] The recurrence of this motif's contour during Gremin's aria in the first scene of
Act 3 is probably coincidental.

Ex. 139

a.

[Who are you: my angel and my keeper, or are you an insidious tempter?]

b.

[As a boy I was captivated by you, not yet knowing the torments of the heart,]

c.

d.

Moderato assai, quasi Andante

Zachem, za - chem___ vï po-se - ti - li nas?

[Why, why have you visited us?]

e.

[Moderato] Meno mosso

Tï v sno - vi - den - yakh mne yav - lyal - sya;
Tvoy chud - ny vzglyad men - ya to - mil;___

[You appeared to me in a dream; unseen, you were already dear to me. Your wonderful glance tormented me; your voice resounded within my spirit!]

ne - zri - my,   tï uzh bïl mne   mil.
v du - she tvoy   go - los raz - da - val - sya!

Tatyana

Akh! Dlya che -vo   ste -

[Ah, why, heeding my soul with groaning, not controlling myself, [did I write my letter to him!]]

-na-nyu vnyavdu - shi   bol-noy,   ne sovla-dav sa-ma   so-boy,   ye-

Onegin

Kogda bï zhizn domashnïm kru- gom   ya   o-granichit za-kho- tel,

[Sometime when I want to confine myself to a domestic circle,]

[Tempo di mazurka] Molto meno mosso

i.

j.   Allegro vivo   [soprano part only]

Andante, quasi Adagio

k.

a piena voce

Lensky

Shto   den grya-dush-chy mne go - to - vit?   Ye -

[What has the coming day in store for me?]

[Allegro moderato] L'istesso tempo   [melody only]

l.

m.   Andante

Tatyana

On strast za - glob-shuyu tak   zhivo voskresil!

[So strongly he has reawakened my dormant passion!]

Allegro non tanto

n.

[etc.]

o.

Andantino

Tatyana

shto   ya   bo - ga - ta   i   znat - na,___   shto

[that I am rich and exalted,]

p.

Andante

Tatyana

Ya   pla - chu!

[I weep!]

Vivace

q.

decided before ever the opera begins, and it is in his part that the motif
first appears when, in his arioso in the first scene, he recalls the time
which had decided his future (Ex. 139b). Its contour is already clearly
present in the latter half of Tatyana's love theme (see *b* in Ex. 137), but
it begins to form itself in its own right early in her letter monologue (Ex.
139d), and its outline recurs in one of the most ravishing moments later
in this soliloquy (Ex. 139e) before reaching its most nakedly expressive
form in Ex. 139a. As, in great confusion, Tatyana waits in the garden
for Onegin's arrival, it creeps into both her line and the orchestral part
as she asks herself what had driven her to write the letter (Ex. 139f),
and Onegin lightly paraphrases it, even adding the little horn
continuation of Ex. 139a, as he launches into his lecture to the poor girl
(Ex. 139g). The lingering effect of Onegin's rejection is subtly
suggested in the introduction to her name-day ball, for while this recalls
the climactic stretch of her letter monologue, the harmonic support is
now that which Onegin had used for his own thoughtless parody of that
same phrase (Ex. 139h). Later the motif's outline is present in the
dance tune (Ex. 139i) that accompanies the Lensky/Onegin quarrel
over Olga during the mazurka (by the end it has taken a form much
closer to the original), hovers behind Onegin's vain attempt to calm
Lensky, and then provides the outline for the final horrified chorus (Ex.
139j). Scarcely adorned, it furnishes the first phrase of Lensky's
farewell aria (Ex. 139k). Again, as the outline upon which a dance tune
is constructed, it underlies the waltz that supports the meeting of
Onegin and Tatyana in the St Petersburg ballroom (Ex. 139l); here the
angular contours of the balancing four-bar phrase also seem distantly
to echo the horn rejoinder to the 'fate embraced' motif in Ex. 139a,
which was also set in D flat.

In the last scene of the opera it shapes the musical phrase when
Tatyana cries out at the pain she feels at Onegin's return into her life
(Ex. 139m). Here it is only part of a whole stretch of music that draws
together earlier threads. The opening music of the scene, which is also
to become Tatyana's tirade of reproach to Onegin, stems from the first
phrase of her husband's love aria. This is in turn partnered by that tiny
three-semiquaver motif of disquiet that has erupted throughout the
opera in moments when inner stress has briefly manifested itself in
outward agitation (notably as Tatyana had stirred herself to begin her
letter to Onegin, later when she gave instructions to her nurse on the
delivery of the letter, in the next scene in the garden as she had entered
in dreadful ferment at Onegin's approach, and (augmented into allegro
vivo quavers) as the chorus in the first scene of Act 2 had reacted in
horror at the impending duel (see Ex. 139j)). In this final scene, as

Tatyana enters, solemn diminished seventh chords recall the opening of the duel scene which had been the terrible consequence of the events of her name-day party. And, as we have already noted, the memory of her earlier young-girl's passion for Onegin brings a last recall of that 'fate in prospect' motif that had so haunted the earliest stages of the opera. Yet in this final scene it is the motif of 'fate embraced' which predominates. Hectically repeated, it accompanies Onegin's impetuous entry (Ex. 139n), crowns Tatyana's bitterly reproachful outpouring (Ex. 139o), and, as she weeps at the thought of lost happiness, it again exhibits its simplest form (Ex. 139p). And, just as the prelude's opening phrase (see Ex. 138b), with its descending six-note span, may have been a forewarning of this motif's appearances in the following opera (this phrase is, in effect, a conflation of the two fate motifs), so the very last desperate sounds of the whole opera are like a final allusion to this motif, its intervals now cramped into semitones and imprisoned in a remorselessly hammered chord of E minor (Ex. 139q), the key of love's pains and sorrows.

Inevitably the crucial importance in *Onegin* of fate as the force which drives Tatyana and Lensky towards their destinies must raise the whole issue of Onegin himself in the opera. Is he merely a catalyst, a cipher to give the illusion of human cause for consequences which in fact stem from forces outside the personalities of the drama? It is a tempting interpretation, but at most only a half-truth. Onegin's problem is that his real self has been stifled by the endless acting out of his social rôle in the St Petersburg haute monde, and by the strangulation of his capacity for response in a hectic round of superficial relationships and sexual intrigue. Finally, world-weary and jaundiced, he has become incapable of that intensity of feeling that is such an engaging attribute of Tatyana and Lensky. Worse still, having lost his capacity to respond, he is unable to develop. The Onegin we meet in the opera scarcely lives, existing as little more than a collection of conditioned reflexes – that is, until the third act, when his slumbering emotions are reawakened by the mature Tatyana.

It is the possession of this capacity for response that permitted both Tatyana and Lensky to grow as persons, but which also rendered them vulnerable to the pains which experience brings. For Tchaikovsky this made them doubly attractive, for while the first quality afforded him a wealth of highly emotional predicaments to stimulate in him a matching creative response, the second fortified this response by also engaging his deepest sympathies.

Yet, however strong his identification with Tatyana and, to a lesser extent, Lensky, Tchaikovsky remained commendably clear-headed about the actual qualities of his characters. He had obviously heeded Pushkin's prediction that Lensky, but for his romantic good fortune in dying young, would probably have grown into the most prosaic of country squires. This ardent swain was Olga's natural counterpart, a simple person who, despite his violent end, is really no tragic figure. Olga's flirtation with Onegin during Tatyana's name-day party was merely a trivial and transitory affair to which Lensky grossly over-reacted. That he should have died in consequence of it is infinitely pitiful, even unnerving, as is a street accident, but his death causes none of that deep shock which comes from watching some great figure caught into a chain of events that builds with seeming inevitability towards an appalling dénouement. Since Lensky is a figure of pathos – neither a coward, nor yet a hero – Tchaikovsky's decision to embody his feelings in simple, sentimental terms was absolutely right, even in the aria he sings when he is about to face Onegin's pistol (Pushkin had been equally careful not to turn Lensky into a great poet at this crisis of his life). The core of Lensky's music is his vocal line – a frank, unsophisticated outpouring, for the most part supported by a simple orchestral accompaniment with none of that harmonic richness that might suggest some significant layer of personality or feeling beneath the surface. But having decided upon Lensky's musical world, Tchaikovsky applied his melodic inventiveness to broadening its natural boundaries to the utmost. Thus Lensky's Act 1 arioso develops a surprising musical weight; even more, his last impassioned cry to the absent Olga in his duel scene soliloquy is supported by the sudden unexpected intervention of an harmonic structure of manifest strength which for a moment steals a little from the lament of another unfortunate in love who had recently touched Tchaikovsky's heart (compare bars 2–3 of Ex. 140 with bars 21ff. of Ex. 124 from *Francesca da Rimini*). Thus Tchaikovsky eloquently disclosed the intensity of the feelings which rack Lensky, without inflating them to epic proportions.

With Tatyana Tchaikovsky was equally successful. The challenge she presented to him was far more formidable, not merely because she had depths which Lensky lacked, but because her development as a personality in the opera is so much greater. A criticism sometimes levelled at Pushkin's original is that the transition from rural ingénue to polished society lady is too sudden. Though Tchaikovsky had at first intended to incorporate Tatyana's passage through the Moscow marriage market, he quickly abandoned this, thus making her transformation in the opera more abrupt, and requiring a particularly gigantic leap by the listener across a chasm of unchronicled event. Yet the dramatic resonances within the orchestral introduction to the

Ex. 140

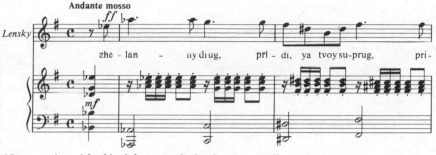

[Come, my longed-for friend; I am your husband, come, come!]

opera's last scene suffice to show that this Tatyana has endured a range
of experience quite unknown to the simple romantic girl who had so
impetuously thrown herself at Onegin at the beginning of the opera.
Haunted musically by the devotion of a husband to whom duty
requires her to be faithful, and by the memory of the duel in which
Onegin had remorselessly slaughtered her sister's betrothed, it is she
who proves the dominant character throughout this final scene, quickly
assuming control from the moment when Onegin surprises her
tearfully pondering his letter.

Throughout much of *Onegin* it may seem that the characters are
projected simply through their emotional worlds as embodied in
Tchaikovsky's music – in other words, that we 'feel' them rather than
perceive them, just as we 'feel' the background against which the
characters are set in the evocative folk-choruses or elaborate dance
movements. This is far from the whole truth, for a little later, as
Tatyana forlornly reminds Onegin of the past, she returns to the scene's
opening music – that close paraphrase (Ex. 141b) of her husband's aria
of devotion from the preceding scene (Ex. 141a) – which now becomes
an explicit musical intimation of the obstacle to the fulfilment of their
desires – an obstacle the memory of which she cannot suppress, and

Ex. 141

a.

Gremin

[All ages submit to love]

b.

Tatyana

[Onegin! I was younger then,]

which she is equally incapable of circumventing. It is a profound piece of musico-psychological illumination. With growing passion and bitterness she questions Onegin's motives for pursuing her, and with infinite pathos recalls how close happiness had once been for both of them. But the firmness with which she now requires him to leave is that of a fully matured woman capable of triumphing, if only with immense difficulty, over the terrible temptation which still claws at her innermost feelings. At this moment Tchaikovsky, again providing a most subtle exposure of Tatyana's complex of emotions, takes her back to the key and phrase in which she had once musically embodied the quintessence of her first passion for Onegin (see Ex. 139a), paraphrasing its contour into a strongly profiled musical declaration which unequivocally substantiates the decisiveness with which she is now rejecting him (Ex. 142) – a decisiveness which gives her confidence to make open confession of her enduring love. Leaving her, as Tchaikovsky did in the definitive version, to issue her final dismissal of Onegin without the supporting intervention of her husband, could only strengthen the image of Tatyana as projected in this last scene.[28]

[28] In fact this change, made for the Moscow production of 1881, was requested by the theatre, and agreed to only reluctantly by Tchaikovsky.

Ex. 142

[Onegin, in your heart is pride and true honour!]

Against such integrity of feeling and openness of character Onegin cannot compete. He labours under the crippling disability that we are told nothing in the opera of that earlier life which has done so much to make him what he is, for such knowledge might win him, if not condonation of his subsequent actions, at least a degree of exculpation. When we first meet him he has already retreated behind a façade of good breeding, and his habitual self-assurance and awesome loftiness are sufficient to bemuse Tatyana into believing that this must be the special being set apart for her by destiny. Accepting this, we must give Tchaikovsky full credit for his projection of some aspects of his nominal hero. There is an apt urbanity in the music which introduces Onegin, and this mood of easy detachment is equally reflected in his conversations with Tatyana, and in his later entrance in the garden scene. Faced with the need to answer Tatyana's letter, he couches his reply in terms that approach the slightly garrulous pleasantries of the drawing-room romance, stooping to Tatyana's musical world in an act of condescension which is absolutely right for this crushing homily. Confronting Lensky on the field of honour, he seems off-hand until, as each combatant is left to his own thoughts while the seconds discuss final arrangements, he joins in canon with his former friend, each man in identical terms, yet in hopeless isolation, questioning the futility of what they are about to do, yet neither capable of acting to break the chain of circumstance into which they are now caught with such dreadful consequences for one of them. Tchaikovsky's handling of the last stretch of this scene is masterly, from this close canon which the combatants share over a remorseless pedal bass, through the fleeting memory of Lensky's early happy love with Olga (now recalled in the fragments of his first scene arioso which break out above the agitated music to which Zaretsky hands the two men their weapons), to the final orchestral coda which, shunning elaborate funereal peroration, allows the first phrase of Lensky's farewell aria to act as a brief requiem to its creator.

It has been observed that in each of *Onegin*'s acts special attention is focused upon one of the main characters. In Act 1 it is Tatyana, in Act 2 Lensky, and in the final act Onegin himself. Certainly the Onegin who apathetically views the dancers in the St Petersburg ballroom begins to disclose an emotional capacity that he had earlier well masked; for one instant, reflecting upon the inescapable anguish that stems from a futile life and a troubled conscience, he fastens upon the 'fate embraced'

Ex. 143

[. . . do not dispel my eternal wearisome melancholy!]

motif (Ex. 143) which, also in the minor key, had intimated Lensky's sorrow in the preceding scene and mourned his end. A little later the tensions within the harmonic structure which companions Onegin's exclamation at the importunate memory of the death he has caused, together with the sharply angular contours of the following orchestral fragment, reveal in him a susceptibility to inner torment to which he had formerly seemed immune (Ex. 144).

Ex. 144

[. . . my solitude, in which a bloodstained phantom appeared to me everyday! I began . . .]

Tchaikovsky's introduction into this scene of Tatyana's husband was a necessary preliminary to the final event of the opera, and the noble aria[29] with which he furnished him provides a worthy musical centre of gravity to the whole scene. Tchaikovsky's creation of the dignified Prince Gremin was a frank sentimentalisation of the blank figure whom Pushkin described simply and unattractively as a 'stout general', but by projecting Tatyana's husband as an adoring and

[29] According to Kashkin, Tchaikovsky stated that what prompted him to compose Gremin's aria was the talent of Mikhail Koryakin, then a student at the Moscow Conservatoire. By the time Onegin was produced, however, Koryakin had left the Conservatoire, and thus did not sing the part.

devoted spouse, Tchaikovsky both emphasised the selfishness of Onegin's subsequent assault upon Tatyana's affections, and brought an extra factor into Tatyana's rejection of her urgent lover. There is perhaps a touch of priggishness in the highmindedness which motivates Pushkin's Tatyana; in Tchaikovsky's opera she is prompted not merely by the conjugal fidelity exacted by principle, but also by the reciprocal loyalty demanded by her husband's love and devotion. From this she gains a small but significant dimension.

But if the awakening within Onegin of a long-dormant capacity for love seems to promise that at least we are to perceive a little of the real man, this last scene of the opera is something of a disappointment. This is not true of the earlier parts, where the pain of regret and reproach predominate (particularly in yet another of those richly ironic touches in which this opera abounds when Onegin, reminded of his rejection of Tatyana, cries out for pity while the orchestra quietly enunciates the phrase to which he had once so blandly told Tatyana that 'dreams and years cannot return'); it is at the end, where he should surely have revealed a stronger, more virile passion than is embodied in his desperate babblings to the object of his desires, that he seems diminished. The Onegin of the final scene ends in cutting a pathetic figure. If Tchaikovsky came to despise him, he took an unfortunate final revenge upon him. What seems much more likely is that Tchaikovsky's own nature stultified his capacity for creating music of truly masculine sexual declaration.

It is sad that an opera that has revealed so much dramatic insight should, in its last pages, slip towards histrionicism. Yet it is a small blemish when set against all that has gone before. Of all Tchaikovsky's works *Onegin* is perhaps the most prodigal in musical riches, and the preceding examination has by no means touched upon all the felicities of the score. To mention but two of these: the brief orchestral prelude to the letter scene – an unsurpassable realisation of tender yearning compounded with the pain felt by youthful emotions stirred for the first time (and yet another manifestation of the 'fate embraced' motif (see Ex. 139c)) – and, in complete contrast, the lovely dawn picture, with its fresh shepherd pipings, which rises in the orchestra as Tatyana draws back the curtains, her writing done.

Of the two masterworks of 1877 there can be no doubt which is the finer. Even if we discount the weakness of the finale of the Fourth Symphony, and even if we admit the remarkable novelty and scope of the experience forged in the first movement, the symphony must still take second place to the opera, for it reveals neither the range of that work nor the expressive equilibrium which the composer so successfully maintained throughout most of *Onegin*, and which ensures that few of the expressive points become blunted or distorted through being thrust forth too forcefully. Only once in the opera, when the trumpet blares out Ex. 139a near the end of the letter monologue, does Tchaikovsky topple into the error of brashness. Caught up in a tale which engaged his inner self more completely than any other subject he ever tackled, and applying his most powerful creativity to the wide range of expressive demands made by the varying situations of *Onegin*, he could in the opera better control those tumultuous eruptions of self that sometimes break through so importunately in the symphony, and instead declare himself vicariously through the feelings of a group of characters whose common misfortune, the agony of a disastrous love affair, he could understand so painfully well.

A Note on the Russianness of *Eugene Onegin*

Except in the explicitly folky elements in the first act of *Onegin*, it might appear to the Western listener that Tchaikovsky's greatest opera is not marked by any quality that is very specially Russian – not, that is, by the kind of national stamp such as Rimsky-Korsakov placed upon *May Night*, or Tchaikovsky himself upon his own *Vakula*. To us in the West Musorgsky's *Boris Godunov* seems so much more thoroughly Russian than *Onegin*: yet the situation may appear very differently to the Russian himself, who does not identify the peculiar quality of his native culture by isolating and defining certain self-consciously national features, but who simply senses that a work is imbued with something of the collective character of his race. Pondering the innate Russianness of Tchaikovsky's music, Stravinsky in 1921 wrote an open letter to *The Times* à propos Dyagilev's revival of *The Sleeping Beauty*: 'Tchaikovsky's music ... is often more profoundly Russian than music which has long since been awarded the facile label of Muscovite picturesqueness. This music is quite as Russian as Pushkin's verse or Glinka's song. While not specifically cultivating in his art the "soul of the Russian peasant", Tchaikovsky drew *unconsciously* from the true popular sources of our race.'[30] Stravinsky had especially strong views on the Russianness of *Onegin* – and so, too, had Prokofiev, a point that is admirably made in one of the reminiscences of Giacomo Antonini, who had known both

[30] Letter to *The Times* of 17 October 1921.

Stravinsky and Prokofiev in Paris between the wars. As he set them down for me, the words of Count Antonini may aptly close this chapter:

Living in Paris, I heard Musorgsky's opera *Boris Godunov* for the first time in the winter of 1932–3, sung by Fyodor Shalyapin. By chance the next day I had lunch with Stravinsky in the studio of Vera de Bosset, his future wife and now his widow, who was a friend of my wife. During lunch I expressed my enthusiasm for the way in which Shalyapin had interpreted the rôle of Boris, and also for Musorgsky's opera. Igor Fyodorovich beamed, smiling at my youthful enthusiasm. He agreed entirely with me about both the performance and the work. But when I said 'I cannot imagine a more Russian opera than *Boris Godunov*,' he at once stopped me and said: 'There, my friend, you are entirely wrong. Our greatest opera composer is undoubtedly Tchaikovsky, and the most Russian opera of all is *Eugene Onegin*, not only because every young Russian woman has something of Tatyana, and in some way dreams of being a Tatyana, but also because from the beginning to the end the atmosphere is intrinsically Russian.'

I knew Pushkin's 'novel in verse', as he himself called the work, but had never heard Tchaikovsky's opera. I listened with interest to what Igor Fyodorovich was telling us, but I have to confess that at the same time, knowing his taste for paradox, I was rather sceptical. Tchaikovsky, as an opera composer, was then new to me as he was to many Western Europeans of my generation.

About a fortnight later, we had dinner with the Prokofievs, who were great friends of ours. I knew from experience that, although Stravinsky and Prokofiev had outwardly good relations and always showed a united Russian front to the French, in private they tended to contradict each other, sometimes in a violent way. Therefore, being curious to know what he thought of Tchaikovsky's *Eugene Onegin* and with youthful facetiousness expecting one of his colourful outbursts, I said to him: 'Now listen, Sergey, to what Igor Fyodorevich said to me the other day concerning *Boris Godunov* and *Eugene Onegin*.' When I had told him Stravinsky's opinion, to my great surprise Sergey Sergeyevich remained for a long time thoughtful and silent; then he said: 'Well, it is maybe not often the case, but for once I entirely agree with Igor Fyodorovich. Tchaikovsky is certainly our greatest opera composer, and *Eugene Onegin* is the most intrinsically Russian opera.' He then went on to tell me that not only Tatyana, but also Olga, Onegin, Lensky, and Gremin corresponded completely to the Russian character, each one in his own way. After a rather long and detailed comment on *Eugene Onegin*, he came back to *Boris Godunov* and said that Western Europeans in general, and the French in particular, had a wrong conception of the Russian character in literature, as in music; they saw the outwardly colourful side and did not grasp the more profound, intrinsic qualities. As Stravinsky had done, he quoted the French view on *Boris Godunov* as an example: 'They forget, or do not know that Musorgsky was what we call a *Slavophile*, that is to say, a reactionary nationalist, fiercely against Poland and the Catholic church; his sympathy was with the Old Believers, as you can see in *Khovanshchina*. Tchaikovsky, on the other hand, was liberal-minded like Pushkin, but nevertheless profoundly Russian.'

He continued, saying that *Eugene Onegin*, which reflects this, had therefore a special appeal for Russians, both those of yesterday (meaning before the 1917 Revolution) and those of the present.

Faced with so unequivocal a pronouncement from two such Russian creators, one may fairly ask: is *Onegin* not only perhaps Tchaikovsky's masterpiece, but also the most deeply Russian of all his works?

6

INTERLUDE
NADEZHDA VON MECK:
BENEFACTRESS AND CONFIDANTE

APART FROM HIS relationships with a very few among the closest members of his family, the most important emotional involvement of Tchaikovsky's life was with a woman he deliberately avoided meeting, and to whom he never spoke. In the preceding pages we have already sampled the first exchange₃ in the platonic love affair between the composer and Nadezhda von Meck, but these were no more than the preliminary signal for a veritable deluge of words which, as published, fills three volumes even larger than the entire present study. Such a corpus of material cannot possibly be ignored, but if the biographer were not to be highly selective in using it, he would quickly find his chronicle swamped by this heaving mass of epistolatory prose. Nevertheless, there are many things which make this correspondence invaluable. It is not merely that we may glimpse a good deal of Tchaikovsky's inner self from his declarations to this correspondent; he was also prepared to be more openly and abundantly confiding to Mrs von Meck about some of his attitudes to life and about his creative processes than to any other person. Since these confidences have little or no relevance to the chronological record of Tchaikovsky's daily life, they are best disentangled from it. Hence this interlude.

Modest conveniently summarised the earlier life of his brother's patroness. Nadezhda Filaretovna (née Frolovskaya) von Meck had been born near Smolensk on 10 February 1831. Fired by the enthusiasm of her father, who was a keen amateur violinist, she acquired a commendable knowledge of the musical repertoire and developed an admirable skill as a pianist. Just before her seventeenth birthday she was married to Karl Fyodorovich von Meck, a 28-year-old engineer in the employ of the Moscow–Warsaw railway. Their early years of marriage were financially difficult, and the arrival of a rapid succession of children made their position even more hard. But

Nadezhda von Meck was an energetic and very determined woman. Persuaded by her to abandon the rigours and frustrations of public service, Karl Fyodorovich found a partner who had capital, and began working on his own account as a builder of railways. His decision proved timely, and during the 1860s he amassed a very large fortune. In 1876, when Nadezhda wrote her first letter to Tchaikovsky, she became a widow. Of the eleven children whom Modest said she bore, seven were still living with her, and she seems to have found satisfaction enough in their company, largely cutting herself off from the rest of the world and devoting herself to managing her own business affairs with the help of a brother and her eldest son, and to conducting the education of her youngest children with the aid of her eldest daughter.

The first letters exchanged by Nadezhda von Meck and Tchaikovsky on the very last days of 1876 have already been quoted (see above, pp.130–1); so, too, have the next two letters written on the last two days of the following February. These exchanges had marked the completion by Tchaikovsky of the first violin and piano transcriptions of his own music requested by Mrs von Meck. The originals of such pieces had, however, been created for others; now, with the swift collapse of reserve between these two correspondents, Mrs von Meck wanted something more personal to herself, and at the end of her letter of 19 March (partially quoted on pp. 134–5) she had asked Tchaikovsky to compose a marche funèbre for piano duet on motifs from his opera *The Oprichnik*. She had drawn a little verbal picture of what she wanted the march to express, and Tchaikovsky did his best to satisfy her requirements. Nine days later it was finished. The lady was enraptured with the result, and within two months requested a second piece of similar kind: a morsel for violin and piano to be called *Reproach*. 'I have a tiny piece of such a sort by Kohne which is called *Le Reproche*, also for violin and piano', she wrote on 12 May. 'I like it very much, but it does not express what I would wish, and moreover it seems to be concerned with personality. My *Reproach* must be impersonal, it may relate to nature, to fate, to myself, but not to any other person. My *Reproach* must be the expression of an intolerable spiritual state, of that expressed by the French phrase: je n'en peux plus!'[1] After adding several further sentences to complete her expressive prescription for the new piece, she ended by offering to send Tchaikovsky this piece and others by Kohne, counselling him to examine further that composer's work.

Now that this relationship was beginning to consolidate, Tchaikovsky clearly became uneasy about some of the trends which were emerging. Despite all the warmth with which he responded to his

[1] *TPM*1, p. 12.

new patroness, he feared the demands which she might make upon his composing time, and he had no wish to place himself in a position where he might have to trade a portion of his creative energies for her bounty. And so in the first of the two letters he wrote on 13 May he excused himself from discharging immediately Mrs von Meck's request, though he showed himself by no means unwilling to profit forthwith from her generosity by a direct borrowing from her. His second letter of the same day is a mixture of genuine embarrassment at the largesse he had already received and of an unabashed determination to ensure that he continued to tap whatever benefits he could from her resources:

With your earlier musical commissions it had occurred to me that you were guided by two motives: on the one hand, that you really wished to have this or that composition of mine in this or that form; on the other that, having heard of my everlasting financial difficulties, you were coming to my aid. The excessively generous payment with which you have rewarded my paltry work compels me to think thus. This time I am somehow convinced that you were guided *exclusively*, or almost exclusively, by the second motive. That is why, reading through your letter in which, between the lines, I discerned your delicacy and kindness, your touching favour towards me, I felt at the same time in the depth of my soul an irresistible *unwillingness* to set to work at once, and I hastened in my reply [written earlier today] to put off the fulfilment of my promise. I should very much wish that there should not be in our relationships with each other that insincerity, that falsehood which would inevitably manifest itself if, not heeding my inner voice, not being inspired by that mood which you require, I were to hurry to fabricate just *something*, to send you that *something*, and to receive from you a disproportionate reward. . . . Let us agree that it is never humiliating for an artist to receive remuneration for his labour: yet, you know, besides labour I must put into a composition, such as you now want, a mood of a certain kind, i.e. what is called inspiration, and this latter is not always at my service – and I should act dishonourably as an artist if, for the sake of improving my circumstances, and by misusing my technical skill, I were to offer you false metal for true. Nevertheless, I do really have a great need of *contemptible metal*. It would take a long time to tell you how and why a man who earns quite enough for a more than comfortable existence should become entangled in debts to such an extent that at times they completely poison his life and paralyse his zeal for work. Just now, when I urgently need to go away and to ensure before I leave that I have the means to return, I have been caught up in a very unpleasant accumulation of financial difficulties from which I cannot extricate myself without outside help.

I have now decided to seek this help from you. You are the only person in the world from whom I am not ashamed to ask for money. In the first place, you are very kind and generous; secondly, you are wealthy. I should like to place all my debts in the hands of a single magnanimous creditor by whom I should be freed from the clutches of moneylenders. If you would agree to make me a loan which would once and for all free me from them, I should be unboundedly grateful to you for this invaluable service. The point is that my debts are very great: something in the region of three thousand roubles. I would repay this sum in three different ways: (1) by various kinds of work – for example, arrangements like those I have already done for you: (2) by assigning you the royalties which I receive from the [theatre] management for my operas: and (3) by a monthly despatch of part of my salary. Regarding the first method of payment, I would ask you to bear in mind that you may apply for any kind of musical work, never feeling in any way embarrassed by the fear of troubling me. Because of my many years of experience, a job like making those arrangements which you commissioned from me costs me very little labour.... A composition like *Reproach* is a very different matter. It requires a certain disposition, the conjunction of certain conditions which is not always possible...

It would be very distressing to me if my request were to appear to you indelicate. I decided upon it above all because it would once and for all exclude the element of money from our relationship.[a]

In the light of Tchaikovsky's later financial relationship to Mrs von Meck, the last sentence is a little droll.

Despite his current absorption in the Fourth Symphony, Tchaikovsky assured his benefactress that he would compose *Reproach*, and he asked her to send him the pieces by Kohne; but on receiving them, he had to admit that he could find nothing to like in them. Fearful that this judgement might seem to be a condemnation of Mrs von Meck's own taste, he hastened to add that he, too, was sometimes captivated by pieces of slight musical value, confessing that Alyabyev's *The Nightingale* still reduced him to tears. In the end, however, his patroness's request went by default, and *Reproach* was never written.

To Tchaikovsky's appeal for financial assistance Mrs von Meck

[a] *TPM*1, pp. 14–16; *TZC*2, pp. 16–18, (with all reference to Tchaikovsky's borrowing omitted).

responded readily and swiftly, and within two days an effusively grateful Tchaikovsky was agreeing to her plea that their correspondence might not be confined solely to practical arrangements between them, but might be more frequent and more personal. Tchaikovsky replied that he would be delighted because it was always pleasant to talk about music generally. Though the correspondence was already far from being purely on business matters, he clearly did not yet envisage this exchange of letters as a way of confessing his own most intimate thoughts and feelings. His encounter with Antonina and his marriage were quickly to change all that. During the next thirteen years some twelve hundred letters were to pass between these two people. Some were very substantial documents, especially those written during the first few years of the correspondence when the exchanges were also most frequent. By mutual consent they never met, and on the rare occasions when they chanced to see each other across a theatre or concert hall, or in the street, they turned away as though there had been no recognition. The closest contact they ever had was at the magnificent von Meck estate at Brailov in the Ukraine. Mrs von Meck had invited Tchaikovsky to use the house when she was absent; if she was in residence he was installed at neighbouring Simaki. On one occasion, in the woods, they met accidentally in a way which made it impossible to pretend they had not seen each other. Even then, however, no word passed between them; Tchaikovsky merely raised his hat, she seemed overcome with confusion, and they passed on. Their 'union' was to be vicariously symbolised when, in 1884, her son Nikolay married Tchaikovsky's niece, Anna Davïdova. That was the closest they ever came to anything physical or truly personal in their relationship. Yet the frankness and fullness of their letters, and the fervour of their prose render this one of the most passionate correspondences of all time.

In recording one detail of Nadezhda von Meck's biography Modest had been less than honest. Her children numbered not eleven, but twelve. Early in the 1870s a young engineer, Alexandr Yolshin, became secretary to her husband. Nadezhda quickly became emotionally entangled with him, and a daughter, Lyudmila (Milochka), was born to them in 1872. For nearly four years Karl von Meck knew nothing of the affair, thinking that Milochka was his own child. Then, on one of his visits to St Petersburg early in 1876, his own daughter, Alexandra, told him of her mother's infidelity. According to the family tradition, it was the shock of this disclosure which caused the heart attack from which he died a few hours later. Was it guilt at this affair which determined Nadezhda von Meck's behaviour towards Tchaikovsky? One suspects that her marriage had had little love in it on her side, yet the continuous train of children shows that her husband's sexual demands had not abated as the years went by. Then suddenly, at forty, her own desire was truly aroused, perhaps for the first time. After this sudden passion had produced an illegitimate child and finally killed her husband, she may well have been terrified that this new man in her life might have for her, if he should possess the potency of his music, an attraction as fatal as that she had conceived for Alexandr Yolshin some six years before. That affair had shown her, too, that there was no more permanent joy to be found in the sudden access of true passion than in the conjugal routine of nearly thirty years. Yet she frantically craved for some sort of partner to whom she could pour out her feelings.

Her response to music was as indiscriminate as it was strong (Tchaikovsky was to have his patience sorely tried as much by her dismissal of Mozart as 'shallow'[3] as by her encomiums of trivial composers like Kohne), and her reactions to Tchaikovsky's own music seem to have been peculiarly violent, to judge from her own words about it; that she should once, to Tchaikovsky's profound distaste, have likened the experience of hearing it to drinking sherry is deeply indicative. Now she discovered a chance to feel that she had a real part in the making of that music by freeing its creator from the need to devote to earning his daily bread those hours which he might otherwise have given to composition. And at the same time, the creator of these musical agencies for delight and emotional release might become her distant, idealised, grateful confidant. For her his letters were, one suspects, the communications of a lover whose infidelity in marrying another was both painful yet irrelevant; for him they became channels for the declaration of personal thoughts and for the confession of inner feelings to an equally distant ideal of womanhood – less a consort than a mother. It is one of the most extraordinary yet fortunate coincidences of history (or, as Tchaikovsky would have put it, of fate) that these two people should have encountered each other at this time.

They exchanged pictures not only of themselves but of their closest relatives. She in particular wanted to bring their families into the relationship, and especially requested portraits of Tchaikovsky's kin. He sent her photos of his twin brothers and of Sasha and her family. All such things were acknowledged with exaggerated expressions of admiration and with a flood of details about her own children and their families. Her letters themselves are flowery, rambling, contain a good deal of nonsense, and reveal a thoroughly muddled, sometimes unbalanced mind quite incapable of distinguishing fact from fiction. At times their emotional pitch is heightened to a degree which verges on

[3] *TPM*I, p. 231.

hysteria. His, conversely, even when he was writing on something on which his own thoughts were not clearly defined or digested, are lucid in exposition and argument. He was thoroughly aware of his reader – at times too aware of what she wanted to read; while her insincerity was guileless, he could plead less innocent intent.

They traded thoughts on the most ordinary, even mundane matters. Doctors, cures for ailments, roulette, flowers (he put some violets in one of his letters to her, though he confessed that his favourite flower was the lily of the valley), brahminism, murder cases, matters of morality, the Imperial family, the books they were reading, the weather: all were subjects for animated exchanges.

With deeper commitment they poured into their early correspondence their mutual involvement in their country's current struggle with Turkey, seething with rage at England's part in the affair, bewailing Russia's reverses and revelling in her successes. When the Russians scored a victory at Plevna in December 1877, she sent him a telegram because she wanted to be the first to tell him the news. The threats to their country from within exercised them as much as assaults from without. With Anatoly employed near the heart of the legal machine in the Russian capital, Tchaikovsky received intelligence of its inner workings as it tried to deal with the wave of revolutionary unrest which erupted as the war with Turkey drew towards its close. Anatoly had observed at first hand the trial of the young Vera Zasulich after her attempt upon the life of the brutal St Petersburg governor, Trepov, and he had become appalled at the cynical self-interest which determined the acts and decisions of all those who had some part in the conduct of the case. 'We are living through a very critical epoch, and God knows how it will all end,' Tchaikovsky wrote gloomily to his confidante on 25 April 1878. 'Anatoly asserts that the student disturbances and the position in general in our internal affairs are very serious, and that we may now expect continually new outbreaks of intellectual ferment among our young people. How one grieves for our poor, good emperor, who so sincerely wishes well, and who encounters such terrible disappointments and griefs!'[4] Thus Tchaikovsky clearly defined his own identification with sentiments which would have found a ready sympathy among the great mass of middle-class Russians of his time, many of whom perceived some at least of the deep flaws and abuses within their society, yet whose sympathy with the aims, if not the means of young idealists was far exceeded by their fear of the dismantling of that hierarchical social

[4] *TPM*1, p. 299; *TLP*7, p. 223; *TZC*2, pp. 160–1.

structure in which their own position was safely assured under, as they saw it, the benevolent rule of the father of them all, their Tsar.

Tchaikovsky wrote her, too, assessments of certain of his friends and fellow musicians. These tell us much of the other side of some of the closest relationships in Tchaikovsky's life – of his extreme sensitivity and of the bitter resentment he perhaps unwittingly nurtured against people who so often had given him great moral support. On one occasion Mrs von Meck asked about Laroche. The cameo Tchaikovsky provided shows both balance and bias: balance in that he endeavoured to look at all sides of the subject matter to present it as clearly as possible, bias in that this subject matter is inevitably filtered through Tchaikovsky's very personal responses (having said this, we might equally have been talking, mutatis mutandis, of Tchaikovsky's compositional process in his most characteristic works). Yet in the end bias wins heavily. After Laroche's great natural gifts have been acknowledged, his character is annihilated in a heartless retailing of his failings:

Unfortunately he is a man weak-willed to the highest degree, languid, idle, and superficial, and despite all the versatility of his abilities, he will never occupy a position commensurate with his talent. When I became acquainted with him he was sixteen, and at that time was already the complete musician to whom all difficulties of musical technique yielded without resistance, of their own accord. Sixteen years have passed since then and he has made *not one step forward*. The *Wunderkind* has remained the same abundantly gifted, but indolent man. Now utter ruin threatens him. . . . Wine, cards, loose women – these are the only subjects which draw him out of his apathy. His friends, and I among them, have many times already tried to raise him up a little, to set him on the right road, to make him work and write, and all this is successful for only a few days. *Le plis est pris*. All that now remains is to give it up as a bad job and wait until either he one fine day comes to his senses or else falls silent altogether.[5]

And so on for many more sentences. Reading such an unloving portrait of a man who had long been one of Tchaikovsky's greatest admirers serves to emphasise the abyss which divided the composer even from those apparently most intimate with him. In the light of this, Tchaikovsky's frequent cries of 'loneliness' become more pointed. Nikolay Rubinstein fared no better. But by far the most fascinating of

[5] *TPM*1, pp. 299–300; *TLP*7, pp. 223–4.

these sketches is that of the Kuchka. By January 1878, when Tchaikovsky wrote it, he had drifted far from the group's musical world and ideals, and its finest days had long passed. Balakircv had withdrawn completely from the musical scene, Musorgsky was sinking deeper into alcoholism, Borodin's creative activities were being increasingly smothered by his official duties; only Rimsky-Korsakov was actively pursuing a composer's career. Tchaikovsky's analysis of each is unsparing, though less merciless than his dissections of Laroche and Rubinstein who, being closer to him, had afforded him greater and more prolonged aggravation and seeded his resentment the more liberally. However eccentric Tchaikovsky's assessments of his fellow composers, there are, within the overall distortions and prejudices, details which are clear and true. His diagnosis of the creative crisis through which Rimsky-Korsakov was passing is very accurate, and he sensed that Musorgsky, the member of the Kuchka with whom he had the least natural sympathy, was perhaps the most creatively talented of them all. But he was quite incapable of appreciating the forms Musorgsky's originality took, badly underestimated Borodin's technique, and did less than justice to Balakirev. Had he looked squarely at his own debt to this extraordinary catalyst, he might have been more ready to recognise how effectively Balakirev had also acted as sire and midwife to the creations of these other composers closer to himself:

All the latest St Petersburg composers are a very talented lot, but all of them are infected to the core with the most frightful conceit and a purely dilettantish confidence in their superiority over all the rest of the musical world. The exception among them in recent times is Rimsky-Korsakov. He is just as self-taught as the others, but he has effected a complete about-turn. His nature is very serious, very upright and conscientious. When he was a very young man he fell into the company of people who first assured him that he was a genius and, second, told him that there was no need *to study*, that training kills inspiration, dries up creativity, and so on. Initially he believed this. His first works bear witness to a very large talent, devoid of any development through [the study of musical] theory. In the circle to which he belonged all were in love with themselves and with one other. . . . Korsakov is the only one of them to whom, some five years ago, the thought occurred that the ideas preached by the circle had, in fact, no foundation, that their contempt for training, for classical music, their hatred of precedents and of authorities were nothing but ignorance. I have one of his letters from that time. It deeply touched and amazed me. He had become profoundly despairing when he saw that so many years had passed uselessly, and that he was going along a path leading nowhere. He then asked what he ought to do. Of course he had to study. And he began to study, but with such zeal that soon academic techniques became an atmosphere indispensable to him. During one summer he wrote countless contrapuntal exercises and sixty-four fugues, ten of which he promptly sent to me to look over. Of their kind the fugues were irreproachable, but I straightway perceived that he had over-reacted. From aversion to training he had, at one go, turned to the cult of musical technique. Soon after this his symphony [No. 3] and quartet [No. 1] came out. Both works were filled with a host of clever things but, as you very rightly observe, they are imbued with a dryly pedantic character. Apparently he is now passing through this crisis, and how it will end is difficult to predict. Either a great master will come out of him, or he will finally become bogged down in contrapuntal tricks.

Cui is a talented dilettante. His music has no originality, but is elegant and graceful . . .

Borodin is a fifty-year-old [in fact, forty-four] professor of chemistry at the Medical Academy. Again he has talent, even a strong one, but it has perished through neglect, because of a blind *fate* which led him to a chair of chemistry instead of into the living profession of music. Thus he has less taste than *Cui*, and his technique is so weak that he cannot write a single line without outside help.

Musorgsky you very rightly call a hopeless case. In talent he is perhaps superior to all the preceding, but his nature is narrow-minded, devoid of any urge towards self-perfection, blindly believing in the ridiculous theories of his circle and in his own genius. In addition, he has a certain base side to his nature which likes coarseness, uncouthness, roughness. . . . He flaunts . . . his illiteracy, takes pride in his ignorance, mucks along anyhow, blindly believing in the infallibility of his genius. Yet he has flashes of talent which are, moreover, not devoid of originality.

The most important personality of this circle is *Balakirev*. But he has fallen silent after doing very little. He possesses an enormous talent which has perished because of certain fateful circumstances which have turned him into a *religious fanatic*, whereas formerly he had long vaunted his utter disbelief. Now he is constantly in church, fasts, bows to relics, and does nothing else. Despite his colossal endowment he has done much harm. For instance, he destroyed Korsakov, having assured him that training was harmful. He is the general inventor of all the theories of this strange group which unites within itself so many undeveloped, undirected, and prematurely blighted forces.[6]

Of the major personal issues which Tchaikovsky and his patroness discussed at some length, religious belief was the first. Nadezhda von Meck claimed to be a 'realist' who had rejected completely traditional religion, replacing it with what she termed an 'ideal materialism' akin to pantheism. Tchaikovsky, who recognised that one factor in his persisting attraction to the Orthodox Church was that it was a part of the Russia he loved, had likewise passed beyond inherited belief, but the poetic atmosphere of the church ritual, and the mystic aura surrounding the image of Christ still claimed a part of him, as he confirmed to Mrs von Meck on 10 November 1877:

On the one hand my mind stubbornly refuses to recognise the truth of the dogmatic side as much of the Orthodox as of all other Christian creeds. For example, however much I ponder the doctrine of reward and retribution with regard to whether a man is good or bad, I can never find any sense in this belief. How can you make a sharp division between sheep and goats? For what is reward given, for what punishment? Equally my understanding is incapable of grasping a firm belief in eternal life. In this regard I submit completely to the pantheistic view of the life to come and of immortality.

On the other hand, education, habit, the poetic notions which have been instilled in me from childhood about everything concerning Christ and his teaching – all this makes me involuntarily turn to him with supplication in sorrow and with gratitude in joy.[7]

Nearly four weeks later he specified more precisely how his responses were reflected in religious practice:

I very often go to mass. The Liturgy of St John Chrysostom is, in my view, one of the greatest of artistic works. If you follow the service attentively, going carefully into the meaning of every act of the ritual, then it is impossible, when attending our Orthodox service, not to be moved by the spirit. I also love very much the all-night vigil. To direct myself on Saturday to some small, ancient church, to stand in the semi-darkness filled with the smoke of incense, to delve deeply within myself in search of a reply to the eternal questions: *to what purpose, when, whither, why?*; to waken from my reverie when the choir

[6] *TPM*1, pp. 135–7; *TLP*6, pp. 328–30; *TZC*2, pp. 72–4; *YDGC*, pp. 161–2 (partial).
[7] *TPM*1, p. 63; *TLP*6, pp. 213–14; *TZC*2, pp. 38–9.

sings 'Many a time have they afflicted me from my youth', and to surrender myself to the captivating poetry of that psalm, to be filled with a certain quiet rapture when they open the central doors of the iconostasis and there rings out: 'Praise God from the heavens!' O, I love all this passionately; it is one of my greatest delights![8]

Within the year Tchaikovsky was to set the Liturgy of St John Chrysostom to music which substantiates his utter surrender to the mystical richness and the emotional sway, if not to the dogma, of the Orthodox ritual. And then, a few lines after the above passage, he confided one thing more which directs a sudden blinding shaft of illumination into the very heart of his inner emotional life. 'Despite the triumphal strength of my *convictions* [that there is no eternal life], I can never reconcile myself to the thought that my mother, whom I loved so much and who was such a wonderful person, has disappeared for ever, and that I shall never again have the chance to tell her that, even after twenty-three years of separation, I still love her...'[9]

Inevitably the exchanges could not long avoid the subject of sexual love. 'Pyotr Ilich,' she addressed him roundly on 11 February 1878, 'have you ever loved? I think not. You love music too much to be able to love a woman.'[10] His reply, composed ten days later, was both direct and evasive:

You ask, my friend, whether I am familiar with *non-platonic love. Yes and no.* If you phrase the question somewhat differently, i.e. if you ask, have I experienced complete happiness in love, then I will reply: *No, no, no!* Yet I think the answer to this question is also contained in my music. If you ask me, do I understand the full power, the full boundless strength of that feeling, then I will reply: *Yes, yes, yes!* – and again I will tell you that more than once I have tried lovingly to express in music the torment and, at the same time, the bliss of love. Whether I have succeeded I do not know – or, rather, I leave others to judge. I completely disagree with you when you say that music *cannot convey the all-embracing characteristics of the feeling of love.* I believe quite the contrary, that *music alone can* do this. You say that here *words* are necessary. O no! It is precisely here that words are not necessary – and where they are ineffectual, the more eloquent language, i.e. music, appears in all its power.... I am glad that you place instrumental music so highly. Your observation that often words

[8] *TPM* 1, p. 91; *TLP* 6, pp. 251–2; *TZC* 2, p. 51

[9] *TPM* 1, p. 92; *TLP* 6, p. 259; *TZC* 2, p. 52.

[10] *TPM* 1, p. 190.

merely spoil the music, drag it down from its unscalable heights, is completely true. I have always felt this deeply, and it is perhaps because of this that I have been more successful with instrumental compositions than with vocal ones.[11]

The Russian scholar, Alexandra Orlova, who once worked in the Tchaikovsky Museum at Klin, and who saw many materials never publicly disclosed in Russia, has revealed in the West a declaration by Modest that his brother was only able to compose *Romeo and Juliet* because he had endured an agonising and unrequited love for his former classmate at the School of Jurisprudence, Vladimir Gerard. This disclosure gives this last quotation special point.

By far the most valuable of Nadezhda von Meck's probings were those which drew Tchaikovsky into talking about his creative processes. When she had sought information on the content of the Fourth Symphony, he had prefaced his reply with some indications of how, for him, a work was born. In succeeding letters he returned to the subject, and these declarations accumulated into one of the most vivid yet credible descriptions ever written of the process of musical conception and gestation. Tchaikovsky was quick to dismiss Mrs von Meck's assumption that some extra-musical factor was necessary to initiate and direct the musical inspiration:

You ask me whether there is a definite programme in this symphony. Usually when I am asked this question in respect of a symphonic work, I reply: *none*. And in fact it is difficult to reply to this question. How can you relate those indefinite feelings which you go through when you are writing an instrumental piece without a definite subject? It is a purely lyrical process. It is the soul's musical confession in which much has been thrown up and which, by reason of its essential character, pours itself out through sounds, just as a lyrical poet expresses himself in verses. The difference is only this: that music has incomparably more powerful means and a more subtle language for expressing the thousand different moments of the inner mood. The *seed* of a future composition usually reveals itself suddenly, in the most unexpected fashion. If the soil is favourable, i.e. if I am in the mood for work, this seed takes root with inconceivable strength and speed, bursts through the soil, puts out shoots, leaves, twigs and finally flowers. I cannot define the creative process except through this metaphor. All the difficulty lies in this: that the seed should appear, and that it should find itself in

[11] *TPM*1, pp. 204–5; *TLP*7, pp. 105–6; *TZC*2, pp. 110–11.

favourable circumstances. All the rest happens of its own accord. It would be futile for me to try and express to you in words all the boundless bliss of that feeling which envelops me when the main idea has appeared, and when it begins to take definite forms. You forget everything, you are almost insane, everything inside you trembles and writhes, you scarcely manage to set down sketches, one idea presses upon another. Sometimes in the middle of this enchanted process some jolt from without suddenly wakens you from this somnambulistic state. Somebody will ring, a servant will enter, the clock strikes and reminds you that you have to go about your business ... these breaks are painful, inexpressibly painful. Sometimes inspiration flies off for a while; you have to go in search of her, sometimes in vain. Very frequently you have to resort to a completely cold, intellectual, mechanical work process. Perhaps this is why you can find moments in even the greatest masters where organic cohesion is lacking, where a seam shows, bits of the whole which are artificially stuck together. But there is no other way. If that state of the artist's soul which is called *inspiration*, and which I have just been trying to describe to you, were to continue unbroken, it would not be possible to survive a single day. The strings would snap and the instrument shatter to smithereens. Only one thing is necessary: that the main idea and the general contours of all the separate parts should appear not through *searching* but of their own accord as the result of that supernatural, incomprehensible force which no one has explained, and which is called inspiration.[12]

'Do not believe those who try to convince you that musical creation is a cold pursuit, governed by the reason,' he continued a fortnight later. 'You can only be moved, touched and shaken by that music which has poured from the depths of an artistic soul stirred by inspiration. There is no doubt that even the greatest musical geniuses sometimes worked unwarmed by inspiration. It is the kind of guest that does not always appear at the first summons. In the meantime you must always *work*.' And then, a few lines later, he turned to the Russianness in his own music. 'Not infrequently it has happened that I have set about a composition openly having in mind the exploitation of this or that folktune which I like. Sometimes (as, for instance, in the finale of our symphony) this has happened involuntarily, quite unexpectedly. As for the Russian element in general in my music, i.e. those elements in the melody and harmony which are related to folksong, this arises because I grew up in the backwoods, from my very earliest childhood soaked up

[12] *TPM*1, pp. 216–17; *TLP*7, pp. 124–5; *TZC*2, pp. 117–18; *YDGC*, p. 174 (partial).

the indescribable beauty of Russian folk music's characteristic traits, because I passionately love the Russian element in all its manifestations – because, in a word, I am *Russian* in the fullest sense of the word.'[13]

Fascinated by all this, Nadezhda von Meck soon returned for more precise details of Tchaikovsky's method of work, and from Kamenka in August he penned the fullest and most illuminating account of his process of composition – an account impressive for its clearheadedness and clean observation. That Tchaikovsky's compositional routine (the word is used deliberately) was thoroughly disciplined, thoroughly systematic, is absolutely clear from all that follows. The conceptual process was one thing, but the vision only became real when it had been embodied in the materials of music, and it was equally essential to have cool, prolonged periods of quiet industry during which emotion might be recollected in tranquillity, and when the forces of his formidable compositional technique might be marshalled to fashion a solid artefact of highly organised sounds to incarnate his inspiration. Final confirmation of the deep objectivity and severity of his compositional vision is provided by his lament at the blemishes he so clearly detected in the finished work. And again, too, he hammered home the need to work at all costs, even when inspiration was lacking, for only thus might he coax it to return.

First of all, he explained to Nadezhda von Meck, it was necessary to recognise two categories in his compositions: the first consisting of works which he wrote from choice or inner compulsion, the second of commissioned pieces. But, he hastened to add, it should not be assumed that works of the latter kind were necessarily inferior to those of the former:

Very often it has happened that a piece belonging to the *second* category has turned out to be completely successful despite the fact that the initial stimulus to its appearance in this world came from outside – while, conversely, a piece which I have thought up for myself has, because of secondary circumstances, been less successful. These secondary circumstances, upon which depends the state of mind in which a work is written, have great significance. Complete calm is necessary for the artist at the moment of creation. In this sense artistic creation is always *objective*, even when it is musical creation. Those who think that the creating artist at the moment of *emotional excitement* is able, through the resources of his art, to express what he feels are mistaken. Both sad and joyful feelings express

[13] *TPM*1, pp. 235–6; *TLP*7, pp. 154–5; *TZC*2, pp. 126–8.

themselves always, one might say, *retrospectively*. Having no particular reasons to be happy, I can fill myself with a happy creative
humour and, conversely, in a happy situation produce a piece which
is imbued with the most gloomy and hopeless feelings. In a word, the
artist lives a double life: that common to mankind, and that of the
artist, and sometimes, moreover, these two lives are not congruous.
However this may be, I repeat that, for composition, the most
important condition is the possibility of separating oneself, if only for
a while, from the cares of the first of these two lives and devoting
oneself exclusively to the second. But I am digressing; I will return to
my subdivision.

For works belonging to my first category there is no need for
anything more than the slightest will-power. It is sufficient to obey
the inner voice, and if the first of these two lives does not, with its sad
accidents, crush the second, artistic one, then the work goes ahead
with quite unbelievable ease. You forget everything, the spirit
trembles with a certain utterly incomprehensible and inexpressibly
sweet emotion, you are absolutely incapable of keeping up *at all* with
your spirit's impulse, time passes literally unnoticed. There is
something *somnambulistic* in this condition. *On ne s'entend pas vivre.* It is
impossible to recount these moments. What comes from your pen, or
what you simply pack away in your head (for very often such
moments come in a situation where you can neither write nor
ponder) is, in such circumstances, always *good*, and if nothing, no
outside jolt recalls you to that other public life, it must turn out with a
perfection as great as that of any artist. Unfortunately these outside
jolts are utterly unavoidable. You have to go out to work, you are
called to dine, a letter arrives, and so on. That is why there are so few
compositions in which the degree of musical beauty is uniform
throughout. It is from this that there come *seams, glueings together,
inconsistencies, discrepancies.*

For compositions of the second category *sometimes* you have *to attune
yourself.* Here you very often have to overcome laziness, reluctance.
Then certain things happen. Sometimes victory comes easily.
Sometimes inspiration slips away, eludes you. But I consider it is the
duty of an artist never to give way, for *laziness* is a very powerful
human trait. For an artist there is nothing worse than to give way to
this. You cannot simply wait. Inspiration is the sort of guest who
does not like visiting those who are lazy. She reveals herself to those
who invite her. Perhaps because of this there are grounds for
accusing the Russian people of a lack of fundamental creativity, for
saying that the Russian is a *lazy* person par excellence. The Russian

loves to postpone; by nature he is talented, but also by nature he suffers from a deficiency of will-power regarding himself, and from a lack of staying power. *You must, you have to overcome yourself* so that you may not fall into *dilettantism* from which even so colossal a talent as Glinka suffered.... What might have happened if this man had been born into a different environment, had lived in different conditions, if he had laboured as an artist who recognised his power and his duty to develop his gifts to the last possible degree of perfection, and not as a dilettante who composed music for want of something better to do!...

I hope, my friend, you will not suspect me of vainglory if I tell you that my appeal to inspiration is rarely in vain. I can say that that power which above I called a capricious guest has now for so long been familiar with me that we live inseparably, and she only flies away from me when, in consequence of circumstances which in some way or other are oppressing my more public life, she feels herself superfluous. Yet scarcely has the cloud dispersed, and she is there. Thus, if I am in a normal state of mind, I can say that I am composing every minute of the day, whatever the circumstances. Sometimes I observe with curiosity that unbroken labour which, of its own accord, irrespective of the subject of conversation in which I am engaged, of the people with whom I find myself, goes on in that region of my head which is given over to music. Sometimes this is some preparatory work, i.e. finishing off details within the accompaniment of some already planned bit, while on another occasion a completely new, independent musical idea appears, and you try to retain it in your memory. Whence all this comes is an impenetrable secret.

Now I will outline for you my process of writing down my music.... I write my sketches on the first piece of paper which comes to hand, sometimes on a scrap of music manuscript paper. I write in a very abbreviated form. A melody can never appear in my head except with its harmony. Both these musical elements, together with the rhythm, can never be separated from each other, i.e. every melodic idea carries its own implicit harmony, and is unfailingly furnished with its own rhythmic structure. If the harmony is very complicated, then in the sketches I may happen to note down details of the part-writing. If the harmony is very simple, then sometimes I set out only the bass; sometimes I figure it, but on other occasions I do not outline the bass at all. I remember it. As for instrumentation, then if I have in mind the orchestra, the musical idea appears already coloured by this or that scoring. Sometimes, however, when I am scoring, my first intention is changed. Words can *never* be written after the music, for as soon as music is being composed to a text, then that text elicits an appropriate musical expression. You can, of course, attach or fit words to a trivial tune, but when the composition is a serious one, such a matching of words is unthinkable.... In exactly the same way you cannot write a symphonic work, and afterwards seek out a programme for it, for here again each episode of the chosen programme elicits a corresponding musical illustration.

This phase of work, i.e. the sketching, is very pleasant, absorbing, at times affords utterly indescribable delights, yet at the same time is accompanied by anxiety, by a certain nervous excitement. During this phase you sleep badly, sometimes you forget completely about food. On the other hand, the realisation of the project and its execution are carried out very peacefully and calmly. Scoring a work which is already ripe and which has been completed in my head down to the finest details, is very enjoyable. The same cannot be said of making a fair copy of piano pieces, songs, and of small pieces in general. This is sometimes boring....

You ask whether I keep to established forms. Yes and no. Certain kinds of composition imply the observance of a familiar form, for instance, *the symphony*. Here in general outlines I keep to the form established by tradition, but only in general outlines, i.e. in the sequence of the work's movements. In details you may diverge as much as you wish if the development of the idea in question demands it. Thus, for example, in *our* symphony the first movement is composed with very decided deviations. The second subject, which should be in the relative major, is in the [relative] minor and thus, in mine, remote. At the recapitulation in the first movement the second theme does not appear at all,[14] and so on. Its finale also consists of a whole string of departures from traditional form. In vocal music, where everything depends upon the text, and in fantasias (e.g. *The Tempest, Francesca*) the form is completely original....

Talking with you yesterday about the compositional process, I expressed myself inadequately about that work phase in which the sketch is brought to fulfilment. This phase is of capital importance. What was written in the heat of the moment must subsequently be critically scrutinised, amended, supplemented, and, in particular, abridged in the light of structural requirements. Sometimes one has to do oneself violence, be merciless and cruel to oneself, i.e. cut off completely bits which had been conceived with love and inspiration.

[14] Here Tchaikovsky was mistaken; the second subject does recur, though the first is drastically shortened.

If I cannot complain of poverty of fantasy and inventiveness, I have, on the other hand, always suffered from an inability to produce a finished form. Only by dogged labour have I now managed to make the form in my compositions correspond more or less to the content. In the past I was too casual, insufficiently aware of the full importance of a critical scrutiny of the sketches. Because of this the *seams* were always noticeable in my work, there was a lack of organic continuity in the sequence of separate episodes. This was a major defect, and only with the years have I begun little by little to put this right, but my works will never be *models of form*, for I can only improve, not completely eradicate the essential characteristics of my musical organism.[15]

If there remains with the reader any lingering trace of the illusion that Tchaikovsky was a neurotic, indiscriminate hysteric whose music gushed from him in vulgar, uncontrollable waves, these declarations must finally shatter it. Inspiration he certainly enjoyed, and this afforded the life force of his best pieces, but at the same time he was in his professional discipline as tireless, as lucid, and as truly self-critical as any composer who ever lived.

[15] *TPM*1, pp. 371–5, 377–8; *TLP*7, pp. 314–18, 320–1; *TZC*2, pp. 182–7.

7

SWITZERLAND AND ITALY:
VIOLIN CONCERTO

WITH THE APPALLING episode of his marriage and the tremendous achievements of the Fourth Symphony and *Onegin*, Tchaikovsky reached the watershed of his life. The catastrophe in his private world was to mark his personal existence for a long while: equally it marked his music. Soon he was composing as regularly as ever and with as much technical finesse, but something had gone out of the creative spirit. Though intermittently works of first-rate quality did come from him, it was not until the Manfred Symphony of 1885 that he truly regained his full stature. Thus the music of the next few years will not detain us as long as some of the most recent works. On the other hand, there is a sudden increase in the volume of documentary evidence from which his personal biography may be reconstructed. Nor is this solely the consequence of his correspondence with his new benefactress; his new circumstances, his growing reputation, and the lengthy periods he spent abroad naturally fostered more active lines of communication with his family, friends, and business acquaintances. In consequence, it is both possible and necessary to chart the course of his personal life in more detail than when dealing with the years preceding his encounter with Antonina. Yet, even allowing for this, the pace of narrative will begin to quicken a little, just as the balance between life and works will change.

The decision that Tchaikovsky, now he was a fugitive from marriage, should leave for Western Europe for an extended stay was as much a social as a medical measure. His precipitate arrival in St Petersburg on 7 October had sent his family and friends into a turmoil of activity to deal not only with Tchaikovsky himself but with all the consequences of his final break with Antonina. In Moscow everybody was gossiping about it. In an attempt to stem the rumours it was put about that there had been no separation, that the couple would be reunited in St Petersburg, and would then go abroad; in St Petersburg it was intimated that they would ultimately leave from Moscow. Tchaikovsky's presence in the Russian capital was played down. Only his stepmother was told the whole truth; as far as possible everything was concealed from Ilya Petrovich and from Zinaida, Tchaikovsky's half-sister, who was visiting their father with her younger children. Secrecy also required the removal of Antonina from Moscow. Not only would her continuing presence help to keep rumours buzzing – there was also a danger that she might begin to talk and thus feed gossip. To forestall this Nikolay Rubinstein and Anatoly gave her three hundred roubles and packed her off quietly to Odessa. Then Sasha undertook to handle her brother's dealings with Antonina, and before the end of October she had gone to the Black Sea resort, scoured it till she had traced her sister-in-law, and borne her back to Kamenka.

While the family was busy coping with the more personal consequences of Tchaikovsky's marital catastrophe, some of his colleagues were equally active in trying to set his future in order. It was desirable that he should have some plausible reason for remaining abroad for a lengthy period, and it was Karl Davïdov, now the director of the St Petersburg Conservatoire, who proposed that Tchaikovsky should be the Russian musical delegate to the Paris International Exhibition of 1878. Nikolay Rubinstein supported the suggestion, and through Anatoly obtained verbal agreement from Tchaikovsky even before the latter left Russia. This appointment might also afford some useful means of subsistence in the future, but there was need for immediate funds. This time it was Nikolay Rubinstein who took the initiative in seeing that his professional colleague should have some of the resources necessary for a prolonged convalescence before undertaking this more official responsibility, and he prevailed upon the Conservatoire to pay their absent professor some twelve or thirteen hundred roubles over the next academic year. Tchaikovsky certainly had good reason to realise at this moment of crisis that he had not only a loyal family but some very devoted friends.

When Anatoly shepherded his brother out of Russia on 13 October, the latter had already made a remarkably good physical recovery from the ordeal which had brought him to St Petersburg only a week before. His mental state was a very different matter. But, exhausted as he was, he recognised that he needed work not only to bring in some money but also to distract his mind. Major composition would still be out of the question for some time, he knew, but if Jurgenson would commission him to make arrangements or translations, or even to compose some little piano pieces or songs, he would very soon be able to respond, and on 17 October, the day after his arrival in Berlin, he hastened to notify his publisher-friend to this effect. Already his appetite had returned and he was again sleeping well, but the horrors of the past months constantly rose up before him, as did the memories of happier times. He paused only briefly in Berlin, and on 19 October he was in Geneva. Two years before he had enjoyed ten days in this city with Sasha and her family. It all came back so vividly now, he wrote to his sister, that he almost expected to meet her, her husband or one of their daughters in the street. 'Tolya and I went twice to look at 26 Boulevard Plainpalais. Your flat looked just the same, even the double windows remained. But it was empty. We looked with emotion and indescribable melancholy at the house where you lived for so long, where I spent several wonderful days, and where *Yury* came into the world.'[1] However, with so little money and a very unfavourable rate of exchange, Geneva proved beyond his pocket, and on 22 October the brothers moved to far cheaper, though very pleasant rooms in a lakeside pension at Clarens, on the outskirts of Montreux. Here they passed the next three weeks.

Exiled and lonely, despite Anatoly's company, Tchaikovsky's flow of letters increased. He was tormented by the fear that he had lost esteem in the eyes of his family, and that they might no longer love him. To Nadezhda von Meck he recounted the last days of his marriage, and made yet another embarrassed application for a loan. He was dreading the time when Anatoly would have to leave, especially since he feared that lack of money would deny him the company of his valet, Alexey Sofronov, as substitute for his brother. One thing delighted him: to hear from Anton Door, his former colleague, that Hans Richter had been much taken by the Third Symphony, and was planning to perform it with the Vienna Philharmonic Orchestra. The symphony was actually rehearsed, but regrettably the Philharmonic Society's authorities cancelled the public performance because the work was difficult and the composer virtually unknown in Vienna. Meanwhile, having as yet received no commissions from Jurgenson, and feeling his nerves were slowly becoming calmer, he resumed scoring *Onegin*, and requested that the unfinished materials of the Fourth Symphony should be sent him from Moscow. As usual when abroad, he had established a regular daily routine, and this included walks in the mountains and along the shore of Lake Geneva. He was feeling, however, that the very majesty of the environment was becoming oppressive, and he dreamed of going to Italy. 'Mountains are very fine, but it's very difficult for a Russian to stand their overwhelming grandeur for long. I'm dying for a plain, for a boundless distant prospect, for an expanse of open country, and for wide horizons,' he wrote to Albrecht.[2]

[1] *TLP6*, pp. 181–2; *TPR*, p. 298.   [2] *TLP6*, p. 195.

News had already reached him of the Conservatoire's generosity; now Mrs von Meck intervened even more liberally. She had answered his earlier letter from Clarens, and her joy at his rupture with Antonina was unconcealed. Feeling her rival to be routed, and realising that Tchaikovsky had now drawn even closer to her, she resolved to bind him yet more tightly by the gift of a thousand roubles which would clear his debts, adding the promise of a future monthly allowance of fifteen hundred. She realised, however, that Tchaikovsky, for all his financial worries, might recoil from indebting himself to a woman in such a way, and she showed considerable astuteness in setting out her reasons:

Perhaps I am not a person who is intimate with you, but you know how I love you, how I wish you all the best of everything – and in my view it is not blood and physical ties that give the right to this, but feelings and moral relationships between people – and you know how many happy moments you afford me, how deeply grateful I am to you for them, how necessary you are to me, and how for me you must be exactly that which you were created to be. Consequently I am not doing anything for you, but everything for myself. . . . And if I should need something from you, you would do it for me, wouldn't you? So this means that we are quits – and so please do not prevent me from giving my attention to your housekeeping, Pyotr Ilich![3]

Tchaikovsky was utterly seduced by these terms. Suddenly all his financial worries seemed to have vanished. His extravagant expressions of gratitude to his benefactress were sealed by a declaration that henceforth every note he set down would be dedicated to her, and he increased her sense of triumph over her rival by providing the description of Antonina for which Mrs von Meck had asked. It was a portrait as unflattering as anything for which she could have hoped, and she could credit it the more because Tchaikovsky did find a very few redeeming features in his wife. It confirmed Mrs von Meck's views upon one thing; she had been right never to send any of *her* daughters to boarding school.

Mrs von Meck's grant was to be of crucial importance to Tchaikovsky, for these monthly payments were continued until 1890, by which time his earnings from his own compositions were more than sufficient for him to live in complete comfort and security. It meant that forthwith he would be able to go where he wished, and that when Anatoly left, he could summon his valet from Russia. Nor need he proceed straight to Italy, and he and Anatoly could gratify their desire

[3] *TPM*1, pp. 51–2; *TZC*2, pp. 34–5.

to visit Paris for a few days, where Tchaikovsky also hoped to consult Dr Saligoux, the physician who had supervised his cure at Vichy the previous year. Fearing, however, that the extra expenditure this wide detour would involve might cause some people to ask how he had financed it in his apparently straitened circumstances, he kept this visit as secret as possible. Just as his correspondence with Mrs von Meck was an utterly private matter, so was the new pecuniary arrangement she had made for him, and only his twin brothers, of all his family, were freely informed of it. Kotek knew, and circumstances soon compelled Tchaikovsky to confess the arrangement to Nikolay Rubinstein (he also agreed that Albrecht, who handled the Conservatoire's financial transactions, might be told if necessary). Sasha and Lev were informed later. But regarding his present position, most other people, even such a close friend as Jurgenson, were to believe that his only regular income was the Conservatoire's monthly allowance of some hundred roubles.

Jurgenson had responded to his request for work by commissioning translations, from Italian into Russian, of the texts of five vocal pieces Glinka had composed in the late 1820s, and in addition Tchaikovsky invented words for a vocal quartet, *Prayer*, by the same composer. But he now demurred when Jurgenson asked him to make piano transcriptions of Glinka's two Spanish overtures, pleading that for such work he had to have a piano available. As for the songs and piano pieces which Jurgenson also wanted, Tchaikovsky postponed the composition of these until the following year. A week or so earlier he had been invited to contribute a piece to a volume that was to mark the unveiling of a memorial to Bellini, but had not been able to set down a single worthwhile note. For the moment the composition even of such a trifle as this was beyond him.

While it is certainly true that his mental condition continued to improve at Clarens, there was no removing the basic causes of his distress, and he was constantly agitated by bulletins from Russia. For all his gratitude to Sasha for taking care of Antonina, he was alarmed by his wife's extended stay at Kamenka. Here lived so many of those most dear to him. Even with no more than they already knew, he felt he would be quite unable to face them, and with Antonina present to poison further their minds, he feared they would spurn him even more. Antonina wrote him letters which alternately accused and cajoled him. Some of her charges were wild; in one letter to Anatoly she even voiced a suspicion that Tchaikovsky's former servant, Mikhail, in revenge for having lost his post through his master's marriage, had had Tchaikovsky bewitched to make him hate her. Such endlessly reiterated reproaches drove Tchaikovsky frantic, and he easily imagined from these something of how she was indoctrinating the Kamenka clan, for she accused him explicitly of using her. He reported her charges to Modest: 'I was a deceiver who had married her *to shield myself*. Every day I had insulted her, I had caused her much suffering, she was horrified at my shameful vice, and so on, and so on.'[4] Constantly in his letters to members of his family he cried out for their continuing love and forgiveness; yet he equally insisted that there could never be any question of the reconciliation with Antonina which both Sasha and Modest were attempting to engineer.

Both she and you, it seems, suppose that a rapprochement will sometime be possible [he wrote to his sister on 7 November]. Now with threats, reproaches, and accusations of dishonourable behaviour – now, conversely, with expressions of love and tenderness (such as today) she is trying vainly to get somewhere. For God's sake let's drop for ever the question of our reconciliation. I'm not in dispute with her. She didn't wish to do me ill, and I'm not accusing her of anything. Even if you're right that she is goodhearted, even if I'm guilty all round because I've not known how to appreciate her, even if it's true she loves me – yet live with her I *cannot, cannot, cannot*. Demand of me whatever satisfaction you will for her: when I return to Russia I'll give her two-thirds of my earnings, I'll hide myself in any backwood you like, I'm prepared to become a beggar – in a word, anything you like – but for God's sake never hint to me that I should return to A[ntonina] I[vanovna]. Very likely I've got an *illness* – but it's an incurable illness. In a word, in the fullest sense of the expression, *I do not love her*![5]

Though once again the magic of Paris worked upon Tchaikovsky, it had insufficient power to dispel his depression. When he arrived there on 13 November he hastened to seek out Dr Saligoux, only to discover that he did not practise during the winter. He approached another doctor about his gastric catarrh, but found the consultation thoroughly unsatisfactory, and within 48 hours he was on his way to Rome. Feeling unwell, he broke his journey for two days in Florence. The physical disorder quickly passed: the sickness of the spirit did not. While Anatoly rushed off for a couple of hours to the Pitti Palace, Tchaikovsky unburdened himself to Mrs von Meck:

When I was living in Clarens in absolute peace and quiet and in a very simple and comfortable situation, I was sometimes melancholy and depressed. Not knowing how to account for these attacks of melancholy, I imagined that their cause was – the mountains!!! How naive! The causes of those very brief attacks of melancholy were purely inner ones. I imagined also that I had only to cross the Italian frontier, and never-ending happiness would begin. What nonsense! Here I am a hundred times more melancholy! The weather is wonderful, by day it is as hot as in July, there is something to look at, something to provide diversion – but a massive, gigantic depression torments me. And the livelier the place I am in, the worse it is![6]

At six in the morning the next day, 19 November, the brothers were in Rome, where Tchaikovsky promptly resumed his lament to his patroness. The city made him even more distraught. 'I literally cannot bear any noise. Both yesterday in Florence and here today, every passing carriage drives me mad, every cry, every sound tears at my nerves. The mass of people moving through the narrow streets begins to irritate me so much that each stranger who comes towards me appears to be a rabid foe.'[7] Worst of all, not a single letter awaited him – only a notification from Clarens that the package containing his Fourth Symphony material had been forwarded to Rome. Realising he could not abide the Italian capital, he conferred with Anatoly. There was no point in proceeding to Naples, they decided, and since in a fortnight Anatoly had to return to Russia, it was essential that Alexey Sofronov should now join Tchaikovsky. To ensure that he might enjoy Anatoly's company to the last possible moment, Tchaikovsky proposed to accompany his brother as far as Vienna where Alexey might meet them. Then he intended to return with his servant to Clarens, where he had been more calm and where he had been able to do some work. For the moment, however, he needed to delay until the packet containing his symphony arrived, as well as the latest instalment of Mrs von Meck's allowance. Then he and Anatoly would spend what time remained to them in Venice, where it would also be quiet and where he hoped some work would prove possible. And he harboured thoughts of a further joy which might await him when he finally arrived in Clarens; perhaps Modest and Kolya Konradi would be able to join him there. But when he proposed to write to Kolya's father for such permission, Anatoly dissuaded him.

Tchaikovsky delayed three more days in Rome, enduring agonies through the delays at the post office, caused, it turned out, through

[6] TPM1, pp. 67–8; TLP6, p. 221; TZC2, p. 40.
[7] TPM1, p. 69; TLP6, p. 223; TZC2, p. 41.

mis-shelving of his mail. Though he said that the rôle of tourist was for the moment abhorrent to him, he visited the Vatican, St Peter's, the Capitol, the Borghese Palace, and the Colosseum. He said he did sightseeing mainly to please Anatoly, yet there is no doubt that his own responses were reviving. He admitted that he was never the most fervent admirer of the visual arts, and that he found a large diet of such riches indigestible. But usually one or two single pieces or places would catch his attention and receive close examination – such as, on this occasion, the statue of the dying gladiator in the Capitol (so much finer, he felt significantly, than the statue of Venus), or Domenichino's *Last Communion of St Jerome* in the Vatican. It was in rather better spirits than on his arrival that Tchaikovsky left Rome on 22 November, with both the symphony and his benefactress's money in his possession.

The quiet of Venice soothed further his nerves, and he found the urge to steep himself in the city's ambience irresistible. Even the narrow streets in this place appealed to him, especially in the evenings when they were illuminated by the gas lights in the shops. Best of all, he found he could work again, and he completed the scoring of Act 2, Scene 1 of *Onegin*. Soon he was debating with himself the possibility of returning here instead of to Clarens after Anatoly's departure. Only one thing really distressed him: the partiality of the Venetian press towards the Turks in their war with Russia, with the newsvendors crying out every evening tidings of Turkish victories. It reached a point where he could bear it no longer. 'Yesterday I lost my temper,' he told Mrs von Meck on 30 November, 'and I accosted one of the shouters: "Ma dovè la vittoria?" It appeared that by "vittoria" he meant Turkish news of some reconnaissance where a few hundred Russians had allegedly been defeated. "Is that really a victory?" I went on to ask him in a stern voice. I did not properly understand his reply, but he stopped shouting about "vittoria".... Today, when I went past the *shouter*, he bowed courteously to me, and instead of "grande vittoria di Turchi", with which the other newsboys were filling the air, he called after me "Grande combattimento a Plevna, vittoria dei Russi!" I knew he was lying, but I liked it as a manifestation of delicacy in an ordinary man.'[8] Had it been ten days later this announcement would have been the truth. Tchaikovsky simply could not see the ridiculous side of this incident, for he was as emotionally involved in his country's struggle as he had been a year earlier when he had composed his Slavonic March. But now his compositional faculties were still too stunned for him to be able to answer Jurgenson's request for another march, this time to celebrate the exploits of General Skobelev against Russia's enemy.

[8] *TPM*1, p. 86; *TLP*6, pp. 243–4; *TZC*2, p. 47.

Tchaikovsky spent nine delightful days in Venice, and before leaving for Vienna on 1 December, he had found accommodation to which he could return with Alexey. Despite his imminent parting with Anatoly, his spirits continued to be good. He remained some twelve days in the Austrian capital, longer than he had expected because certain formalities had delayed the departure of Alexey from Moscow. Part of the time had to be devoted to putting the final touches to the fourth scene of *Onegin*, the score of which Anatoly was to take back to Moscow. Tchaikovsky had no wish to meet the local musicians, especially Door, and so he did not appear at any concerts where he might be recognised. But in the darkness of the opera house it was easier to remain hidden, and he saw Cherubini's *Les Deux Journées*, an opera he did not know, and which delighted him. Even more was he enchanted by the ballet which followed. 'Never before has there been a ballet with such grace, such melodic and rhythmic richness, such superlative scoring,' he enthused to Mrs von Meck two days later. 'Without any false modesty I tell you that *Swan Lake* is not fit to hold a candle to [Delibes's] *Sylvia*.'[9] To Taneyev he was even more severe on his own work: 'If I had known this music [*Sylvia*] earlier, I would not, of course, have written *Swan Lake*.'[10] Seeing *Die Walküre* confirmed in him his own earlier judgement that Wagner was really a symphonist by nature. Another musical experience which gave him no pleasure was playing through Brahms's recent First Symphony with Kotek in the arrangement for piano duet. 'God, what a loathsome thing it is!' he exclaimed to Kashkin. 'I think that music's whole future is now in *France*.'[11] Kotek was also in Vienna, and having his unexpected company was another of Tchaikovsky's pleasures. Then, on 11 December, despite Tchaikovsky's prediction that his valet's utter ignorance of any language except Russian would produce many 'tragi-comic episodes' on the way, Alexey arrived safe and sound, and Anatoly could now delay his return no longer. The next day he departed. The day before, Tchaikovsky had been overwrought at the prospect of separation, but this was as nothing compared to his distracted, even hysterical state once his brother had gone. He lingered two further days to look after Kotek, who was indisposed, and to please Alexey, and then returned to Venice. However, before leaving Vienna, he did one thing which he hoped might bring him future happiness. Now that Anatoly was no longer present to restrain him, he wrote to Konradi senior, asking him to allow Modest and Kolya to come to Western Europe.

[9] *TPM*1, p. 96; *TLP*6, pp. 256–7; *YDGC*, p. 156.
[10] *TLP*6, p. 294; *TPB*, p. 578; *TTP*, p. 21.
[11] *TLP*6, p. 260.

The journey back to Venice was terrible, especially since Tchaikovsky found himself in the very same train compartment in which he had travelled to Vienna with Anatoly. On arriving in Venice he felt so overcome by misery that he got thoroughly drunk, repeating this exercise more than once in the following days. Yet the most terrible evidence of just how deeply disturbed he was at this moment is provided by something found in Tchaikovsky's own library after his death: a copy of three Euripides tragedies in a Latin edition printed in Antwerp in 1581. Inscribed in Tchaikovsky's own hand is the following: 'Stolen from the library of the Palace of the Doges in Venice on 15 December 1877 by Pyotr Tchaikovsky, court counsellor and professor at the conservatoire.'[12]

Tchaikovsky returned to Venice nearly destitute. Always improvident and generous, he had doubtless ensured that Anatoly was well provided for on the journey to Russia. In order to return to Venice, however, he had to borrow from Kotek, and when he arrived back in Italy he had only thirty lire in his pocket. In Venice another misfortune awaited him: Mrs von Meck had not sent his December allowance, and soon his funds were down to only three lire. Nevertheless he managed to continue the work he had already begun on the Fourth Symphony, and completing this from his sketches was his main occupation during the next weeks. Again his daily routine became fixed. He got up at eight, drank tea, worked till eleven, and then breakfasted. There followed a walk with Alexey till one or one-thirty, and work until five, when dinner was served. Finally a walk by himself until eight, after which tea. Though Alexey usually retired to bed early, Tchaikovsky often remained up until the early hours reading journals and books (currently he was immersed in Thackeray's *Pendennis* and an illustrated biography of Napoleon), and writing letters. The volume of his correspondence, already considerable in Clarens, continued to swell, for in this he could find emotional release. Some of his letters to Mrs von Meck in particular were becoming longer and more personal; religious belief and (on her side) disbelief had already become a special subject of confession and debate. For Anatoly he began to compile a diary.

A more settled personal state was also fostered by news from Kamenka. While he was still in Vienna he heard that Antonina had finally become too much for Sasha and Lev, and that the sympathy which Sasha in particular had been inclined to show to her sister-in-law had cooled. They wanted to be rid of her, but Antonina proved reluctant to be dislodged, and Lev had asked Anatoly on his return to

---

[12] *TPM*1, p. 577. 'Court counsellor' was the civil service rank to which Tchaikovsky was entitled by his final examination performance at the School of Jurisprudence.

Russia to journey to Kamenka and conduct her back to Moscow and her own family. Now, in Venice, Tchaikovsky himself received letters from both Sasha and Lev which made it clear that he was fully redeemed in their eyes. Once Antonina had left Kamenka he knew there would be one place in Russia where he would be able to find a haven.

Meanwhile Alexey's cheerful personality, and the ease and contentment with which he had settled into his Venetian existence gave Tchaikovsky much pleasure and reassurance. There was both reassurance and delight, too, in hearing from Albrecht that his Moscow colleagues were enchanted with the first act of *Onegin*. Then only two days after his return to the Italian city came a telegram from Modest to say that the elder Konradi had agreed that Modest and Kolya should spend some time in Europe. Venice itself could regain from time to time something of its charm for Tchaikovsky; only the persistent smell remained intolerable. At last on 18 December he received a double instalment of his allowance from Mrs von Meck, and within a week Modest notified him that Sanremo had been chosen as the place where he and Kolya were to settle first, and that they were to leave Russia on 1 January. Tchaikovsky promptly set his own departure for 28 December so that he might arrange their lodgings in Sanremo. The day before, his conscience uneasy that he had not delivered any of the promised translations to Jurgenson, he sat down to finish what he could. For all his veneration of Glinka, he could find little to praise in these pieces, and some of the work Jurgenson had requested of him he declined to do, considering that it would be performing no service to Glinka's reputation. Tactfully he asked to be excused such toil in the future.

On the way to Sanremo Tchaikovsky paused briefly in both Milan and Genoa. Milan Cathedral he judged one of the most beautiful things he had ever seen, and he climbed to the top to enjoy the view of the city and the surrounding countryside. An abominable performance in Genoa two evenings later strengthened his opinion that Meyerbeer's *L'Africaine* was a dreary opera; again he found pleasure in climbing a church tower for a panoramic prospect of the city. At Sanremo, where he arrived the next evening, he quickly settled down to proceed as far as he could with the symphony before Modest and his charge arrived.

Hardly had he begun than he was distracted by other business. On 2 January there arrived the official notification of his appointment as delegate to the Paris Exhibition. That Tchaikovsky now found himself embarrassingly cornered was entirely his own fault. While in Venice he had been formally asked whether he would accept the appointment if offered, but by now he was unenthusiastic at the prospect, and he had replied that acceptance would be possible only if a fee were paid him. He thought this condition would close the matter; now he was told that he would receive a monthly allowance of one thousand francs for eight months. Dismayed at what was required of him and by the need to leave promptly for Paris, but tempted by the fee offered, he first thought he would have to accept, then vacillated for two days, drank a lot, and finally decided.

'I *cannot* go to Paris. It's not *cowardice*, it's not *indolence*, but I can't,' he wrote to Nikolay Rubinstein on 4 January. 'All these three days, from the moment I received news of my appointment, I've been thoroughly ill, I've been going out of my mind.... I cannot *see people*.... Quiet, quiet, quiet and work – these are the two things I now need.'[13] Rubinstein, because he had been a party to securing Tchaikovsky's appointment in the first place, was furious, and was to accuse Tchaikovsky of preferring to be the plaything of a wealthy woman. Tchaikovsky was even to entertain a suspicion (quite unfounded, as it turned out) that Rubinstein, being convinced that Mrs von Meck's generosity was ruining the composer, had told his benefactress that he knew of her arrangement with Tchaikovsky, and had attempted to persuade her to cut off his funds. His suspicion of Rubinstein's malevolence was to be further fostered by the director's angry response to his dereliction of the Paris delegateship. Deeply offended by Rubinstein's accusations and insinuations, and with his indignation exacerbated by discomfort at his own conduct, Tchaikovsky was to berate Rubinstein, and defend himself furiously.

His resentment at what he felt to be Rubinstein's autocratic (and certainly, at times, tactless) attitude towards him had already found expression in a verbal portrait in an earlier missive to Mrs von Meck, and this fresh evidence of the Moscow despot's imperiousness was to be the subject of much bitter comment in Tchaikovsky's letters from Sanremo, especially in those to his patroness. But Rubinstein's anger had much justification. Except for Mrs von Meck, no one felt Tchaikovsky had behaved irreproachably, and both Albrecht and Kashkin were to join their reproofs to Rubinstein's wrath; the repercussions of his withdrawal were to ring in Tchaikovsky's ears during the weeks ahead. For the moment, however, although his conscience was much troubled by his retreat, he hoped that the matter could be considered closed, and he once again buried himself in the symphony. When he had first resumed work upon it in Vienna it had proved merely hard labour, but by now he was revelling in the piece,

[13] *TLP6*, p. 325; *TPM1*, p. 579; *TZC2*, pp. 71–2; *YDGC*, p. 161 (partial).

and he attributed his sudden surge of good morale to the joy he was finding in his work upon it. On 7 January it was done.

The matter of the Paris delegateship was not the only thing to trouble Tchaikovsky during his first days alone at Sanremo. Anatoly had at last managed to remove Antonina to Moscow, but a new horror arose in Tchaikovsky's mind – that she might still be there when he returned to the Conservatoire the following autumn. More tormenting still was the absence of any communication from Mrs von Meck. Had she found out about his homosexuality? 'Of course, with my characteristic suspiciousness I already suspected she had fallen out of love with me, that she knew about *that*, and wished to break off all relations,' he wrote to Anatoly on 5 January,[14] having that morning at last received a letter from her. Then came a message from Milan. Modest and Kolya had arrived, but the latter was ill. The next day, 8 January, Tchaikovsky rushed off thither.

Tchaikovsky's relationships with each of his twin brothers were quite distinct. Though Anatoly frequently solicited and received vast doses of moral support from him, he felt that he could in turn lean upon Anatoly, especially during these difficult months, gaining assurance and some sense of protection from the company of this brother who possessed qualities he himself did not. Certainly Anatoly had an authority with him which was lacking in his twin. Modest, homosexual also, was more like Tchaikovsky himself, who recognised this and experienced both comfort and exasperation in consequence of it. Once he had privately admitted that he preferred Anatoly, yet he does not seem to have achieved with him that particular closeness he found possible with Modest. For all the tensions and anxieties Anatoly experienced in his government service, he was by nature gregarious and socially confident, and he possessed no real talent for music. He could sing a little, but his violin playing was 'extremely bad', Tchaikovsky unsparingly told Mrs von Meck, though he had a certain amount of taste. By contrast, Modest, while not musically endowed, was a private individual like Tchaikovsky himself, and artistically far more sensitive than Anatoly. With Kolya present they could make up a kind of family, with Tchaikovsky as father and Modest in the rôle of mother. It was the nearest Tchaikovsky was ever to come to satisfying his yearning for an ordinary, domestic life. The degree to which this little deaf-mute was to arouse his tender responses is clear from his report to Mrs von Meck on 13 January 1878:

[14] *TPM*1, p. 579; *TPR*, p. 343; *TLP*6, pp. 336–7 (with the veiled reference to his homosexuality omitted).

Kolya makes me infinitely happy. It was lovely to observe how, even in those few months since I last saw him, he has already managed to achieve a great deal both in verbal pronunciation and in grammar under the guidance of my brother. He has developed a lot. His ability and, in particular, his memory are amazing. It's very interesting to observe such a clever child in such an exceptional position as a result of his handicap. As for his disposition, his goodness, his sweetness, his tenderness, he is one of the very best human characters I have ever seen. All in all, he is a being created to inspire love and tenderness in all around.[15]

There were disturbing signs of a homosexual undertone in the relationship, too, for on the same day he wrote in less bridled terms to Anatoly. 'What a joy to have near such a child; how nice it is to cherish and caress him!'[16]

Reunited with Modest, Tchaikovsky again visited Milan Cathedral and the convent of Sta Maria delle Grazie to see Leonardo da Vinci's *Last Supper*. Deprived of the chance of attending the first night at La Scala of Gounod's *Cinq-Mars* because of the death of King Victor Emmanuel II, and the consequent closing of the theatres, they proceeded to Genoa for a day before settling in at Sanremo on 12 January.

At the Italian resort their 'family' life continued, and in such domestic closeness Tchaikovsky's nerves grew calmer still, and his mental state became yet more composed. Modest and Kolya were delighted with Sanremo, but Tchaikovsky was less contented; in particular he could not bear the olive trees that covered the surrounding hills. He would have much preferred to be in Clarens. He continued his diary to Anatoly, chronicling their excursions on foot or by donkey into the hills and their walks along the shore, their ailments, his visits to the opera with Modest, as well as all the minutiae of daily living. The relationship between Modest and Kolya was frequently tempestuous, for the frail deaf-mute's impediment to self-expression caused vast reservoirs of frustration to build up within him, and a mild reproof could precipitate a violent emotional outburst, screams, and a flood of tears. But reconciliation always followed swiftly between master and pupil. Often, when Tchaikovsky was working, Kolya would come into his room and ask innumerable questions about the score, questions which Tchaikovsky was always ready to answer, especially since he was finding it more and more easy to understand Kolya's speech. He took immense pleasure also in Modest's efforts as guardian and teacher –

[15] *TPM*1, pp. 143–4; *TLP*7, p. 13.
[16] *TPM*1, p. 580; *TPR*, p. 345; *TLP*7, p. 18 (with the second sentence omitted).

and discovered yet another cause for pride when Modest suddenly produced part of a novel he had been writing and read a couple of chapters to his brother. Tchaikovsky, greatly impressed by these signs of talent and diligence, made Modest promise to complete this literary prodigy before he returned to Russia.

Now that the Fourth Symphony was finished, his own efforts were focused upon *Onegin*, and he completed it in three weeks. As for the symphony, he had posted the score of that to Rubinstein from Milan, and he offered the work to Jurgenson free of charge, together with the Rococo Variations and the *Valse-scherzo* for violin and orchestra. Even for *Onegin* he told Jurgenson he would accept only the royalties on performances.

His own financial affairs were in fact in utter chaos, largely due, it would seem, to Alexey. Shortly after they had settled in Sanremo it had been discovered, to the brothers' horror, that the valet had contracted a venereal disease. While in Florence they had suspected him of amorous escapades; now the consequences revealed themselves, and Tchaikovsky and Modest bore a protesting and badly frightened Alexey off to a doctor. His treatment would delay their departure, and he had to be removed to a maison de santé where the additional rental and the medical expenses made unforeseen inroads into Tchaikovsky's exchequer. The crisis was greatly alleviated when Mrs von Meck sent him fifteen hundred francs to defray publication costs of the symphony. Tchaikovsky immediately drafted a thousand of these towards his current expenses, and set aside five hundred to commission a piano-duet transcription of the new work; yet it seems that finally this money, too, was swallowed up by more pressing personal needs. Nor was this the end of Mrs von Meck's openhandedness: three weeks later she sent him another double instalment of three thousand francs augmented by a further thousand.

Such gifts merely restored the situation briefly. Despite this, Tchaikovsky's personal insolvency never seemed to have the slightest effect upon his generosity to others. Before leaving Moscow he had committed himself to helping a young student violinist, Alexandr Litvinov, and he insisted upon continuing this subsidy. Such help to young students was to be repeated on future occasions. He showed equal liberality in the monthly allowance he proposed to make to Antonina. During all the time since he had left her, even when her behaviour was causing him most distress because it was driving a wedge between him and his sister, he insisted that she was blameless, that the responsibility for the marriage ever having taken place was his alone, and that he must give her proper alimony, so long as she would leave him alone and make no effort to contact his relatives. By now, however, his pity was turning to contempt, and when Jurgenson, who, with Rubinstein, was attempting to keep some control over Tchaikovsky's financial affairs in Russia, commented that Tchaikovsky's allocation of one hundred roubles a month to his wife was very liberal, the composer disclosed a less laudable motive for his generosity. 'Only with money can I buy myself the right to *despise* her as much as I *hate* her!' he confessed on 13 January.[17]

Tchaikovsky and his companions remained some five and a half weeks in Sanremo, with a break in Nice from 3 to 5 February (days most memorable for the journey along the Corniches, and for a visit to the menagerie so that Kolya could see the animal-trainer), and a day-trip on 14 February to Monaco to avoid having to meet Mikhail Azanchevsky, the former director of the St Petersburg Conservatoire, now living in Nice. Tchaikovsky was still possessed by a horror of meeting people, and hearing of Azanchevsky's intention of coming to Sanremo to see him, he instructed his hotelier to tell the unwanted guest that he had left for Genoa two days before. He was the more horrified to discover, on returning from a delightful day in Monte Carlo, that Azanchevsky had taken a room for the night at his hotel. Tchaikovsky evaded his pursuer successfully, but being fearful that Azanchevsky, whom he liked, would discover the truth, he resolved to write him a letter of confession when they arrived in Florence.

On 19 February Tchaikovsky and his companions set out for Pisa. He described the improvement in his health to Anatoly on the eve of his departure:

Thanks to the regularity of my life, to the sometimes tedious but always inviolable calm, and above all, thanks to time which heals all wounds, I have completely recovered from my *insanity*. There's no doubt that for some months on end I was a bit *insane*, and only now, when I'm completely recovered, have I learned to relate *objectively* to everything which I did during my brief insanity. That man who in May took it into his head to marry A[ntonina] I[vanovna], who during June wrote a whole opera as though nothing had happened, who in July married, who in September fled from his wife, who in November railed at Rome and so on – that man wasn't I, but another Pyotr Ilich.[18]

The good spirits he bore away from Sanremo were, however, briefly

[17] *TLP*7, p. 17; *TPJ*1, p. 27.
[18] *TLP*7, p. 98; *TPR*, p. 367; *YDGC*, p. 170 (partial).

clouded by sad news from Russia. On 25 January Zinaida had died in Orenburg. For her children, whose father had died two years before, Tchaikovsky felt a deep sorrow, and an even deeper anxiety over the effect upon his father when the news was at last broken to him. Tchaikovsky himself had never been close to his half-sister. She was eleven years older than he; the eldest of her six children were all but grown up, and he had not seen her in fifteen years. He could not pretend that his own grief was profound or long-lived, and in Pisa he forthwith engaged in a vigorous round of sightseeing of the sort from which he had shrunk only a couple of months before. His ultimate goal was Florence. Just as in 1876 he had delighted in watching Modest's reactions to new environments and experiences on the latter's very first trip abroad, so now he wanted to observe his brother's delight in the artistic cornucopia of this wonderful Italian city. They paused only two days in Pisa, admiring the cathedral and, above all, the famous leaning tower which they climbed for the spectacular view. On 21 February they were in Florence. 'What a nice, sympathetic city!' Tchaikovsky wrote to Nadezhda von Meck that evening. 'I experienced a very pleasant feeling as I entered it and recalled how I was two months ago in this same Florence. What a change there has been in my spirit since then! What a pitiful sick man I then was, and how hale and hearty am I now!'[19]

Once again, in response to a distraught letter from Anatoly, he displayed that admirable capacity for fraternal advice which had been of such service to the twins in the past. Recognising that Anatoly was not a person out of the ordinary, he told him so with infinite tact, and counselled him to abandon any unrealistic hopes he might have for spectacular success in the eyes of the world. Instead he urged him to place his trust in the breadth of his talents and in the abundance of sympathetic qualities in his own character. All his more capable friends, he said, had endured the same sort of doubts and torments which Anatoly was suffering, and he supported his advice by reference to his own experience:

There are no sufferings more fruitless than those caused by excessive self-esteem. I say this because I myself constantly suffered from it, and was likewise never satisfied with those results which I did achieve. Perhaps you'll say that because they write about me in the papers, I am well known, and must be happy and contented. Yet this is of little importance to me – et j'ai toujours voulu péter plus haut que mon cul. I wanted to be not only the first composer in Russia but

[19] *TPM*1, p. 201; *TLP*7, p. 103; *TZC*2, p. 107.

in the whole world. I wanted to be not only a composer, but also a first class conductor. I wanted to be *unusually* wise and a *person* who knew a colossal amount. I wanted also to be elegant and fashionable, and to be able to shine in salons. There was little I did not want. Only bit by bit, at the price of a whole series of unbearable sufferings, did I come to a realisation of my true worth. . . . How many secret torments did I endure before I was convinced that I was quite incapable of being a conductor! How much time was needed for me to arrive at the conviction that I belonged to the category of *people who are quite intelligent*, and not to those whose mind has some outstanding feature! How many years did I need to realise that, even as a composer, I'm just a talented person, and not some exceptional phenomenon![20]

Yet a man who, now in early middle age, can write so openly and objectively about his own disappointments and frustrations, must also be a man who has come to be fully confident in his own abilities, who is fulfilled by, and satisfied with his own achievement. In fact his self-depreciating assessment was at least a little disingenuous, as he himself must have recognised, for to Mrs von Meck he wrote another letter in which without diffidence he described to her the fame he had already achieved in Western Europe, and expressed his high hopes for the future of his own music. On this European trip he had seen much evidence that his compositions were gaining wide currency. In Vienna he had discovered his own works in arrangements about which he knew nothing – such as the Andante cantabile of the First String Quartet arranged for flute. A pirated edition of some of his piano works had appeared in Leipzig, and he had found German editions of his songs. He had good grounds for confidence, and he knew this perfectly well.

Tchaikovsky's delight in Florence continued throughout his fortnight's stay. He explored its glories in leisurely fashion, being especially impressed by the chapel of the Medicis which led him to draw a comparison between Michelangelo and Beethoven. But while Modest, who was a voracious devotee of the visual arts, could not have enough of the city's galleries, palaces, and churches, Tchaikovsky gained an equal pleasure from simply strolling round the streets and in the city's outskirts. Since there was currently no opera to be heard in Florence, the brothers patronised the spoken drama for their evening entertainment, visiting spectacles which ranged from a production of *Hamlet* to a curious melodrama-cum-harlequinade of local provenance.

Tchaikovsky's time was not entirely devoted to self-gratification, however. While completing *Onegin* and the Fourth Symphony he had

[20] *TLP*7, p. 115; *TPR*, pp. 373–4 (with French quotation omitted).

been sometimes compelled to create a modicum of new music, but this had been merely to supplement or realise more fully the existing sketches. In Florence, on the second day of his stay, he wrote a completely new song on Lermontov's 'The love of a dead man'. At last, after a gap of many months, he was beginning to compose again. Tchaikovsky had brought with him to Western Europe no store of Russian poetry, and his choice of text for this new song had been determined by circumstances; it was simply that Mrs von Meck had quoted Lermontov's poem in one of her letters as evidence to support her opinions on the relationship between poetry and music. The Tchaikovsky whose conceptual faculties had remained so long incapable of creating anything from the promptings of his own inner life must have been almost surprised by the sudden strength of his own response to this grim outburst from another man struck down by fate. The tread of a stepwise bass, ascending and descending remorselessly, and a vocal line which mingles a leaden monotone with cries of powerful anguish, provide a sternly austere but forceful rejoinder to Lermontov's monologue of a dead man recollecting the joys and still living passions of his vanished life. Spurred on by this proof that his creative faculties could be reawakened, Tchaikovsky asked Mrs von Meck to hunt out and send him more texts to set out of the works of Alexey Tolstoy, Fet, Mey, and Tyutchev. A similar request was sent to Kashkin.

Before leaving Florence on 7 March Tchaikovsky had composed at least two more pieces. One was a trifle for the piano, *Rêverie interrompue* (later published as No. 12 of Twelve Pieces (moderate difficulty), Op. 40), which employed a tune Tchaikovsky had noted down from a street singer in Venice two months before. Since on 26 February Tchaikovsky had declared to Anatoly his intention of composing a piano piece each day, it is probable that others of the Op. 40 set were finished in Florence. The remaining piece known to have been conceived in Florence was also based upon an item in the repertoire of a street singer. During his brief stay in the city in the preceding November Tchaikovsky had been profoundly stirred by the accomplishments of a boy of about eleven, Vittorio, who performed to a guitar accompaniment. 'He sang with a marvellous, rich voice, with a finish and warmth such as one rarely encounters in professional artists,' he had written to Mrs von Meck.[21] Now – and it is evident that Tchaikovsky's sexual nature played a part in this – he confided to Anatoly that to find this captivating singer was his main aim in

---

[21] *TPM*1, pp. 124–5; *TLP*6, p. 309. Another boy singer, Amici, is briefly mentioned in Tchaikovsky's letters from Rome in March 1880.

Florence. Finally, having enlisted the aid of a local inhabitant, he located the boy, and a meeting was arranged.

Precisely at nine o'clock I went to the place where the man who had promised to find him was to await me [he wrote to his brother]. The man was there, and a group of other men were also awaiting me with curiosity – and in the centre of all this was our boy. The first thing I noticed was that he had grown a little, and that he was *beautiful*, whereas before he had seemed to us to be plain. Because the throng was still growing and it was a crowded spot, I set off a little in the direction of the Cascino. On the way I expressed doubt as to whether it was he. 'When I sing you'll know it's me. On the previous occasion you gave me a silver half-franc piece.' All this was spoken in a wonderful voice, and penetrated to the depths of my soul. But what became of me when he sang? It's impossible to describe. I do not believe that you get greater pleasure when you are listening to the singing of P[anayeva]. I wept, broke down, languished with delight. Besides the song which you know, he sang two new ones of which one, 'Pimpinella', is delightful.[22]

Two days later he saw Vittorio again. 'He appeared at midday *in costume* on account of it being the closing days of the carnival, accompanied by two moustached minions, also in costume. Only then did I examine him. He is positively *beautiful* with an expressibly sympathetic look and smile. He is better when heard in the street than in a room; there he is cramped, and doesn't fully open up his voice. I wrote down all his songs. Then I took him off to be photographed.'[23] Tchaikovsky arranged that two days hence, on the eve of his departure, Vittorio would come to him again and sing. But the boy did not appear; he had a sore throat, and Tchaikovsky had to leave Florence, taking with him as the fruits of this encounter the transcriptions of Vittorio's songs. Within a week he had used 'Pimpinella' as the basis of a romance. Though in the sharpest possible contrast to 'The love of a dead man', 'Pimpinella' likewise sprang from a creativity prompted by outside stimulus, not this time the impact of a poem, but the magic of a personality. Yet Tchaikovsky was not so bemused by this enchanting

[22] *TLP*7, p. 134; *TPR*, p. 379; *TPM*1, p. 585; *TPB*, p. 151. Alexandra Panayeva was a soprano with whom Anatoly was currently emotionally involved. Tchaikovsky was to dedicate to her his Seven Romances, Op. 47. The text of this letter, as printed in *TLP*7, reveals that Tchaikovsky had 'with difficulty' to extricate himself from an 'amorous rendezvous' to meet Vittorio; mention of this is excluded even from the normally far more complete text of *TPR*.

[23] *TLP*7, p. 134; *TPR*, pp. 379–80; *TPB*, p. 152. See illustrations following p. 192.

singer as to be a slave to the original tune as he noted it down in his letter to Mrs von Meck of 4 March, and he modified it, changing the phrase ends to introduce a mild declamatory element totally absent from the original (Ex. 145a) but which is, regrettably, more feeble as

Ex. 145

melody (Ex. 145b) than the source tune. No better is the original music he devised for verse three, though it widened a little the expressive world of Vittorio's song; nor had the sudden tonal twist at the end of the fourth and final verse anything to do with the musical world of Florentine street singers, but was simply a kind of chromatic shock treatment Tchaikovsky had used before to animate the codas of his large formal dance movements, most recently in the swing towards D flat and the succeeding chain of secondary dominant cadences in the peasants' choral dance in Act 1 of *Onegin*. 'Pimpinella' is a slight song of some charm.

When Tchaikovsky had arrived in Italy his enchantment with that Mediterranean land had prompted him to set Naples as his next destination. But the strains imposed upon his finances by Florence compelled him to turn his thoughts to a cheaper resort, and the sort of sightseeing which he would wish to enjoy in Naples would have been difficult with Kolya. And so once again Clarens claimed him. There was the added attraction that it was more accessible from Berlin, whither Kotek had returned to continue his studies with Joachim. Thus, after a night in Geneva, which seemed by comparison with Florence to be utterly prosaic, he settled himself back into the lakeside pension where he had found such solace with Anatoly. Modest, who in Florence had begun to worry his brother by devoting more attention to the city's artistic riches than to Kolya's education, returned to his proper duties, and Tchaikovsky tried to establish a daily production of one piano piece, a self-imposed discipline he had attempted in Florence but had found impossible owing to the Florentines' endless propensity to sing at all times, and of English lady guests at the hotel to practise the piano endlessly. No such yield was possible, however, and it was not until nearly the middle of May that the Twelve Pieces, Op. 40, were completed. In any case, other far more ambitious compositional matters quickly engrossed his attention, for on 13 March, only four days after returning to Clarens, he had set about a piano sonata. Four more days, and he had begun his Violin Concerto.

Tchaikovsky's delight in his Clarens pension was unbounded, and besides the excellent food, accommodation and service, he had a good piano available. With the piano sonata he was once again attempting major composition, but from the beginning the work did not go well. For a day or two he forced himself to proceed with it. In the meantime he had by telegram notified Kotek of his presence in Clarens, and on 14 March his violinist friend arrived from Berlin, bringing with him a whole pile of piano-duet and other arrangements of recent pieces which he and Tchaikovsky immediately set about investigating. It was probably playing through the *Symphonie espagnole* by Lalo the day after Kotek's arrival that sowed in Tchaikovsky's mind the idea of himself composing a large-scale work for violin and orchestra. 'It [the *Symphonie espagnole*] has a lot of freshness, lightness, of piquant rhythms, of beautiful and excellently harmonised melodies,' he wrote to Mrs von Meck later that day. '. . . He [Lalo], in the same way as Léo Delibes and Bizet, does not strive after profundity, but he carefully avoids routine, seeks out new forms, and thinks more about *musical beauty* than about observing established traditions, as do the Germans.'[24] He might almost

²⁴ *TPM*1, p. 234; *TLP*7, p. 153; *TZC*2, p. 126.

have been writing the prescription for the violin concerto he himself was about to compose. However, the following day he was still labouring on the sonata. 'I neither know, nor can I understand why, despite such favourable circumstances, I am not *disposed* to work,' he lamented to Anatoly. 'Am I played out? I have to squeeze out of myself weak and worthless ideas, and ponder every bar. But I shall achieve my goal, and I hope inspiration will dawn upon me.'[25]

The urge to set about the concerto proved irresistible, however, and only the next day he started upon it, finding such instant joy in this new project that he laid aside the sonata. In addition, he wished to avail himself to the full of Kotek's presence while the latter remained in Clarens. Progress upon the work was swift and steady; above all, he had rediscovered his inspiration. By 23 March he had reached the slow movement, and three days later had set about the finale. On 28 March the sketches of the whole concerto were complete. Both Modest and Kotek were enthusiastic about the outer movements, but had reservations about the central one, doubts which the composer himself shared. On 5 April he composed an entire new slow movement which satisfied both his critics as well as himself. He did not feel that the discarded movement merited complete oblivion, however, and it was to become *Méditation*, the first of the three pieces for violin and piano, *Souvenir d'un lieu cher*, Op. 42. Kotek was now delighted with the whole work. 'How lovingly he's busying himself with my concerto!' Tchaikovsky exclaimed to Anatoly on the same day on which he completed the new slow movement. 'It goes without saying that I would have been able to do nothing without him. He plays it marvellously!'[26] Tchaikovsky wasted no time in starting upon the orchestration of the work, and on 11 April all was done.

Early in 1877 Tchaikovsky had written a slender concert piece for Kotek, a *Valse-scherzo* for violin and orchestra. However, it was not Kotek who gave the first performance of the piece; that was to be another of Tchaikovsky's Conservatoire pupils, the young Pole, Stanislaw Barcewicz, at an RMS concert on 13 December 1879. Nor, for all his help to Tchaikovsky during the composition of the Violin Concerto, was it to be Kotek who would first play that work in public – nor even, indeed, be the one to whom Tchaikovsky was to inscribe the piece.

The man chosen as dedicatee was Leopold Auer, for whom Tchaikovsky had composed his *Sérénade mélancolique*, also for violin and orchestra, and who Tchaikovsky hoped would introduce the work to

[25] *TLP*7, p. 151; *TPR*, p. 386; *TPB*, pp. 153–4; *YDGC*, p. 175.
[26] *TLP*7, p. 194; *TPR*, p. 396; *TPB*, p. 159.

the musical world. In fact, what would have been the first performance of the concerto was actually advertised in St Petersburg for 22 March 1879. The circumstances which caused the cancellation of this première must have brought back sour memories of the early history of the First Piano Concerto. Tchaikovsky alluded to the matter briefly in the course of his *Autobiographical description of a journey abroad in 1888*. 'I do not know whether Auer was flattered by my dedication – only that, despite his sincere friendship towards me, he never wanted to master the difficulties of this concerto, deemed it awkward to play – and that a verdict such as this from the authoritative St Petersburg virtuoso cast my poor child for many years into the abyss, it seemed, of eternal oblivion.'[27] Auer himself, writing thirty years after Tchaikovsky's death, by which time he had played the concerto many times, excused himself on the grounds that he wished to make revisions to the solo part before attempting it publicly, but that the pressure of other commitments so delayed this work that Tchaikovsky two years later transferred the dedication to Adolf Brodsky after he had given the work its first performance in Vienna at a Philharmonic Society concert conducted by Hans Richter on 4 December 1881.[28]

But Auer's rôle in the concerto's fortunes on the road to performance was certainly less immaculate than he would have us believe. Only days after its Austrian première, Jurgenson was reporting to Tchaikovsky that Auer had attempted to dissuade Émile Sauret from playing the concerto in St Petersburg, saying that he would 'do himself à mischief'.[29] It appears that Tchaikovsky had hoped that Kotek would introduce the concerto to their homeland, but the latter had procrastinated, and it was again Brodsky who gave the first Russian performance at a concert in Moscow on 20 August 1882. The Russian audience's reception of the concerto was thoroughly enthusiastic, very different from the one it had faced in Vienna. On that occasion Brodsky, making his Viennese début, had been warmly received, but the concerto had provoked violent extremes of opinion, both in the hall and in the press. From Hanslick it drew one of the most notoriously damning of all reviews, in which he declared that Tchaikovsky's concerto demonstrated how there were pieces of music in which you could 'hear how they stink'.[30] Modest believed that his brother had never been so wounded by any review since that which Cui had accorded Tchaikov-

[27] *TMKS*, p. 340; *DTC*, p. 464.
[28] In a letter of 8 January 1882 Nadezhda von Meck alluded to a performance of the Violin Concerto given by Leopold Damrosch in New York in 1879. There is no other evidence to confirm this alleged performance.
[29] *DTC*, p. 468; *TPJ*1, p. 217.
[30] *TZC*2, p. 503.

sky's graduation cantata in 1866; to the end of his days Tchaikovsky could recite Hanslick's diatribe by heart. Most of the Viennese press came down on Hanslick's side, only two critics—so Modest said—giving the concerto a real welcome. Brodsky, however, had faith in the work, and was soon playing it in Germany, where it rapidly achieved success.

In character and quality no works could be more dissimilar than the two large-scale pieces upon which Tchaikovsky worked at Clarens. He admitted that the sonata had to be fabricated, and nothing demonstrates more clearly the prevailing emptiness of his emotional life. His rapid transference of attention to the concerto, and the sudden profuse feeling which sprang into life in this work signified a sudden change in his spiritual condition patently precipitated by something very special – and this was clearly the arrival of Kotek, for whom Tchaikovsky's feelings had certainly once been sexual. The fact that he had wished to dedicate the concerto to the young violinist but, as he confided to Jurgenson, had decided against it because it might provoke gossip, is one indication of this; another is found in Tchaikovsky's own words. 'I love him very much – but by now quite differently from before,' he confided to Anatoly four days after Kotek's arrival in Clarens.[31] Yet if homosexual passion had now cooled, it is manifest that Tchaikovsky felt an unusually strong attraction to the young man. Equally we can see from some of Tchaikovsky's letters that there was a strain in the relationship at Clarens – a strain which emanated, at least in part, from Tchaikovsky's disapproval of Kotek's overwillingness to continue living on money from his father. Thus the relationship had a particular tension. Out of this emotional world came the Violin Concerto, with Tchaikovsky's lingering passion for Kotek, spiced by the personal factors that were tending to keep them apart, surely accounting for the vibrant and varied lyricism which is one of the most precious qualities of the work.

In the first movement Tchaikovsky attempted none of the stupendous architectural daring which is so crucial a part of the massive experience afforded by the first movement of his most recent instrumental work, the Fourth Symphony. He did not even try to build a less complex, though admirably original structure of the sort he had essayed so successfully in the first movement of the First Piano Concerto. The development of the Violin Concerto contains nothing as sophisticated as the impressive chain of thematic metamorphoses which had followed upon the central ritornello in the corresponding section of that work. In fact, in the Violin Concerto nothing at all new is

[31] *TPR*, p. 388.

added after this ritornello, for when the soloist re-enters, it is simply to present an ornamented review of a substantial portion of what the orchestra has just played, the whole development being rounded off with a written-out cadenza interpolated between the dominant preparation which forecasts the recapitulation, and the recapitulation itself, exactly as in the E minor Concerto of Mendelssohn. In the exposition, as in those of the piano concerto and the two most recent symphonies, there are three distinct themes, but the first two are simply successive parts of the first subject and are set in the same key, while the third theme follows as the second subject in the conventional dominant. Yet to dismiss this movement as trite on the evidence of such an apparently threadbare structure would be a sad error, for this artless scheme simply provides a frame upon which may be deployed a rich and carefully organised flow of lyrical invention and brilliant passage work which represents Tchaikovsky's powers at their best. Such an alliance of simple melody and complex pyrotechnics was, of course, the recipe for countless virtuoso concerti of the nineteenth century, but in none of these is the melody on a higher level, or the display element more judiciously employed or more naturally integrated into the flow of lyrical ideas – nor is the structural bracing of musical expanses so secure.

The introduction to the first movement, whose elegant opening phrase and methodical dominant preparation might lead the listener to suspect that a neo-classical piece like the Rococo Variations is beginning, is not as closely linked to the following thematic material as had been the far more extensive introduction to the First Piano Concerto. Yet this introduction contains hints of things to come, not only in the intimations, in its very first phrase, of tiny but significant elements of the two main subject themes of the movement (the opening of the first subject is further unveiled in the dominant preparation which follows), but also in the two-quaver figure which forms the links in a chain of repetitions occupying the three bars before the soloist's first notes – a figure which is to be taken up at far greater length in the second half of the movement's central ritornello (bar 141), and which is also audible in the dominant preparation before the soloist's cadenza.

The exposition repays close examination for the evidence it yields of Tchaikovsky's admirable capacity, revealed as early as the slow movement of the First Symphony, for combining the most fertile, free, and vastly deployed melodic flow with an equally decisive focusing upon certain recurrent features which integrate the whole expanse – features in whose recurrence there is not a hint of fabrication or mere doctrinaire intent. We have observed this technique, for instance, in the central theme of *Francesca da Rimini* (see Ex. 124), where it is used as a way of integrating a single huge melodic span, but in the first movement of the Violin Concerto it is employed to relate a succession of different melodic ideas from which an even longer stretch of music is created. Thus the points at which both subjects break into their respective rhetorical climaxes are closely connected in content (Ex. 146), and the redistribution of the ingredients – an upward rushing demisemiquaver scale passage and a repeated three-note rising figure – in no way masks this relationship. More important still is the way in which the three-note shape heard in both the fifth and sixth bars of the first subject (see *a* in Ex. 147a) acquires by the end of the eighth bar a completely new rhythmic character simply by the repetition of the second note. This immediately generates a tailpiece made from swift repetitions of this figure, and in so doing it creates the rhythmic mould for the new second theme of the first subject, a theme which emerges seamlessly out of the restatement of the first theme (see Ex. 147b). This join is deftly managed – indeed, so deftly that the listener is hard put to identify precisely where the second theme begins. Is it where the orchestra joins in during the second bar of Ex. 147b, or where the new rhythmic figure emerges in the following bar, and where the harmony resolves to the tonic chord? Such teasingly delightful ambiguity is in extreme contrast to the appalling woodenness of the piano sonata's rhythmic world and phrase-structure. In the Violin Concerto there is little contrast in character between the subjects, the second adding no more than a little fervency to the open-hearted sentiments of the first. The sedately balanced proportions at which Tchaikovsky aimed in this concerto are well served by an almost wholesale repetition of the exposition by way of recapitulation, the only adjustment being the deflecting of the second element of the first subject into G to ensure that the second subject will arrive in D.

The slow movement (significantly labelled *canzonetta*) is the most consistently and wholeheartedly melodic Tchaikovsky had composed since the Andante cantabile of the First String Quartet. And, having drawn this comparison, we have a clue to the striking intensity of feeling within this uncomplicated piece. If the emotions raised by Kotek were one source of the concerto's inspiration, the other was Tchaikovsky's burning love for Russia. Increasingly in his letters over the last few months there had been cries of longing for his homeland, and this canzonetta breathes a melancholy as deeply Russian as the folksong-based quartet movement of seven years earlier. There had already been something of this quality in the rejected slow movement, but there it had been diluted and a little sentimentalised. When

Ex. 146

Ex. 147

[a.]

[b.]

Tchaikovsky came to replace this movement he had already composed the rondo finale, the Russian-peasant quality of which some critics were quick to recognise. Having conjured for himself a vivid evocation of a slice of pure Russian life, he found his longings fed by his own creation, and returned to compose afresh the slow movement with his urge to create both more focused in intention and heightened in intensity. Ternary in design, with a more ardent middle section, the canzonetta is framed by a wind theme which is also enunciated quietly by the strings as the solo violin winds its way decoratively back to its opening theme. Just as the introduction to the first movement had adumbrated the opening of the first subject, so this wind theme hints, in its fifth and sixth bars, at the first notes of the canzonetta's opening theme. The slow movement and finale, which Tchaikovsky linked together most felicitously, are thus complementary, the one inwardly yearning, the other vividly pictorial in the best sense.

The main theme of the finale is immensely athletic, the second sturdily robust, with a double pedal which suggests peasant bagpipes beneath a gypsy violin (Ex. 148a). Tchaikovsky dwells especially upon this second, most Russian of themes, taking its second half (Ex. 148a,

Ex. 148

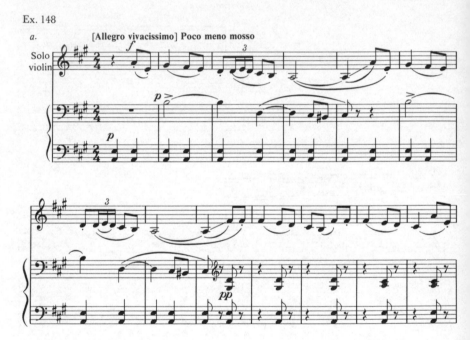

bars 9–17) and decorating it with different backgrounds as Glinka might have done, then suddenly slowing the pace to produce a form in which earthy vigour has given way to a more tender, feminine persuasiveness (Ex. 148b). Except, perhaps, for the finale of the Third String Quartet, it is the closest Tchaikovsky had come for six years to the musical world of the last movement of the Second Symphony, and, like that movement, it must count as one of his most successful finales.

8

RETURN TO RUSSIA:
BREAK WITH THE CONSERVATOIRE

THE VIOLIN CONCERTO, the child born of twin longings in those early spring days at Clarens, admirably reflects the brief, inwardly calm phase in Tchaikovsky's life when, with Kotek, Modest, and Kolya around him in the most quietly congenial surroundings, he could look forward to returning to his native land without, as yet, being forced to face the problems and strains which would attend his joy at being back home. When Tchaikovsky left Clarens on 17 April, six days after completing the scoring of the concerto, he took with him other congenial memories besides those connected with this piece and with his close companions. There were the two enigmatic but charming Russian ladies also staying at the pension who would only speak French and who were promptly joined by a Frenchman whom Tchaikovsky at first took to be their lover. There was also the amusement of Alexey's flirtation with one of the maids at the pension (though Tchaikovsky was to find discomfort in the result which arrived nine months later), and a diverting incident when some of the hotel servants appeared one evening, the men and the women having exchanged clothes. And there were the walks and expeditions to visit beauty spots and places of interest whenever the weather permitted – and, since the latter was often bad, there were the hours of music-making with Kotek.

There is no doubt that it was a very long time indeed since Tchaikovsky had been so untroubled in spirit. But most of these pleasant recollections belonged to his earlier weeks in Clarens, and as the time approached for his return to Russia, his mood began to shift. His more tense personal condition was exacerbated by other causes for disquiet – by Anatoly's continuing misery over his unrequited passion for the soprano, Alexandra Panayeva, by some less encouraging news of the Russo–Turkish dispute and the consequent fall in the rouble, and by anxiety over Modest's relations with the Konradis. With Mrs Konradi Modest was now on thoroughly bad terms, and for one wild moment he even thought of attempting to assume legal guardianship of Kolya, the more so since neither parent showed much affection for the child. Then there was concern for Kotek, who seems to have suffered some crisis of confidence, and on whose behalf Tchaikovsky endeavoured to negotiate, but without success, a post as teacher of violin at the St Petersburg Conservatoire.

There was one piece of intelligence, however, which really did boost his morale as he was preparing to return; not only did he receive some long-awaited news of his friends' reactions to the Fourth Symphony after its première in Moscow, but he also heard that *Francesca da Rimini* had been a great success when St Petersburg heard it for the first time on 23 March. And there was the added bonus of learning of Cui's hugely enthusiastic endorsement of the First Piano Concerto after Rubinstein had played it in the Russian capital. This great virtuoso was now making amends for his initial rejection of the work by performing it frequently, and during 1878 he played it not only in Moscow and St Petersburg, but also twice at the Paris Exhibition.[1] But Tchaikovsky's growing reputation both at home and abroad could not help in what would confront him when he returned to Russia, and the fundamental cause of his apprehension remained: how would it be when he was once again face to face with his family and friends? On 15 April the Clarens party began to break up. Modest and Kolya had to visit Lyon so that the latter's progress might be monitored at the deaf-mute institute. Tchaikovsky passed a last desolate day in Clarens, and then left for Lausanne, where he was rejoined by Modest and Kolya. Via Zurich and Vienna, they headed for Russia.

There was nothing romantic about Tchaikovsky's return to his native land. He had expected it to be accompanied by 'a strong and sweet sensation', but the reality was bitterly disenchanting. The more mundane, coarser side of Russian life had not changed, and he listed his unfavourable first impressions to Mrs von Meck on 24 April, the day after his arrival:

A rough and drunken gendarme who for a long time would not let us through because he simply could not make out whether the number of passports I handed over corresponded to the number of people to whom they belonged; a customs' official and porters who rummaged in our bags and made me pay fourteen gold roubles on a dress costing

[1] In addition to playing the solo part in the First Piano Concerto at the Paris Exhibition, Rubinstein conducted Tchaikovsky's *The Tempest*, *Sérénade mélancolique*, and *Valse-scherzo* (with Stanislaw Barcewicz as soloist); the latter was receiving its première. Rubinstein also played the piano piece, *Chant sans paroles*.

seventy francs and bought on the orders of my sister; an officer of gendarmes who eyed me suspiciously and scrutinised me for a long time before deciding to give me back my passport; the dirty carriages; a conversation in Zhmerinka with some persistent gentleman who assured me that nothing was more humane than England's politics; a mass of dirty Yids with that poisonous atmosphere which accompanies them everywhere; seeing a big hospital train filled with typhoid victims; a mass of young recruits who accompanied us in one train, during which journey at each station there occurred scenes of farewell with their mothers and wives; all this poisoned for me the pleasure of seeing my own passionately loved native land![2]

But the reception at Sasha's home could not have been more understanding.

All day yesterday I was agitated in anticipation of my arrival at Kamenka [he continued]. We were met by my sister and the rest of my relatives. They all expressed so much love and concern for me that I very quickly calmed down and began to feel that I was in a world favourable and sympathetic towards me. Because my sister's home is congested, she has prepared for me very nice and completely separate accommodation. I shall be living in a most clean, comfortable peasant cottage, some way from the main habitation ... with a view on to the village and on to the river meandering in the distance. The garden is thickly sown with sweet peas and mignonettes which in a couple of months will be in flower and will give off their wonderful smell. My cottage is arranged very conveniently and comfortably. They have even got me a piano and put it in the little room alongside the bedroom. Working will be good for me.[3]

Because of epidemics in St Petersburg and Moscow, it had been decided that Modest and Kolya should also go to Kamenka, and this had delayed the parting which Tchaikovsky was so much dreading. His joy was even more increased when Anatoly appeared on a few days' visit only 48 hours after his own arrival. Tchaikovsky promptly discussed his matrimonial affairs with his brother, and together they finalised a divorce strategy and full proposals for a financial settlement about which Anatoly straightway wrote to Antonina. Worried at the weight of work he would have to bear at the Conservatoire when he returned that autumn, Tchaikovsky had written to Rubinstein, who

[2] *TPM*1, p. 297; *TLP*7, p. 221 (with 'Yids' missing); *TZC*2, pp. 158–9.
[3] *TPM*1, p. 297; *TLP*7, pp. 221–2; *TZC*2, p. 159.

now readily agreed to lighten his load. The very uniformity of life at Kamenka, broken in his first weeks there only by Sasha's name-day party at which he danced furiously and untiringly (mainly, he admitted, because he then did not have to carry on conversations), helped to maintain his equilibrium of spirits, and work progressed steadily. Tea first, followed by a short walk, and then composition until dinner, after which letter-writing, proof-reading, another walk by himself, and then the evening spent with his sister's family playing the piano: this was his daily pattern of activity. Within less than three weeks the piano sonata was completely sketched, and he had added five piano pieces to the seven he had already completed at Clarens, thus making up the Twelve Pieces, Op. 40; the next day he started upon some children's pieces. In addition, on 6 May, on the eve of his thirty-eighth birthday, he composed a *March for the Volunteer Fleet* for piano, another piece which sprang out of Russia's patriotic fervour in its dispute with Turkey. The piece had been requested by Jurgenson, and Tchaikovsky stipulated that all the proceeds from it should go to the fund for building cruisers. He also insisted that his own name should not appear on the published work. It was left to Jurgenson to devise a pseudonym, and he chose 'P. Sinopov', after the Turkish Black Sea port of Sinop where the Russian Navy had destroyed the Turkish Fleet in 1853. Tchaikovsky's head was also filled with future schemes. There were to be a set of romances, some violin pieces, church music, and an opera. His choice of subject for the last was, surprisingly, *Undine*, that very same subject upon which in 1869 he had already composed an opera which he had later destroyed. Browsing through his sister's library he had come upon Zhukovsky's translation of de la Motte Fouqué's tale, had been completely captivated by it again, and had asked Modest to prepare a scenario. But within a week or two an alternative subject for an opera had supplanted this one, and *Undine* was forgotten.

There is something seriously amiss when a major composer, feeling himself to be in good spirits and applying himself systematically to work, can express himself satisfied with works which are patently commonplace and, worst of all, dull. That Tchaikovsky could, in the piano works he finished at Kamenka, have felt that he was composing successfully is a telling sign not merely of the emptiness in his own creative store, but also of how paralysed was his self-criticism. True, in the past he had written pieces in which there had been no significant element of self-declaration – in most movements of the first two string quartets, for instance – but in some of these more anonymous movements he had at least shown himself capable of producing a stream of fresh and attractive ideas. No such claim can be made for the Piano Sonata. At Clarens, where he had started upon it, he had been all too aware of the problems it was posing, but when he picked it up at Kamenka these difficulties seem to have disappeared and he proceeded to finish it off fluently. After completing the sketches by 12 May he laid it aside for a while. The labour of realising the work fully was begun on 27 June, was concluded on 7 August, and the first performance was given by Nikolay Rubinstein on 2 November 1879 in Moscow. Tchaikovsky was not present, but Kashkin hastened to telegraph the composer news of Rubinstein's magnificent performance and of the work's success. A week later, when Rubinstein played the sonata to Tchaikovsky, the latter was equally unbounded in his admiration for his friend's execution of 'this somewhat dry and complicated piece'.[4] By now Tchaikovsky himself was realising something of the work's lack of allure, and one can only suppose that it was Rubinstein's phenomenal pianism, rather than the sonata's intrinsic appeal, that won it such warm public approval.

In fact, the Piano Sonata is a strong candidate as the dullest piece Tchaikovsky ever wrote. When he was composing for the orchestra, his natural flair for exploiting the vastly varied colour potentialities of the medium could usually ensure that the sound was attractive even when the musical substance was dreary or slight. But the piano in no way stirred his aural imagination, and his use of it was, at best, efficient. His pianistic model was less Liszt than Schumann at his most turgid. Worse still, Tchaikovsky's ideas in the sonata are never more than second-rate.

The predominant impressions left by the first movement are of sterility – of chunkily chordal, rhythmically square, short-winded phrases, monotonously patterned accompaniments, tedious sequences, noisy posturing (notably in the development), bloated dynamic climaxes (the end is especially gross), and a dispiritingly mechanical structure, all of which is relieved only by the watery charm of the second subject, which also offers some remission from the textural congestion.

The main idea of the slow movement is almost a thematic non-event (see Ex. 152b), so little happens above the step-wise descending bass foundation which Tchaikovsky had already found of such efficacy when churning out romances. One need only look at Chopin's well-known prelude in the same key of E minor, a piece which must surely have been lurking at the back of Tchaikovsky's mind, to see how this particular type of melodic-harmonic synthesis may be used so very

[4] *TPM*2, p. 240; *TLP*8, p. 403; *DTC*, p. 518; *YDGC*, p. 220.

much better, for Chopin, having opted for the same two-note restriction initially used by Tchaikovsky, finally allowed the melody to burst into a strongly profiled climax before subsiding into its former manner. Nothing as epic as this happens in Tchaikovsky's opening theme. Liszt as much as Schumann stands godfather to the evolution of a good deal of the other music in this rather haphazard succession of loosely strung sections. Only in the C major moderato con animazione section does any significant expressive life begin to stir, but the attempt to rewrite this $\frac{9}{4}$ idea in the $\frac{9}{8}$ coda is ineffective.

The scherzo is by far the best movement, partly because it is the shortest, though a lighter textural touch is really needed if material as fleet as much of this is to be heard to best advantage. The last movement, a rondo of the simplest ABACABA design, aspires to some of the hectic rhetoric of the first movement, but is less disfigured by congested climaxes, and despite an impoverished opening theme, it has some moments which arrest the attention. One is in the first episode, where the accompaniment is suddenly reduced to a sustained pedal note against which a thoroughly Russian phrase exposes itself momentarily (Ex. 149a), while another is in the coda, where the tune which had afforded the central episode is furnished with a tonic pedal and a

Ex. 149

chromatic inner part (Ex. 149b) which provide support so much more distinctive than the crudely simple harmonies that had attended this same tune's noisy delivery on its first occurrence.

In this sterile sonata Tchaikovsky's neo-classical line came to an inglorious end. Rococo stylisations were still to appear in his work, but none of these had anything to do with sonata structure. In future, when he wanted a multi-movement instrumental vehicle for his more poised and objective musical invention, Tchaikovsky shifted his attention to the orchestral suite in which, as he himself said, he was freed from the obligation to observe established rules.

If the Twelve Pieces, Op. 40, which Tchaikovsky also completed at Kamenka, are not open to the charge of grandiloquence, most are certainly equally mediocre. No. 2 is the well-known *Chanson triste*, one of the better pieces in the set. There is some evidence of life also in the two Russian stylisations, *Au village* (No. 7) and *Danse russe* (No. 10; this is a reworking of the Russian dance from *Swan Lake*), but the only item which really arrests the attention is the last, *Rêverie interrompue*, which was among the first to be composed (the very earliest in origin was the *Valse* (No. 9), which was a reworking of a piece Tchaikovsky had written down in one of Taneyev's music manuscript books on 16 July 1876). *Rêverie interrompue* was written on 24 February 1878 in Florence, and was based, as has already been observed, upon a popular song Tchaikovsky had noted down some two months before. 'In Venice a certain street singer with his little daughter sometimes came to our hotel in the evening, and one of their songs I liked very much,' he had written to Mrs von Meck on 28 December 1877.[5] It can hardly have been the musical distinction of the tune which attracted Tchaikovsky to it, yet so much did he like it that he had written it out in full in his letter, even sketching in an accompaniment. Now he used it not only in *Rêverie interrompue*, but also in *L'Orgue de barbarie*, the piece which Tchaikovsky initially intended should be the last of the Twenty-four Children's Pieces, Op. 39. In the Op. 40 piece Tchaikovsky first fragmented the opening phrase to build the beginning of an andante un poco rubato introduction (Ex. 150a and b), and then paraphrased the contour of the tune's second half to continue this preliminary section (Ex. 150c and d), using an harmonic language full of acerbities and almost searing chromatic progressions, out of which the little sentimental Venetian theme steals most naturally and wistfully, as though a tormented mind, anguishedly brooding on a half-heard melody, suddenly turns to contemplate the fairer reality outside itself. In Tchaikovsky's emo-

[5] *TPM*1, p. 125; *TLP*6, p. 310.

Ex. 150

tional biography *Rêverie interrompue* is of some genuine, if modest interest.

There is a greater abundance of appealing fare in the Album for Children: Twenty-four Easy Pieces (à la Schumann), Op. 39, upon which Tchaikovsky embarked on 13 May. In February he had declared to Jurgenson his intention of composing such a collection, and by the time he came to carry out this project he was so full of ideas that he shaped out an average of six pieces a day. By 16 May, all 24 were sketched. The Schumann model was not *Kinderszenen* but *Album für die*

Jugend, for these pieces are not about children, and Tchaikovsky made no attempt to emulate that marvellous ability displayed by Musorgsky in his *Nursery* cycle for conjuring musical imagery which projects the world of childhood with dazzling precision. To exhibit on the concert platform such pieces as these of Tchaikovsky would be inept; it would be equally a mistake to dismiss them as mere childish prattle. In identifying with a musical world suitable for young children, Tchaikovsky showed not a touch of condescension, and these miniatures have a genuine creative life which stems patently from the strong mutual attachment between the Davïdov children and Uncle Pyotr.

Several set borrowed tunes. *Kamarinskaya* turns up as the *Chanson populaire* (No. 13), and echoes from Glinka's epoch-making orchestral treatment of this tune are audible in Tchaikovsky's setting. Tchaikovsky had already nearly ten years earlier arranged the folksong used in the *Chanson russe* (No. 11) as the second of his Fifty Russian Folksongs, and the tune upon which he had based the Neapolitan dance in *Swan Lake* turns up again in *Chanson napolitaine* (No. 18). A French chansonette, 'Mes belles amourettes', from which he was to make the minstrels' chorus in Act 2 of *The Maid of Orleans*, is the basis of No. 16, *Mélodie antique française*. As already noted, a Venetian tune is used for *L'Orgue de barbarie* (No. 23), while another item from the repertoire of Vittorio, the boy street singer from Florence, appears modified in the *Chanson italienne* (No. 15). But it is not the varied dressings of these borrowed melodies, nor the dance movements in this collection, which afford the most attractive music. This is to be found in some of the character pieces – in the brisk, spry little phrases precipitated by a bracing winter's morning (No. 2), in the merry clatter of the little horseman (No. 3) and the lively marching of the wooden soldiers (No. 5), in the plaintive portrait of the sick doll (No. 6), its solemn miniature funeral (No. 7), and in the vignette of its delicately vivacious successor (No. 9). Or, from the more adult world, there is the tender portrayal of mother (No. 4), and the sketch of the accordion-playing peasant (No. 12) who seems to have mastered little more than tonic and dominant seventh chords and whose instrument finally sticks on the latter. There is the nurse's tale (No. 19), obviously spiced with a few thrills from the world of the supernatural, and there is Baba Yaga herself (No. 20), nothing like as intimidating as Musorgsky's witch, but definitely grotesque. A lark twitters prettily in No. 22. And just as the day had begun with a simple prayer (No. 1), so it ends in church (No. 24)[6] with solemn chanting and a dying descent from celestial regions to a close in earthly peace.

[6] In Tchaikovsky's original sequence this had been No. 23 (the set had ended with

Immediately upon his arrival at Kamenka Tchaikovsky had been pressed by Mrs von Meck to spend some time on her splendid estate at Brailov, near Zhmerinka. The invitation had been extended to Lev and Sasha also, for Mrs von Meck was anxious that Tchaikovsky's brother-in-law should admire the running of the Brailov organisation (in fact, when Lev was given some statistics of the estate's economy, he was convinced that the whole was being maladministered, and that its owner was being cheated). But Tchaikovsky wished to make the visit alone, and his patroness, appreciating his need for solitude, issued the necessary instructions: the guest was to be given absolute freedom, his wishes were to be satisfied to the letter, and he was to be undisturbed if he so wished, with Alexey acting as an intermediary between his master and the Brailov staff. The latter were clearly mystified by the identity of this new arrival, and they finally concluded that it could only be a fiancé of one of their mistress's daughters. Meanwhile the mistress herself revelled in the feeling that, because her friend was living in her very own home and enjoying the things and places which gave her pleasure, he was being drawn closer to her in yet another way. On 25 May Tchaikovsky, Modest, Sasha, and five children arrived in Kiev for a few days. The next evening, while Uncle Pyotr remained at the hotel to put the children to bed, Sasha and Modest went to the theatre to see *Romeo and Juliet*. Having safely stowed his charges, Tchaikovsky was moved to share their experience by reading the Shakespeare play for himself. The result was instant excitement:

> Since I read *Romeo and Juliet*, Undine, Berthalda, Huldbrand seem to me the most childish nonsense [he wrote excitedly to Modest on 6 June from Brailov, where he had arrived eight days earlier]. Of course I'll compose *Romeo and Juliet*.... It will be my most monumental work. It now seems to me absurd that I couldn't see earlier that I was predestined, as it were, to set this drama to music. Nothing is more suitable to my musical character. There are no kings, no marches, there is nothing of that which constitutes the routine belonging to grand opera. There's love, love, and love! And then, what a delight are those secondary characters: the nurse, [Friar] Laurence, Tybalt, Mercutio.... From children heedlessly intoxicated by love, Romeo and Juliet became *people*, loving, suffering, who found themselves in a tragic and hopeless position. How much I want to set about it straight away![7]

L'*Orgue de barbarie*) When the set was published a number of other changes were made in the order of pieces.

[7] *TLP*7, p. 281; *TPR*, pp. 416–17; *TZC*2, pp. 174–5; *TPB*, pp. 168–9; *YDGC*, p. 182.

There were other more pressing projects to complete, however, and in the ensuing delay his ardour for again tackling this Shakespearean subject began to cool. Although he was to return to it in 1881, and again in 1893, even on one of these occasions sketching a duet for the lovers, the opera was never composed. Having only recently, in *Onegin*, set a subject which abounded in those human qualities of character and feeling which he now also discovered in *Romeo and Juliet*, Tchaikovsky's attraction to this Shakespearean subject occasions no surprise. It is the more strange, therefore, that within a year he should have set the grandiose and misconceived libretto which he himself freely devised from Zhukovsky's translation of Schiller's *Die Jungfrau von Orleans*.

Tchaikovsky's first impressions of Brailov were not without reservations. To its mistress he was all enthusiasm, and he described for her the details of his daily routine in that rapturous tone which he knew would please her. To Modest he was more frank. The house was magnificent, the furnishings luxurious, the comfort limitless, but its situation was less attractive, and the garden neither picturesque nor sufficiently shaded. In this respect Glebovo and Usovo were preferable. For the first day he was still without Alexey's services and company, and this aggravated the loneliness he felt after parting with Modest in Kiev. He had shed many tears after this, he confessed, but was comforted by the thought that his brother would rejoin him later in the summer. There was some good news from the matrimonial front. Antonina had (for the moment) agreed to a divorce, and this intelligence so excited Tchaikovsky that he had to pace the garden for an hour and a half to release his agitation. Mrs von Meck had a splendid library, an impressive collection of music, and a number of good instruments, including an excellent harmonium. Hearing of Tchaikovsky's delight in this last, she subsequently offered to give him one of the two harmoniums she had in her Moscow home, an offer which Tchaikovsky gratefully accepted. The country around Brailov he found delightful, and he explored it to the full, sometimes in Alexey's company, sometimes alone. The solicitous and unobtrusive attention of Marcel, Mrs von Meck's chief servant at Brailov, was a source of constant gratitude, while the luxury of having at his disposal a carriage with several attendants was almost embarrassing. He found a rather special pleasure in the services at the nearby nunnery which had a good choir capable of reading music, and which was well directed. And he developed a passion for collecting mushrooms and for taking his tea in state during the course of his various expeditions.

The sheer peacefulness of his present daily existence enabled him to make easy progress with composition, and the awareness of the divorce preliminaries which would very soon face him in Moscow strengthened his zeal for putting in order his current creative projects. He added two more pieces to the discarded slow movement of the Violin Concerto to make up the set, *Souvenir d'un lieu cher*, for violin and piano, Op. 42, and he proposed to leave these behind for his benefactress as a token of gratitude for this interlude at Brailov. Though in his letters to the family he pictured himself as the slave of idleness, he had obviously been working steadily, for on 8 June he could inform Mrs von Meck that he had not only completed the Six Romances, Op. 38, but had sketched his entire setting of the liturgy of St John Chrysostom.

Though neither the set of songs nor the liturgy is among Tchaikovsky's more important works, both contain some music more significant and more alive than that in their immediate predecessors for solo piano. Two of the romances, 'The love of a dead man' (No. 5) and 'Pimpinella' (No. 6), were fruits of his stay in Florence in February and March. The remaining four are all settings of lyrics by Alexey Tolstoy drawn from the anthology of poetry which Mrs von Meck had sent Tchaikovsky at Clarens in response to his request for texts. Neither 'It was in the early spring' (No. 2) nor 'O, if only you could for one moment' (No. 4) has any notable mark either of character or quality to lift it above the general run of Tchaikovsky's romances (the second of these, for baritone, might well have been written under the shadow of Onegin's rejection of Tatyana in Scene 3 of the opera), but the remaining two are far more important. The lyrics of both are amorous declarations; in one a rumbustious Don Juan vigorously summons his Nisetta to come out on to the balcony, in the other a pensive lover recalls the happy voice and sad eyes of a beautiful woman glimpsed across a crowded ballroom. Both songs gain much of their distinctive character from features within their rhythmic world and phrase structure. 'Don Juan's serenade' (No. 1) uses a three-bar phrase length throughout the piano introduction and interludes (which perhaps owe something to Glinka's *Jota aragonesa*), but exhibits within each group of three $\frac{3}{4}$ bars a 2 + 2 + 2 + 3-crotchet subdivision. The singer inclines initially towards four-bar phrases, though by interpolating extra bars for the piano between the phrases (as at bar eleven of Ex. 151), and by overlapping some phrases of singer and pianist, squareness is skirted, and the infectious variety within the metrical life of this two-strophe piece is greatly enhanced. Much is added, too, by the piano, here a spirited ally of the rake's amorous sally – a racy guitar, perhaps, bringing substance and atmosphere to a warm-blooded Mediterranean world. Surrendering himself absolutely to the merry vigour of the Don's technique of courtship, Tchaikovsky produced a serenade which is

Ex. 151

[The golden bounds of distant Alpujarra fade]

among the most engaging and deservedly popular of his songs. The
rhythmic variety within 'Amid the din of the ball' (No. 3) is far more
gently projected, and vigorous extraversion gives place to quiet
contemplation, the piano now sounding, as it were, from within the
singer's inner world, echoing, underlining and sustaining the thread of
feeling that flows from his musings. The delicate, sighing ebb and flow
of the melody within its prevailing sixteen-bar periods, and the soft
insistence with which the opening vocal phrase recurs like an
irrepressible recollection combine to make this melancholy waltz song
linger in the memory as persistently as the image of the lovely woman
haunts the thoughts of her adorer. A comparison of 'Amid the din of the
ball' with the other two Tolstoy settings which flank it in this collection
brings home how narrow can be the dividing line between the
memorable and the prosaic.

No work of Tchaikovsky had greater problems in gaining admission to the world at large than the other composition finished at Brailov, his setting of the liturgy of St John Chrysostom. In February he had broached the subject of composing church music to Jurgenson. 'Write and tell me generally, my friend, what sort of small-scale pieces I can particularly oblige you with. I'm very disposed now as relaxation to busy myself with all sorts of small-scale work.... Don't you need some *sacred* pieces? If so, then indicate which texts. Would it pay you to print an entire liturgy of my composition? That's work which would be particularly congenial to me! Can you print sacred music, and can you expect to find a market for it?'[8] In the event of Jurgenson acceding to this suggestion, would he please send Tchaikovsky a copy of Lvov's settings for the ordinary of the mass.

Shortly before his departure for Brailov Tchaikovsky set out more precisely for Mrs von Meck his reasons for wishing to tackle the composition of church music; he also outlined the difficulties which he now knew could confront his work when it came to be published:

[In church music] the composer has a huge and as yet scarcely touched field of activity. I concede there is some worth in Bortnyansky, Berezovsky and such like – but how little is their music in harmony with the byzantine style of architecture and ikons, with the whole structure of the Orthodox service! Did you know that the composition of music for the church is a monopoly of the Imperial Chapel's musical establishment, that it is forbidden to print and to sing in churches everything not included in the list of compositions printed in the editions of the Chapel, which jealously guards this monopoly and flatly refuses to allow new attempts to set sacred texts? My publisher, Jurgenson, has found a means of getting round this strange law, and if I write something for the church, he will then publish my music abroad.[9]

Having sketched his setting of the liturgy at Brailov in May and completed the work by 5 August, Tchaikovsky sent the score to Jurgenson, who had now revised his plan of campaign, and had decided upon a head-on challenge to the law: he would publish in Russia. In early October the Moscow censor passed the text, and before the end of the year the Liturgy was in print. Immediately Nikolay Bakhmetyev, the director of the Imperial Chapel choir, responded; copies were confiscated, and a lawsuit between an outraged Chapel director and an

[8] *TLP*7, p. 120; *TZC*2, pp. 114–15; *TPJ*1, p. 33.
[9] *TPM*1, p. 314; *TLP*7, p. 238; *TZC*2, p. 163.

equally obdurate publisher was set in motion. For over two years the
case was argued until, in May 1881, judgement was given in Jurgenson's
favour. In the meantime, in June 1879, the Liturgy was sung in the
university church in Kiev, and on 30 December 1880, a special
dispensation having been made by the Holy Synod to permit a concert
performance, the work was given by a choir under the direction of Pyotr
Sakharov at an RMS concert in Moscow. Despite the difficulties of
mounting a convincing performance of the work outside the framework
of the liturgy itself, it was enthusiastically received.

The liturgy of St John Chrysostom is the form of mass most
generally used in the Eastern Orthodox Churches. The eucharist itself
is only the third and final part of an extensive ritual in which a
substantial proportion is allocated to responsorial dialogue between
officiating clergy and the choir. A body of traditional chant was the
foundation of such dialogues, and Tchaikovsky followed these melodies
scrupulously, rarely departing either from the cantus fermi or from the
chordal style of accompaniment prescribed by tradition. Tchaikovsky
set all these responses, often indicating that one harmonisation was to
be used for as many as nine successive occurrences of the same text.
Even with such economy much remained to be done, and he wrote over
two dozen different settings of the words 'Lord, have mercy' to cover
some seventy appearances of this phrase during the entire service.
Besides a multitude of such fragments (Amens, doxologies, and so on),
there are a half-dozen freely composed pieces, including a Creed (No.
8) and the Lord's Prayer (No. 13), and, most substantial of all, a
Cherubim's Song (No. 6). Both the Creed and the Lord's Prayer adhere
to the strictest homophony, as does No. 14, *Praise ye the Lord* (except for
the concluding alleluia). *Thee we hymn* (No. 10) employs some gentle
imitation between tenor and soprano, but without breaking the
prevailing four-voice texture, and *Meet it is indeed* (No. 11) uses brief
antiphonal rejoinders between the upper and lower pairs of voices
before breaking into quasi-imitative entries at the opening of the second
half (and, again, between tenor and soprano near the end). There is
some loosening of the note-against-note manner in portions of the
Cherubim's Song, in the largely contrapuntal alleluia at the end of
Praise ye the Lord, and momentarily in the 'Holy, holy, holy' section of
No. 9. But otherwise the almost rigid block-chord manner, often made
more sonorous by division of the individual voices, prevails throughout
the entire Liturgy. The most distant ancestor of this is a very generalised
late Renaissance style, though rarely does Tchaikovsky come at all
close to the true manner of the original (the opening of the alleluias in
the Cherubim's Song might just credibly be a re-working for a single

choir of a bit from a double motet), for his harmonic palette includes various seventh chords and moderate chromaticisms of later vintage, and much of the treatment of harmonic progression is from later periods. The other stylistic element is sharply contrasted — a contrapuntal manner which might be described as 'broad eighteenth century'; for instance, a passage which sets 'invisibly escorted by the Angelic orders' in the Cherubim's Song, or the opening stretch of the alleluia in *Praise ye the Lord*, might momentarily suggest a fragment filched from a mass of Haydn or Mozart.

That such a mixture of styles should occur in this setting is a sign of the uncertainty with which Tchaikovsky approached the musical treatment of the liturgy. He was not to be blamed, for there was no truly indigenous tradition for the musical adornment of the service texts. At the very end of his life Glinka had addressed himself to the problem, and had even gone to Berlin to study the church modes and contrapuntal technique for this purpose, but his brief efforts show no sign that he was more than on the threshold of inventing a new, appropriate style. Like Glinka, Tchaikovsky recognised that alien Western elements had contaminated the style of Orthodox church music (he was particularly offended by the use of dominant seventh chords), and in his Liturgy he attempted to do something about it. For all the censure that Tchaikovsky's treatment (especially his handling of the old Church Slavonic words) drew from some pundits, most writers have acknowledged warmly the pioneer value of his relatively small contribution to the corpus of Orthodox church music. And, unsure as his style is, the strength of his emotional response to the service in general, and to certain texts in particular, is clearly audible, above all, in the slow, quiet majesty of the first section of the Cherubim's Song (Ex. 152a), an opening so much better than that of the Piano Sonata's slow movement (Ex. 152b), with which it appears to have some relationship. But this movement of the Liturgy is marred by the stylistic jar in its final quick section. Such incongruity does not occur in the Lord's Prayer, nor in *Thee we hymn*, a little piece which, skirting the cloying sentimentality which tinges the former, displays that brand of simplicity which is such a precious quality in music which seeks to address even the humblest heart among the worshippers while remaining worthy of the noble ritual which it is to enhance.

Tchaikovsky had never before lived in such pampered conditions as during this fortnight at Brailov, but as the day of his departure for Moscow approached, his unqualified delight in his life-style was tempered by growing anxieties about what he was soon to face. Having entrusted the manuscript of *Souvenir d'un lieu cher* to Marcel to hand over

Ex. 152

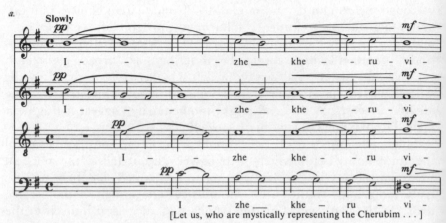

[Let us, who are mystically representing the Cherubim . . .]

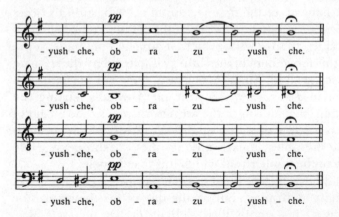

to his employer, Tchaikovsky himself set out for Moscow on 11 June. Arriving two days later, he had immediately to endure a host of those social reunions which he had so dreaded, but which sooner or later he would have to face. Anatoly met him, and before the end of the day he had seen Taneyev, attended a musical gathering at the Jurgensons', and dined with Bochechkarov, whom he did greatly enjoy meeting again. The next day was Rubinstein's birthday with its obligatory communal breakfast to attend. The social round of the third day was as hectic. Tchaikovsky sensed that Rubinstein had not forgiven him the affair of the Paris delegateship 'which, as he [Rubinstein] sees it, I ought to have accepted as an unspeakable boon. He always dislikes people who do not consider themselves to have been done a great favour by him,' he added to Mrs von Meck. 'He would like everyone around him to consider themselves his creatures.... In a word, I annoy him – this he could not, or did not succeed in concealing from me.'[10] Whatever Rubinstein's lingering anger, Tchaikovsky was less than fair to his colleague.

Far more deeply distressing was a visit to one of his pupils, Mariya Golovina, who was dying of consumption. Yet most harrowing of all was the interview with the secretary of the Consistory about his divorce. The cynical farce of certain parts of the divorce process, and the blatant practice of bribery among the officials repelled him. Over the last few months a possible scheme for a marriage settlement had been drawn up in consultation with Anatoly and Mrs von Meck. Again his benefactress was acting as his dea ex machina; she would settle upon

Antonina 10,000 roubles in return for a divorce. But it was vital that the origin of this money should be concealed. Thus Antonina and the world at large were to believe that its source was Lev Davïdov, while Lev and Sasha were to be told that it came from the RMS. To reassure Antonina, the settlement sum was to be deposited, pending the divorce, with someone both she and Tchaikovsky could trust, and it was agreed that this should be Jurgenson. Finally Tchaikovsky would take all blame upon himself, would defray all the legal costs, and would repay a 2,500 rouble loan which his wife had raised against the woodland she had inherited from her father. As we have seen, it appeared that Antonina had finally assented to these conditions. Now, in Moscow, Tchaikovsky was told the formal procedure for divorce. He would have to appear to commit adultery (exactly how he never specified); a witness would then write to his wife of this, whereupon she would submit a divorce petition to a senior member of the clergy. It was here that Tchaikovsky suddenly perceived a difficulty; while Antonina apparently saw her position as that of the innocent party being cajoled into an unwilling divorce, she would have to appear before the court and its officers as the plaintiff irrevocably committed to seeking a dissolution of her marriage. Until she could be relied upon to do this convincingly – and Tchaikovsky was so persuaded of her stupidity that he was sure someone would have patiently to process her for this suppliant rôle – it would be disastrous to proceed with the case. There was a further reason which threatened delay. Antonina had suddenly disappeared, whether deliberately or not Tchaikovsky could not determine. Convinced, therefore, that nothing could be done at the moment, Tchaikovsky seized the excuse for fleeing from Moscow, and on 16 June, only three days after his arrival, he and Anatoly headed for Kondratyev's estate at Nizy. He would set in motion his divorce proceedings when he returned to the Conservatoire in the autumn, he decided. Meanwhile Jurgenson would, when the truant Antonina had been located, train her for the part she would have to play.

As he was to remain only a few days at Nizy, Tchaikovsky resolved to contain himself in the face of the excesses of Kondratyev's servant, Alexey, whose drunkenness had driven him from the estate two years before. One pleasure which he could enjoy here which was not available at his sister's home was river bathing. But Kamenka was where he really wanted to be, and on 25 June, after a day in Kiev to revisit much-loved places and to buy some cartridges in anticipation of hunting forays, he and Anatoly were again with Sasha and her family. The remainder of the summer was spent here, at nearby Verbovka, at Nizy, and at Brailov. Compositionally Tchaikovsky confined his

activities during the first six weeks to realising the final versions of the
pieces he had sketched earlier in the year. On 10 August he could write
to Jurgenson listing a full six new works with proposed terms:

1	For the [piano] sonata	50 roubles
2	For the 12 pieces [for piano] at 25 roubles a piece	300 roubles
3	For the children's album at 10 roubles a piece	240 roubles
4	For 6 romances at 25 roubles each	150 roubles
5	For the violin pieces at 25 roubles each	75 roubles
6	For the liturgy	100 roubles

Total: 915 roubles

– or, in a round figure, 900 roubles – but seeing I have written so
much at one go, I will let you have the lot for 800 roubles.[11]

These figures are interesting as indicating the relative commercial
value of such pieces. A large work like the Piano Sonata would achieve
only a very limited sale, as would even a fine piece like the Violin
Concerto for which, in the same letter, Tchaikovsky asked only fifty
roubles. On the other hand, piano pieces and romances would find a
ready market in domestic circles. It was with such things that
Tchaikovsky might hope to gain the widest reputation, and thus more
quickly achieve financial solvency as a composer. This fact was a
powerful incentive to his systematic operation, over the last months,
of his production line for manufacturing short pieces. He was not,
however, prepared to do just any kind of lowly musical work for money
or to broadcast his name more widely. In May 1877 he had prepared a
second set of arrangements of children's songs on Russian and
Ukrainian folk tunes for Mariya Mamontova (the first set had been
done in 1872). He had now mislaid the manuscript. Having found the
work so unpalatable that he could not bear the thought of doing the
entire job again, he asked to be released from this new labour. Since the
lady had already made some caustic remarks about how 'routine' had
been some of Tchaikovsky's accompaniments in the earlier set, there

[11] *TLP*7, p. 351; *TZC*2, p. 191; *TPJ*1, p. 46.

was no difficulty in breaking the relationship, except that Tchaikovsky had to return the hundred roubles she had already paid him. He tried also (unsuccessfully) to have his name expunged from the title page of later editions of the first collection.[12]

In the meantime Jurgenson had tracked down Antonina, who had changed her mind, and who proved thoroughly uncooperative. She had even written to the priest who had married them, telling him that it was his responsibility to persuade Tchaikovsky to live with her again. By now this poor, disturbed woman was completely confused, feeling that everyone was against her and that she was a victim of conspiracy. To Jurgenson's assurance that she would not have to perjure herself before the court, that Tchaikovsky's infidelity would be attested by another, she had calmly rejoined '*but I will prove the contrary*'.[13] With such an ominous hint that she would expose his heterosexual incapacity, Tchaikovsky dare not proceed; Antonina's 'granite wall of stupidity', as he put it in his reply to Jurgenson of 28 June,[14] blocked the route to divorce. His best hope for the present was to remove Antonina from Moscow before his own return became due, and he turned to his patroness for funds with which he might clear Antonina's 2,500 rouble debt and also provide her with some extra money upon which she might live, this money to be accepted by Antonina as a lump sum advance payment on a series of monthly allowances which would run for the next few years; in return she would give written agreement to live away from Moscow for the term of these allowances. Meanwhile he informed her that she had lost for ever the chance of receiving the 10,000 roubles, though his willingness to divorce her on his remaining terms still stood. But the initiative would now have to be taken by her.

Tchaikovsky remained a fortnight at Kamenka before he and the whole Davïdov establishment migrated to the neighbouring estate of Verbovka. Here he did not have such private quarters, but the whole environment was pleasanter, and when in the evenings he was overwhelmed by a disinclination to talk or listen to anybody, a glass of wine proved very beneficial. As always he enjoyed the Davïdov life-style: the opportunities to shoot duck or bustards, to read (he was especially engrossed by eighteenth-century matters; for some months now Nadezhda von Meck had, at Tchaikovsky's request, been sending him copies of the periodical, *Russia in olden times*), to participate in amateur theatricals, and to play the piano for dancing and family

---

[12] After Tchaikovsky's death the manuscript of his second set of arrangements was rediscovered.
[13] *TPM*1, p. 364; *TLP*7, p. 304.
[14] *TLP*7, p. 306; *TPJ*1, p. 41.

celebrations. This summer the Davïdovs had been joined by Ekaterina Peresleny, Lev's elder sister, and her three children, Sasha, Dima, and Kolya, and their corporate amusements were also shared by a variety of neighbours, friends and senior personnel of the Kamenka estate:

During this past week I've turned myself completely into some Goddess Diana [he wrote to Modest on 19 July, giving a lively picture of their domestic diversions]. I go hunting almost every day. On Sunday there was a big shoot with Vishnitsky, Volokhov, Roman, Tikhon, etc. Quite a lot were killed – but I, as usual, just *blasted away*. Rehearsals for our performance [which Tchaikovsky was producing] started yesterday.... Lev doesn't want Tanya to play the matchmaker [in Gogol's *The Marriage*]. Sasha [Peresleni] has taken her rôle. Dima, for want of anybody else, is playing *Yaichnitsa*. Vl[adimir] Andr[eyevich] declined to take part in the performance. Besides *The Marriage* we're putting on two scenes for Tanya and Sasha: (1) the scene of the two women from *Dead souls* [by Gogol] and (2) the scene of the two women from [Molière's] *Misanthrope*. Yesterday's rehearsal showed that Nat[alya] Andr[eyevna] will be delightful. ... but her delivery is a bit monotonous. Sasha plays the matchmaker superbly. Though Kolya Peresleny overacts, he still isn't bad as Zhervakin. Tolya played Podkolesin very respectably: Biryukov didn't know his part . . . '

The day before yesterday we went to the Verbovka wood to collect mushrooms. There we found *aspen-mushrooms* in such quantity as I have never before seen anywhere. The same day Sasha went with the three youngest children and Miss *Eastwood* to the Rayevskys', and had a whole series of adventures. On the return journey they were overtaken by a storm, Sasha was almost killed by the horses, they were all drenched, somehow or other got back to Kamenka, and arrived here when it was already late evening, where they found us all in great agitation.[15]

As when he had fled to Kamenka a year earlier after his marriage, Tchaikovsky's ability, even when beset by the most monumental personal problems, to immerse himself in this family life at Sasha's home as though he had no care in the world, seemed absolute.

The theatrical performance was to take place two days before Anatoly's departure on 30 July. To muster an audience peasants from the estate were invited, and the scenes were given in the open air on the balcony of the house, with Tchaikovsky as prompter. Sadness at

[15] *TLP*7, p. 333; *TPR*, pp. 427–8.

Anatoly's going was partially offset by pleasure at the arrival of brother Ippolit and his wife, and by the prospect of Modest joining the party very soon. It was some time since Tchaikovsky had seen Ippolit, and he deliberately delayed his departure for a second sojourn at Brailov so that he might enjoy both brothers' company. When Modest arrived on 3 August he came alone, for despite his attachment to Kolya, he had need of a break from his tutorial duties. Nevertheless, the perpetual swarming of people at Verbovka was beginning to become unbearable for Tchaikovsky. Even his zest for hunting was going. 'This shows that my natural misanthropy is beginning to make itself strongly felt, and that I need to be alone for a bit,' he wrote to Anatoly on 9 August.[16] Yet he realised that, wherever he was, it was his nature never to be thoroughly content. 'To regret the past and to hope for the future, never being satisfied with the present: that's how my whole life is spent,' he added self-perceptively a week later.[17] Despite increasing nervous symptoms he remained at Verbovka until 17 August, when he set off for a day in Kiev, and then directed himself not to Brailov, but to Kondratyev's estate at Nizy for two days so that he might be able to have Modest's company till the last possible moment. On 23 August he was in Brailov alone.

During the next week Tchaikovsky buried himself much in books. De Musset had long been one of his favourite authors; now, finding a de Musset edition in the Brailov library, he spent a lot of time exploring its contents. 'Today ... I was carried away by his play, *André del Sarto*, and I simply squatted on the floor until I had read it all the way through,' he informed the book's owner on 26 August, by way of illustrating the attraction de Musset had for him.[18] More pointed still are his observations of two days later. 'Pay particular attention to *Caprices de Marianne*, *On ne badine pas avec l'amour*, and *Carmosine*,' he counselled Mrs von Meck. 'Tell me, do not all these cry out to be set to music?'[19] To substantiate this belief he straightway decided to use *Les Caprices de Marianne* for an opera, and when he returned to Verbovka on 31 August, he asked Modest for his opinion on the relative merits of this play and *Romeo and Juliet*. It was upon the problem of devising a satisfactory scenario that this project foundered. Yet for the rest of his life de Musset continued to tantalise him, and only a few weeks before his death *Carmosine* was the object of his interest as a possible opera subject.

Such reading, together with bathing and walking, sometimes

[16] *TLP*7, p. 349; *TPR*, p. 432.
[17] *TLP*7, p. 357; *TPR*, p. 434; *TPB*, p. 172.
[18] *TPM*1, p. 411; *TLP*7, p. 368; *TZC*2, p. 197.
[19] *TPM*1, p. 413; *TLP*7, p. 370; *TZC*2, p. 198.

accompanied by a whole army of dogs – above all, solitude: these were the special joys Brailov offered on this visit. Having just completed the fair copies of his recent compositions and corrected the proofs of *Onegin*, he had intended in the quiet of his benefactress's country house to rest completely from musical labours. Yet only recently had Tchaikovsky admitted to Nadezhda von Meck that he found creative inactivity difficult to endure, and after four days, on 27 August, he was composing again. 'This morning I so much wanted to sketch an orchestral scherzo that I could not resist it, and spent a couple of hours working,' he confided to his patroness.[20] The work he had begun was finally to emerge as his First Suite. Within days of his swift return to Verbovka he had roughed out three movements, and made some sketches for a fourth, but this was as far as he could proceed for the moment. His present stay at Verbovka was brief, for he needed to visit St Petersburg before settling in Moscow for the new Conservatoire session. On 9 September he left his sister's house. In Fastov, on the way to Kiev, he read a scurrilous newspaper article on the Moscow Conservatoire. 'At one point the article talks about the professors' *love affairs* with girls, and adds at the end: *Love affairs of another sort also go on at the Conservatoire, but of these, for a very understandable reason, I will not speak,* and so on. It's clear what this hints at,' he wrote to Modest in alarm.[21] Focusing his thoughts on his own position in that institution, he came to a decision: he would resign his professorship – not forthwith, because this would cause too much chaos, but at Christmas. Passing through Moscow he chanced to meet Modest at the station, and in consequence he spent a further night in that city. On 13 September he was in the Russian capital.

The main purpose of this visit was social – to see Anatoly and their enfeebled father, as well as other relatives. For all the strains which some of these meetings occasioned him, Tchaikovsky's concern for the close members of his family was such that he made a point of several times visiting his niece, Anna, at her school so that he might reassure Sasha that her daughter was well, had endeared herself to everybody, and was not fretting too much. Memories of his own boarding-school misery far from his own parents must have played a large part in prompting this generous attention. To see friends he was less keen. On the final stage of his journey he had spotted Apukhtin on the train, had endeavoured repeatedly to avoid meeting him, but had finally been cornered. Now that the ice was broken, however, Tchaikovsky met his old friend each day in St Petersburg, and admitted he much enjoyed

[20] *TPM*1, p. 412; *TLP*7, p. 369; *TZC*2, p. 198; *YDGC*, p. 186; *DTC*, p. 385.
[21] *TPR*, p. 442.

these encounters. But haunting him all through this visit were thoughts of his now firm intention to leave the Moscow Conservatoire, and he decided he must prepare his benefactress for this step. In one of the longest and most consistently gloomy letters he ever sent her, penned over a period of seven days, he set out his reasons for resigning – the offensive newspaper article which hinted at him, the dreadful experience of overhearing (so he alleged) during the journey from Kiev to Kursk strangers talking about his marriage and 'madness', Rubinstein's despotism, the whole intolerable oppression of his Conservatoire duties. He harped upon how prejudicial his teaching commitments were to his creative work, how much more and better he might compose if only he were completely free to live with Sasha, at Brailov, or in such places as Clarens or Florence. 'And so, my friend, what would you say if I were to quit the Conservatoire? I have by no means decided to do this,' he added mendaciously. 'I am going to Moscow, and I shall try to accustom myself to it. But I must know for certain how you regard this. Not for anything in the world would I wish to act other than according to your counsel and instruction. Please give me your answer.'[22] He did not for one moment doubt her reply.

Besides Apukhtin, the only other outsider whose company he really enjoyed during this week in St Petersburg was Karl Davïdov, the director of the Conservatoire there, who now offered him a professorship of free composition. The terms, as recorded by Tchaikovsky, were almost unbelievably generous: a salary nearly double what he was currently receiving, in return for only four hours' teaching a week. There is no doubt that Davïdov, who had recently quarrelled with Nikolay Rubinstein, was deliberately trying to poach one of the biggest fish in Rubinstein's pool – and Tchaikovsky was perfectly well aware of this; yet it was immensely gratifying to have further positive proof of how his stock was rising in Russian music generally. That he should accept the offer Tchaikovsky found unthinkable, for he feared giving mortal offence to Rubinstein who was, after all, at that very time handsomely advocating Tchaikovsky's cause at the Paris Exhibition. But the offer sorely exacerbated his already deep despondency at returning to his obligations in Moscow. He arrived there on 18 September, and the next day gave his first class of the session.

During the last twelve months Tchaikovsky's life had come full circle. In September 1877 he had returned from Sasha's home to Moscow to face a critical decision. For some six months after this he had slowly recovered from the nervous havoc of his marital calamity. But when he had left Clarens in April 1878 his anxieties had already

[22] *TPM*1, p. 431; *TLP*7, p. 386.

again begun to increase, for he knew that in Moscow in September he would again enter a situation of stress, and that to escape would again require of him an act of will which would cost him dearly in nervous capital. The profound distaste he now felt for Moscow and for his Conservatoire teaching permeates his letters to his twin brothers. 'Words cannot express my aversion to everything to do with the Conservatoire: to its walls, its people, its professors, its students,' he wrote to Anatoly after his first class. 'I escaped from the place as from some loathsome, stinking, stifling dungeon, and went to the Neskuchny Gardens, where I spent a couple of hours by myself.... How can I explain to you the state of my spirits? One thought has gripped me, absorbed me, obsessed me so that there is room for nothing else. I'm not depressed because I know I shan't have to remain here long – but somehow I'm edgy and impatient.'[23] Five days later he amplified his feelings in a second letter:

> I'm utterly dispirited, and regard everything around me with cold loathing. Moscow is thoroughly offensive to me.... I try to avoid all society and all encounters with people. Everybody I see, except for Nik[olay] Lv[ovich Bochechkarov], I find intolerable, and this includes Kashkin, Albrecht, Jurgenson and Laroche.... In the Conservatoire I feel like a visitor; it's become something so alien to me that I no longer get angry about it, nor do I get worked up during my classes, but view my students and their work with stolid aversion.... I go straight to my class when I arrive at the Conservatoire, and I leave it forthwith after the class, trying not to talk with anybody or encounter anybody. To various greetings such as 'Hullo' or 'Who's that I see?' I respond with a sweet-and-sour face, and immediately rush off in another direction.... I walk for a couple of hours and go home to dine, almost always with Nik[olay] Lv[ovich] as my guest.[24]

As usual, when under stress, he was drinking a lot, and he had absolutely no inclination to compose. Only one piece did he strain out of himself: an additional aria for Vyazminsky in *The Oprichnik*, written at the request of the baritone, Bogomir Korsov, who was to sing the rôle in Moscow. By the terms of his contract with Bessel Tchaikovsky was obliged to respond to such requests, and his reluctance to compose was the greater because of his total detestation of *The Oprichnik*. So unwilling

[23] *TLP*7, p. 393; *TPR*, p. 446.
[24] *TLP*7, pp. 399–400; *TPR*, p. 447; *TPB*, p. 174; *YDGC*, p. 189 (partial). On the same day he wrote an almost identical letter to Modest.

was he that he suggested to Korsov that another composer, the young Grigory Lichine, should be invited to compose the piece. But in the end there was no evading his obligation, and the aria (now lost) was written.[25]

Antonina's behaviour was one matter about which he could not complain. In accordance with the terms of his recent financial arrangement, she appeared to have left Moscow: at least, if she was still in the city, she kept out of sight. Instead, it was now his mother-in-law who was tormenting him with expressions of affection and of a hope that Tchaikovsky would agree to act as sponsor at her younger daughter's wedding. 'She also urges me in one letter to live "with a certain person", and promises me *complete happiness*,' a bewildered Tchaikovsky wrote to Nadezhda von Meck.[26] The latter had offered Tchaikovsky the freedom of her house in Moscow, but Bochechkarov had arranged a flat for him. To please his patroness he did, however, twice visit her home so that he could pour out to her the rapturous expressions of appreciation which he knew she wished to hear from him. For nearly a fortnight all he could do was to await Rubinstein's return from France. At last, on 4 October, this propagandist for Russian music in Paris sailed into Moscow, to be greeted in style:

> The Conservatoire's reception of him was full of solemnity. At six o'clock we dined him at the Hermitage. There were speeches. Rubinstein's first speech was in my honour. He said that my compositions had made a great impression in Paris, and how fortunate the Conservatoire was to possess such a celebrity as I. Everyone congratulated me.... I decided after all this that, for the present, when je suis censé être si reconnaisant et si indebted to Rubinstein, it would be embarrassing if I were to start talking about my intention of leaving the Conservatoire very soon.... I returned home very melancholy, and today I awoke with despair in my heart at the thought that I would have to postpone my retirement until next year.

But, as he explained to Modest in the very next sentence, the matter was virtually taken out of his hands:

> Fortunately Rubinstein, seeing me at the Conservatoire, himself

[25] In fact, though there was advance press notice of its performance, the aria was not included in the opera. It was to have been inserted in Act 2, Scene 2.

[26] *TPM*1, p. 446; *TLP*7, p. 409. 'A certain person' was the term by which Tchaikovsky habitually designated Antonina in letters to Nadezhda von Meck.

requested a few minutes of confidential conversation, and started asking me what I was doing and how I felt. I straightway blurted out that I would not stay longer than December. I carried on the conversation in the most amicable tone, and after an hour of chatting, we parted with long and friendly embraces. And so I've got to hold out until December, and then at last I shall be free like a bird on the wing. A load has been taken off my mind. Now I feel absolutely calm. For God's sake not a word of this to anyone. I want to leave here unnoticed as though I was going on leave.[27]

Rubinstein may have been a difficult character, and his pride in Tchaikovsky as one of the finest ornaments of his Conservatoire was certainly great, but he was too perceptive not to see that the composer simply could not be restrained any longer. Forthwith the two men devised a strategy which would make Tchaikovsky's departure as discreet as possible. Only four days after their conversation Rubinstein proposed that Taneyev should be invited to undertake a temporary piano class at the Conservatoire; then, when Tchaikovsky slipped away, his former pupil could quietly take upon himself Tchaikovsky's theory class. 'I shall go off to the country as though on family business, and from there I'll write that I can't return because of illness,' Tchaikovsky confided to Taneyev. 'Thus, so that no one may guess the purpose of your appearance among the throng of Conservatoire teachers, it will be very useful if for a while you put up with piano lessons.'[28] The same day he heard that Nadezhda von Meck fully approved his intention. Already he was scheming to make his departure earlier than December, for now that Taneyev would replace him, there was no reason for delay. 'I've been taking absolutely no account of the fact that in essence there is nothing particular to bind me to the Conservatoire, nor is there any particular need to tread delicately,' he wrote, self-persuadingly, to Anatoly on 14 October. 'Today I informed Rubinstein that I was leaving at the end of the week.'[29] Four days later he made his last ever appearance as a Conservatoire teacher. The next day, 19 October, he dined with his old friends, Rubinstein, Albrecht, Jurgenson, Kashkin, and Taneyev. 'Despite all my joy at my longed-for freedom, I experienced some sadness at parting from people among whom I have lived for more than twelve years,' he admitted to Mrs von Meck. 'They all seemed very

[27] *TLP7*, pp. 405–6. Again Tchaikovsky wrote an almost identical letter to his other twin brother.
[28] *TLP7*, p. 410; *TTP*, p. 39.
[29] *TLP7*, p. 418; *TPR*, p. 450; *TPB*, p. 177; *YDGC*, p. 190 (partial).

grieved, and this touched me.'[30] He had spent much of the rest of that day in putting in order his correspondence. The forthright opening of the letter he now wrote to the woman who had made his independence possible carried a far greater depth of grateful emotion than all the extravagant expressions of thanks with which he had so constantly, and often with such difficulty (as he himself admitted), charged his earlier letters to her. 'Yesterday I gave my last lesson. Today I leave for St Petersburg. Thus I am a *free man*.'[31]

The watershed, which in Tchaikovsky's inner life had been passed in July 1877, had now been reached in his day-to-day world. For some twelve years he had been forced to earn his daily bread, and to tie himself for the greater part of the year to Moscow. Now, with Nadezhda von Meck's allowance, he would never again have to procure his living by anything except his own compositions. He was free to go where he wished, to compose whenever he wished. Liberated from the need to have a permanent home, he entered his years of wandering. If he had a home at all, it was at Kamenka with Sasha; otherwise he moved restlessly round Europe until, in 1885, he took a house at Maidanovo, just outside Moscow. Here, and finally at neighbouring Klin, he found a haven of his own where he could take his leisure in private when not composing or travelling the world on the concert tours which claimed more and more of his time as his international reputation grew.

What of his international standing as he entered this new state? Little more than a month after this momentous break, Turgenev, who had witnessed the impression created by Rubinstein's exertions at the Paris Exhibition, wrote to Tolstoy from Paris. This purely personal communication between two people, who had no reason to view Tchaikovsky and his art other than objectively, speaks eloquently. 'The name of Tchaikovsky here has grown much greater since the Russian concerts at the Trocadéro. In Germany it has long enjoyed, if not esteem, then attention. In Cambridge one Englishman, a professor of music, told me very seriously that Tchaikovsky is the most remarkable musical personality of the present time. I gaped....'[32] Whatever Tchaikovsky's personal problems, the prospect for his music was full of the highest promise.

And what of the man to whom Tchaikovsky saw the Moscow branch of the RMS offer his vacant Conservatoire post? As he cast his mind back to the St Petersburg musical scene during his own student days fifteen years before, and as he recalled that period ten years before when

[30] *TPM*1, p. 454; *TLP*7, p. 424; *TZC*2, p. 215.
[31] *TPM*1, p. 452; *TLP*7, p. 420.
[32] *YDGC*, p. 192.

a musician far more famed and powerful than he had cajoled him into composing his first masterpiece, *Romeo and Juliet*, he must in October 1878 have felt a significant sensation, and some provocative thoughts must have stirred in his head. For the man to whom the RMS now first decided to offer Tchaikovsky's vacant post was: Balakirev.

INDEXES

INDEX OF WORKS

304 TCHAIKOVSKY

Souvenir d'un lieu cher for violin and piano, Op. 42 (1878): 280, 285, 289
1. *Méditation*, 261
2. *Scherzo*
3. *Mélodie*

PIANO WORKS

Chant sans paroles (No. 3 of *Souvenir de Hapsal*, Op. 2) (1867), 271
Valse caprice, Op. 4 (1868), 66
Six Pieces, Op. 19 (1873), 125
The Seasons, Op. 37b (1875–6): 56, 122–25
Janvier: Au coin du feu
Février: Carnaval
Mars: Chant de l'alouette
Avril: Perce-neige
Mai: Les nuits de mai
Juin: Barcarolle
Juillet: Chant du Faucheur
Août: La moisson
Septembre: La chasse
Octobre: Chant d'automne
Novembre: Troika
Décembre: Noël
Funeral March on themes from the opera, *The Oprichnik* (1877) [lost], 221
Piano Sonata in G, Op. 37 (1878), 66, 260, 263, 265, 273–6, 285, 287, 289
Album for children: 24 Easy Pieces (à la Schumann), Op. 39 (1878): 273, 277–8, 289
1. *Prière de matin*
2. *Le matin en hiver*
3. *Le petit cavalier*
4. *Maman*
5. *Marche des soldats de bois*
6. *La poupée malade*
7. *Enterrement de la poupée*
8. *Valse*
9. *La nouvelle poupée*
10. *Mazurka*
11. *Chanson russe*
12. *Le paysan prélude*
13. *Chanson populaire (Kamarinskaya)*
14. *Polka*
15. *Chanson italienne*
16. *Mélodie antique française*
17. *Chanson allemande*
18. *Chanson napolitaine*, 80
19. *Conte de la vieille bonne*
20. *La sorcière (Baba Yaga)*
21. *Douce rêverie*
22. *Chant de l'alouette*
23. *L'orgue de barbarie*, 276, 279
24. *À l'église*
Twelve Pieces (moderate difficulty), Op. 40 (1878): 260, 273, 276–7, 289
1. *Étude*
2. *Chanson triste*

STAGE WORKS

CHORAL WORKS

SONGS

ARRANGEMENTS

MAJOR LITERARY WORKS

INDEX OF PERSONS